DOUGLAS THOMPSON is the *Sunday Times* bestselling author of many non-fiction books covering an eclectic mix of subjects from major Hollywood biographies to revelatory bestsellers about remarkable people and events. Four of his books are at present being developed for global television, another, *Devil's Coin*, for film in Hollywood. With Christine Keeler, he wrote her revealing memoir *The Truth At Last*. That instant bestseller was revised as *Secrets and Lies: The Trials of Christine Keeler* and the audio version recorded by actress Sophie Cookson who played Christine to critical acclaim in the successful BBC television series. His works, published in a dozen languages, include the television-based anthology *Hollywood People*, and worldwide-selling biographies of Clint Eastwood, Madonna and John Travolta. He collaborated with Michael Flatley on the bestseller *Lord of the Dance*. He divides his time between a medieval Suffolk village and California, where he lived as a Fleet Street correspondent and columnist for more than twenty years.

www.dougiethompson.com
@dougiethompson

It was a bright cold day in April, and the clocks were striking thirteen.

1984, George Orwell, 1949

INSIDE OUT

The Extraordinary Legacy of

APRIL ASHLEY

Douglas Thompson

First published in the UK in 2024 by Gemini Adult Books Ltd,
part of the Gemini Books Group

Based in Woodbridge and London

Marine House, Tide Mill Way,
Woodbridge, Suffolk IP12 1AP

www.geminibooks.com

Paperback ISBN 9781802471755
eBook ISBN 9781802471847

A CIP catalogue record for this book
is available from the British Library.

Every reasonable effort has been made to trace
copyright-holders of material reproduced in this book,
but if any have been inadvertently overlooked the publishers
would be glad to hear from them.

Printed in the UK
10 9 8 7 6 5 4 3 2 1

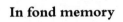

In fond memory

CONTENTS

AUTHOR'S NOTE

'Buy the ticket, take the ride.'
Fear and Loathing in Las Vegas, Hunter S. Thompson, 1971

With the increasing hysteria around the sexual identity politics of the world, recalling April's story gave me pause. What terms might offend in the telling of a story which began so many decades ago? Are you true to the times or must you levitate to what is considered proper in modern debate. There was much guidance offered but, as work developed, April's adventures told themselves as she had in conversation. April's advice long ago was: 'You're always going to offend someone, darling.' I hope I haven't but if so, sorry, the intent was to establish a memoir of a rather remarkable woman who lived as she wanted, or could afford, while helping, often by osmosis, countless others to become the person they wanted to be; to transform their lives, as she had, to be her true self. April was a pioneer in more perilous times. To paraphrase her friend Simon Callow, the sheer brass neck of her ambition. I consulted Bev Ayre, who with Lou Muddle, keeps April's road open for others to follow by preserving her archive and her comforting memory and Bev was encouraging because her advice was doable: 'I do think the only thing you can do is to use her own words to be guided by. You can't argue with

April. We might argue with your opinion, we cannot argue with April's opinion of herself.'

Suffolk, England, July 2023
www.dougiethompson.com
@dougiethompson

Preface

ARTISTIC LICENCE

'Dance first, think later... it's the natural order.'
Waiting for Godot, Samuel Beckett, 1953

Her one-liners were larcenous. A look could leave an exit wound. She insisted that when she lowered her gaze, her fluttering eyelashes made her appear as Madama Butterfly and encouraged by substantial champagne corkage, she'd pirouette and mime the Puccini geisha's most tragic moments. '*Un bel di, vedremo*' ('One fine day, we'll see') was *her* aria, *her* party piece. She also did an impressive Marlene Dietrich, particularly in a martini bar near the seafront in San Diego, California. It's the sort of joint where it's midnight by mid-afternoon. Reluctantly, and protesting outrageous casting, I'd play Charles Laughton's role of the defence lawyer Sir Wilfrid Robarts who's discombobulated in a barroom meeting by Dietrich as the incognito *Witness for the Prosecution* in the 1959 film. She'd seen the movie in Paris aware of the concept that clever makeup and a costume change can bring a remarkable metamorphosis.

Twilight was her colour. Play-acting made her memories visible, and she enjoyed the show, the flourish of personality, but present was the perpetual watchfulness of the abused child. That was something she could not disown.

Yet, that ever-glancing, expecting the unexpected, established her as a proficient sales lady – *salesperson, darling* – at an art gallery in San Diego, perfectly placed at a spot where a freeway sped you to Marine World and yachts across the Pacific. She never missed a potential tourist-customer meandering to her door along the pink stone path in the coastal enclave. *'Eyes in the back of my head, darling.'* On the gallery walls were images of California sunsets, wet set dream locations, colourful cabañas and endless ocean panoramas. It was a quiet afternoon and we were deep in conversation about her life story when a family wearing dollar signs wandered into the gallery. She stood up. But… one more question…

'Can't you see I'm selling ART!' I raised an eyebrow. In return, a withering look, and *'Darling,* I know it's not *the Louvre.'*

She was a conjurer of illusion, presenting an unflappable carapace to most, reserving her fears, and the acute moments of emotional turmoil, for herself and, with passing time, an ever-dwindling coterie of intimate confidants. Oh, she made new friends often and quickly, people liked her, and she them if they survived their roustabout audition. There was some comfort in strangers and, if anxiety intruded, she'd turn to escapism. She'd tell her rakish stories, tales of fearless adventure and louche locations, deal gossip about kings and queens and any number of society and theatrical characters across the dinner table like a pack of cards, expertly grasping the moment, like a falling trapeze artist, for a sizzling pay-off. If she did so in new company, it was an entertainment to watch the listeners' faces display the wonderment that so much can happen to one person in one lifetime.

She had, of course, been reborn.

Yet, that's not what made her special. That was time – past, present, and future – which always seemed to be racing to catch up with her.

Prologue

BORN AGAIN

'After all, tomorrow is another day.'
Final line, film version *Gone with the Wind*,
Vivien Leigh as Scarlett O'Hara, 1939

April Ashley was born, aged twenty-five, on 12 May 1960. It was a difficult birth at the Clinique du Parc on rue Lapébie, a back street, running parallel to the admired avenue d'Amade in Casablanca, on a day when the Moroccan sunshine was behaving the way the guidebooks say it should. It was hot and uncomfortable inside the clinic, which had remarkable medical expertise but little air conditioning.

Yet, Dr George Burou, wrapped in charisma and Caron fragrance, with a windsurfer's tan and the sultry appeal of the French New Wave cinema idol, was cool and, most vitally, confident. His English didn't stretch far, golf and gynaeco-logical terms, but his manner spread comfortably across his patient's bedside.

It wasn't their first encounter. They'd met for moments when, after a sleepless night in a narrow bed in her cut-price Casablanca hotel room, April arrived early on 11 May 1960 and was signing in at the clinic's reception. She'd felt his gaze as puzzled, he looked at her, and smiling, asked: 'You've already had surgery?'

He was gone before she could tell him she hadn't even troubled too much about her makeup and the strings of pearls were artificial. Her intent was not.

Dr George Burou discovered that a little later during their initial interview in his study-style consulting room in the avenue d'Amade section of the clinic. He asked April, who'd already passed his vital, personal test of looking like a woman, if she knew she might die under the knife; he had only per-formed eight such surgeries: it was early days, she was *another guinea pig.* He showed her explicit photographs of his previous, bloodied rearrangements of the human body. She told me only a true transsexual would stay put. Ditherers, seeing the graphic images, would race for the exit. Dr Burou asked when she'd like to *transfer from monsieur to mademoiselle.*

Immediately, she said.

To her incredulity, expecting protracted mental and physical examinations, he asked her to move into the clinic that evening, he would operate *at 7 a.m. tomorrow.*

It was, appropriately, being Casablanca, the beginning of a beautiful friendship, of another chapter in what being human can be all about. April Ashley, who was born a boy, would become one of the most talked about women in the world.

PART ONE

In The Beginning

'It always makes me laugh when people say I was born a man. I was born a baby, not a man. From the year dot, I knew I was female, so as soon as I could kneel to say my prayers, it would be, "God bless Mummy, God bless Daddy, and please let me wake up and be a girl."'
April Ashley, *Daily Telegraph*, **London, 2009**

One

Prime Target

'It's no wonder that I feel abused, I never got a
thing that ain't been used.'
'Secondhand Rose', Grant Clarke,
James F. Hanley, Fanny Brice, 1921

As Mrs Ada Jamieson [née Brown] would later explain,
she didn't enjoy hitting little George, but he was so bloody
irritating it was something to do. Ada, not one ever inebriated
by the wine of maternal love, was a sixteen-year-old bride and
quickly had six children and suffered several miscarriages. She
disdained constantly being pregnant, her Roman Catholic
husband Frederick, his Church, and her children.

Not always in that order.

George Jamieson was born on 29 April 1935, and although
number four in the line-up, between Rod, Theresa, Freddy and
then Ivor and Marjorie, was first in the battering order. Ada,
short, wiry and strong, with impressive biceps from hefting
sacks of potatoes about for a small wage at the local greengro-
cer shop, regularly hoisted toddler George up by his ankles and
repeatedly thumped his head on the ground like a workman
with a pneumatic drill. It was cruel, illogical, a certain madness.
George learned not to complain, that brought another bashing,
or to cry, and that was pure defiance, for Ada wanted a reaction
and when she didn't get it her onslaught was more frenetic.

Her sensitive son's body was a rainbow of new and fading bruising and a calcium deficiency meant it didn't need a hard knock to jigsaw a brittle bone. He was a regular at the pioneering Alder Hey Children's Hospital in Liverpool. It remained forever close to April's heart and, if mentioned, she'd boast to anyone within earshot that 'in my time' penicillin was first used at Alder Hey in 1944, saving a child perilously close to death from pneumonia.

Often George would be too fragile for the journey to hospital and Ada, reluctantly, carried him. It was very much a loveless obligation, and, like a delinquent child, she was surly during the trips; no comfort, no smiles of encouragement, no words at all. April thought many years later that thin-lipped Ada simply couldn't cope with family life and wrapped a scarf of scorn around herself. It kept emotions elsewhere. With an unhealthy misfit in the household, Ada was suspicious, wary, she knew George was different and her ignorance and fears prompted her to bully him mentally and physically.

From George's toddler days neighbours exasperated her by asking: 'Is it a boy or a girl?' *It* was an outlier, and a target. April's conversations about the hurt and pain of childhood were warm, spoken of fondly, as if it was all jolly fun and games, and jam and jelly and ice cream for tea. It's a puzzle why this childhood horror story, and it was a constant, did not appall her thoughts of her mother or early life in Liverpool. Often, in the tone of April's telling, it was an Ealing script, eccentric, a time presented through Vaseline-smeared memory, in flickering, nostalgic black-and-white; a story for which she wrote her own, always witty lines.

Her father's drunkenness was set off as an incorrigible affability, excused by his dark, attractive eyes and handouts of out-of-date chocolate when he returned from voyages as a Navy cook, often elevated in April's conversation as a *Royal Navy chef*. She recalled the darned and patched hand-me-down clothes, feeling like a reshoed horse in the second-feet, worn-down wooden clogs with bashed in metal rims (*Perfect for tap dancing, darling*), the bed-wetting until she was fourteen years old, and a daily battle with food – she didn't like to eat.

Over the years she talked about this part of her life as if it involved another person and, indeed, for the April I knew and spoke with, George Jamieson was a separate entity, tragically someone too painful for her to embrace. Nevertheless, it was George who endured life in wartime Liverpool and April's surprise and pride was in George's survival, for it was touch and go.

Ada's violent tantrums didn't rival Hitler's, but for young George Jamieson it was a combination punch. Ada would have her daytime moments, and, in the night, there were the bombs dropping on Liverpool, the most attacked area of Britain outside London. Shipping was the Nazi target, and the Jamieson family were easily within the couple of dozen miles of dockland comprising the German pilots' bullseye.

After birth, at Liverpool maternity hospital on Oxford Street, George had joined Rod, Theresa, Freddy, and his mother at grimy Pitt Street, a no-go area for anyone valuing their wallet and general wellbeing. By wartime, the family had flitted three miles to more council housing in Norris Green, to 51 Teynham Crescent, where for safekeeping they kept the coal in the bath and, as much as possible, George in his tiny room. The neighbourhood had moved with them: the secret of Norris Green was not to get off the bus there. The bombs didn't know that. Details of the damage inflicted by the German blitz of Liverpool, home of the Cunard-White Star passenger lines, and the port of registry for the *Titanic* and *Lusitania*, was censored to avoid boosting the enemy or souring the morale of Liverpudlians. The Jamiesons, like all families trapped by that geography, saw, and felt the impact.

The out-of-place George Jamieson became more disorientated. Ironically so, for Liverpool of all places, was then and remains, a salute to diversity, home to multiple religions and cultures and orientations, with the oldest Chinese community and black African community in Europe, a city over which many cultural flags flutter in unison. Unknown to all but himself, George Jamieson was more on the edge, very different emotionally and physically. He wanted to be a girl, and had no inkling why, and that meant the turmoil of struggling to be a boy, a boy from a family of scouser sailors, the kind all the sailors like.

> I was born strictly as a boy. There was an enormous battle going on inside me, in that I knew I was growing up to be one thing and yet I was supposed to be another.

An absentee father, Fred Jamieson insisted his children be brought up as Roman Catholics and George was hauled off by the ear to St Teresa's primary school, Norris Green, where tolerance wasn't high on the curriculum or a priority for fellow pupils, the teachers and administrators. Conservative, for protection as much as by nature, young George learned his Latin and prayed more than was compulsory and kept his befuddled head down. It didn't save him from the politics of the playground where anyone different got picked on. George was a target for older boys showing off their bullying skills and classmates with their name-calling. They had no clue of what troubled or marked out George but had no need for reason. Someone to make fun of and taunt, helped pass the time and added excitement to the day.

On 28 April 2015, the day before her eightieth birthday, April was given a grand tour of St Teresa of Lisieux Catholic primary school and St Teresa of the Child Jesus church in Norris Green. At the front of the church she recalled for Father Chris Fallon, the parish priest, the days before she fell out with God.

> I was terribly religious, I went to mass at 6 a.m. every day, before having tea or anything to drink, until the age of thirteen. I used to go round the stations of the cross

and I knew all the prayers and responses, all the missal, and everything was in Latin. I learned it all in Latin. It stays with you forever.

To prove it, she spontaneously sang '*Adeste Fideles*', the Christmas carol 'O Come All Ye Faithful', in perfect and tuneful Latin:

Adeste Fideles laeti triumphantes,
Venite, venite in Bethlehem.
Natum videte, Regem Angelorum;
Venite adoremus,
Venite adoremus,
Venite adoremus
Dominum!

Father Fallon was visibly impressed, and with the story of how benevolent priests rescued little George from 'rough boys' who would regularly tie him face down by his feet and arms to a bunk in the air-raid shelters, his face mashed into the metal springs of the bed frame. It was not the discomfort so much as the marks on the face. It was good to hear, said Father Fallon, that the priests, who made a post-school tour of the shelters, had been of help. April thought about this.

Yes, but the priests all got terribly drunk on Fridays.

This is presented in a haughty voice, one called *fruity* in theatrical yesterdays, and echoing the post-war BBC Light Programme radio stars, not the elocution of a Liverpool slum; she had a careful voice which, so very often, had to catch its breath. As it did so, Father Fallon, perhaps wary of more stories about over-imbibing priests, thought it time to visit the primary school. There, April regaled the staff with her well-honed story about being forced to polish the floors by skating along with dusting cloths tied to her clogs. If, she told them, you didn't whiz along fast enough the nasty nuns took a ruler to your legs, which was extremely painful. They were, she said, unpleasant times and she had her repertoire of stories to prove it.

The headmaster was foolish enough to take on Ada Jamieson in a battle of wits and slaps (Ada doing the slapping) about the face when she went for him after he pushed her son around. Ada won. April enjoyed the story of her tormentors battling each other, part of her doing her best to put a blue sky over her schooldays, but they were miserable. Fifty years later, April, gazing out to the Pacific one early evening, acknowledged the irony of her mother 'rescuing' her.

My mother hated me. She called me 'it'. I'd ask her why she hit me, and she'd shrug and say in case I did anything. Anything? Anything at all. Breathing could be a crime. She never wanted children. She was a Protestant. She pitted one against the other and she was wicked to everybody. The headmaster came into the class, and we were all there and he said he could hear someone whispering at the back. Then he pointed to me and said, 'Come here you.' He then said, 'How are you whispering when I'm in the class?'

I said, 'I'm sorry, sir, it wasn't me. I didn't whisper.'

'Oh yes it was,' and he hit me in the chest so hard it knocked me to the ground.

I was a fragile little thing. So, I ran home to my mother. It was the only time in her life when she ever … she wasn't doing it for me, she was doing it for herself. She was angry.

She said, 'He hit you and knocked you to the ground? You come with me.'

I said: 'No, Mother, please, please. No.'

He was still in the classroom. She went in, and she was tiny, and said, 'You hit my child for nothing?'

'Don't you dare speak to me like that, madam,' and she kicked him so hard she almost knocked him down.

She said, 'Don't you dare touch my children.'

He was speechless. The whole class was screaming with laughter. It was so funny.

When I got older, I realised that it wasn't for me, it was for herself. She wanted to give someone a good thump. My mother was tiny but boy, was she strong. She could swing a sack of potatoes across the shop like mad. Incredibly strong. It was a wonderful sight the way she jumped up and really let the headmaster have it. The only time she fought for me, but it was, as I say, totally for herself. I never learned anything from her. She would never speak to me. The only thing that I found out how I could punish her was to get the strength not to cry. It would drive her into a frenzy and make her hit me ten times more, but I would never cry in front of her. I would just look at her and she would just hit me until I was black and blue. I would not cry.

The other children? She wasn't kind to them either. She was tough on them but always, always tougher on me. Once, she was threatened with prison, for she had beaten me within an inch of my life. In those days, you never heard of anything about child abuse. But she had taken a belt to my back and hit me so many times that the doctors could put a thumb in the hole in my back and touch my spine. They told her if they found another mark on me the police would be called and she would go to court – and prison. My mother was furious, and she let me have it, a good couple of whacks across the face, once we got outside the hospital, the Alder Hey Children's Hospital, which was becoming a second home. She was a very strange woman. When there is a movie of my life, whomever plays her should get an Oscar, because if it is written properly, she is the most extraordinary character.

The world outside the classroom windows was also horrid but, for this fearful child, not as terrifying as the inner conflict. Anti-aircraft guns were placed in school playgrounds and, alerting all to the possibility of enemy planes dive-bombing, were the giant silver balloons flying over the prime target areas. Incendiary bombs were a constant, as was the anti-aircraft flak and the danger of death by accident, from ricocheting detritus, and flying rubble and shards of glass cascading from bombed buildings. The odds were greater than being hit by a German bomb despite the continual onslaught, the night after night of bombing raids to the soundtrack of sirens. While some feared being bombed to bits by the enemy, George anticipated the horrors of friendly fire in the supposed haven of the air-raid shelters.

The war was another confusion in young George's life, one more thing to endure, but the inner conflict dominated even with a world trying to destroy itself all around and the person who should have cared for him and sheltered him from the torment, the tempestuous Ada, carrying on like an undertaker's helper. George did find some sympathetic souls, especially a young local lad, two years older, called Tommy Robbins, from Toxteth, who showed an exceptional understanding and always encouraged the down-in-the-dumps George. Another pal, school friend Vincent, brought playtime happiness – and then guilt. Vincent died in a cruel way: on a hot day he drank water retrieved from a river and was poisoned. For that, and her own torments, April said she was angry – why him, not me? – at religion and, at age fourteen, had enough of it.

God was playing silly buggers with me.

April insisted she knew her hormones were muddled in the womb about the time she could walk. She never tired of patiently trying to explain those feelings to me, to all who would listen and attempt to understand, an epic task. Somehow, miraculously, she wanted us to *know* how *she* felt. She didn't disagree with the suggestion that she was, decades later, still trying to explain to herself why her stars were so cruelly misaligned.

I think I was three years old, maybe younger – it's a long time ago, darling – when I knew I was different. It came very, very early. There was nothing obvious in my behaviour. I never played with dolls; my favourite character to read about was Edgar Rice Burroughs's Tarzan; another book I read again and again was *Huckleberry Finn*. It was the adventure of it all that I adored. And I loved history beyond words. I didn't like Beatrix Potter and all of that. Yet, from the beginnings of my memory, people were always asking what sex I was. Maybe I should have been screaming from the cot telling them. I didn't understand why. I couldn't understand why. My life was unbelievably confusing. As I got older, I knew what I wanted to be, but there was nobody I could talk to and say, 'What is wrong with me? Why do I want this? Why am I not like my brothers?' Yet, my only dreams were about growing up to be a woman. I knew that if I was to live it could only be as a woman. In those days, there was nothing you could do about that.

In my sort-of belief in God, I simply believed that it would happen one day. Something extraordinary would happen or I would kill myself. I couldn't have lived on. It was clinical, with all sorts of thoughts: Well, I'll give it until such and such a time and then I'll kill myself … Then nothing happens and you don't know what to think. Later, I would give myself 'death deadlines'. I'm not being melodramatic. It was the way I felt, the way it was. I knew even then that I could not live my life as a man. My childhood was difficult, painful, with no love from the usual sources – from my mother or brothers and sisters.

My father loved me, but in a maudlin, drink-sodden way. He was not the person to give understanding counsel – he was the one that needed social services.

Loneliness is just one of those things you must learn to live with. In the end, it rescues you. It prepared me for my life, enabled me to fight my corner on my own. I wasn't accustomed to help, so I never looked for it. I just fought on. People were recovering from the war and were not interested in peculiarities like me. Even now I sometimes feel as though I'm from another planet. That I'm not a human being at all – just a space alien visiting. I'd have these wonderful dreams where I would be a beautiful woman – Cinderella at the ball and midnight would never strike. I also dreamed that people would stop hurting and chasing me. There was nothing sexual about the dreams. I would dream and I would hate to wake up because I was having such a lovely, happy life in my sleep.

In today's world of self-realisation, when all the closet doors are wide open, when there's sex-change on the National Health and gay weddings down the guildhall, it is hard to imagine the isolation. It's still with me, too. I have failed throughout my life to be an ordinary person. Now, at my grand age, that is clearly beyond me. The physical torture went on at home – and at school. I was supposed to be one thing and I was turning into another. It was a sensation more than something in my brain. I felt it rather than thought it. Of course, I had no understanding of it. That was the fearsome bit. It was as if I was growing up in a deep, narrow tunnel.

A tunnel which didn't even offer a glimmer of light at its end.

I don't think there was a day went by without sort of being beaten up. Simple as that. I once was held down while they jumped on my legs and I was crippled for four months. There was no 'nice day' where you, sort of, felt good, you know, you were made aware of it every single day of your life. I think that gave me the strength to go on and carry on regardless of what people think of me.

The bombs stopped and that was a relief, but the personal battles intensified. George was, in twenty-first-century jargon, *vulnerable*, at high risk. He was ten years old when the Second World War stopped on 2 September 1945, and that day began holiday work at the now long-gone St John's Market in Liverpool. By bicycle he delivered enormous joints of bacon for a couple of shillings for a very long day's work. He was trusted and trusting and ever willing. He made deliveries all over Liverpool, a city filled with empty warehouses and factories, bombed-out streets littered with debris and a council struggling to decide on a plan to renew the blitz-ruined city centre. There was other wreckage for George to get around. April told me about this more than fifty years after the events, a memory which never stopped troubling her. Why she'd kept it to herself, she couldn't explain, but one evening by the fireside at my home in England she felt comfortable to speak about it.

Family life was hell, but my situation was made much, much worse. I became a victim of what today we call child abuse. The perpetrator – I presume he was a paedophile – was the husband in a couple my family were very close to. I adored them, for they were always very kind to me. When I first lived with them on and off, I thought I had died and gone to heaven because they treated me so beautifully and I had a chauffeur-driven car to the cinema. I was allowed to have a small whisky before dinner and a tiny, tiny little glass of wine with dinner and those sorts of thing. It was quite a schizophrenic upbringing because, with them, I would have all these civilised things and then I would go home, and I'd be lucky to have a glass of tap water put in front of me. My mother, yelling and screaming and shouting. So, you go from a chauffeur-driven car to having to get on a tram car. It came as such a shock when I discovered Jack was like that.

It started when I was aged eleven and went on for more than a year. I've never told anyone before, never once mentioned it. Jack would make me masturbate him and try other sorts of things. I was so innocent. I'd never seen a grown man's willy. It was a shock. He wanted me to perform oral sex on him, but I never could. When he tried to force me, I'd be sick – truly sick as a dog. It never stopped him trying to make me do it, though. Masturbating him became the easier option for me, although I felt so terribly, terribly sordid. When you're a child and somebody you love very much abuses you, it puts you in the worst position in the world – you don't want to rat on them because you love them so much, and yet you feel like a dirty little thing all the time. The conflict of my emotions, my needs, were overwhelming.

I was already isolated from my own family; this made me become even more isolated. I was terrified of losing the friendship of Jack and his wife Helen. I was just in the worst position. I trusted Jack. Yet I was abused and betrayed by him. It was so ugly. I was trapped. Something had to happen, because I went into the most incredible depression, though I didn't recognise it as such at the time. My life was a total turmoil. I was struggling with my own sexual identity and at the same time had this sick man preying on me. Yet I loved him. The sense of betrayal was horrendous. Well, one day, Jack said he and Helen never wanted to see me again.

I said, 'What?'

He told me, 'Go home now to your parents and ...'

'You can't do that,' I cut in. 'I love you and Helen.'

At that moment, Helen came into the room, and it all came out. She already knew about what he had made me do to him, the constant abuse – he had told her. There was an almighty explosion. Then Helen pulled him aside and said to him, 'You have to be very careful; if he tells his mother, we're in serious trouble.' So Jack decided that I was not to be banished from their lives after all. He was horrible. I was such an innocent child. I didn't have lots of friends like all the other boys and girls. I didn't know all about sex talk that went on. I was an isolated child to begin with. The sexual abuse made me even more isolated and devastated. All the magic had gone. Then to find that Helen took his side rather than mine … I was the one being used. I didn't think of it as abuse because the word didn't exist in those days. But I was the one being wronged. When Helen took his side, it was the final straw, it was simply devastating. I loved these two people beyond words. I felt more betrayed by Helen than by Jack.

When the abuse was going on, I always said to myself, 'Well, at least Helen will stick up for me' – she would know that this was not right. I was an innocent lad, but I knew instinctively that this was wrong. Jack would say to me, 'Oh, don't worry … everyone does this.'

I wouldn't believe him and then I closed all the walls and became a depressed child. I became even more isolated than I was before. Nobody could get me to talk. There came a point when I couldn't speak for three days, and everyone said I had had some kind of trauma. Then, when I did speak, it was in a fractured voice. It remains with me to this day. It's not a natural voice. I had obviously done something to myself; it did have terrible effects. I never think about it without guilt. I still feel guilty about it. Why is that? After all, I was the one being abused.

I never hated Jack. It's a funny thing. When it was all over, I never hated him – I just couldn't bring myself to do that. I suppose it's the Catholic thing that you've got to forgive everybody. Whenever I spoke about him in life – and never to anybody about his behaviour before, not to a single soul – my thoughts were always fond of him and his wife. Yet, what torment I went through with him. How can kindness suddenly turn and break your heart? I will never know the answer. Probably there isn't one. I don't think victims of abuse ever get over it. It becomes part of your life, part of your personal history. It also makes you so much more aware of other people and more understanding of their problems. I can't see even a total stranger cry without imagining what had caused it and what might help. It's sad to contemplate. It's a dreadful way to learn compassion for others. But learn it I did. The hard way.

It didn't get easier. The teenaged George Jamieson had no body or facial hair. While schoolmates were shaving and growing wispy moustaches to prove how macho they were, George had no need of a razor. His traumatised voice didn't break naturally. April's sometimes quivering vocal pitch was the result of self-inflicted, torturous punishment by George of his larynx to drop his voice; that attempt to be identified more as a man, a bid for the protection of 'normality', was rather cancelled out when, by the age of fifteen, George began developing breasts. The horror was to be thought a freak.

The greatest fear was to be ridiculed. I wanted to hide from the world. Or run away from the one I was in, which I did.

Two

Valley Of The Dolls

'There is nothing more enticing,
disenchanting, and enslaving than the life at sea.'
Typhoon, Joseph Conrad, 1902

Despite his brother Freddie telling him he should be in the circus, the teenage George Jamieson ran away to sea and the experience, troubled as it was, was the making of a lifetime love. April forever saw escape on the waves. So much so that in later life some of her friends believed she'd become obsessive.

'We thought April had gone quite insane,' remembered the actress Shirley Anne Field, when her friend announced, in 1996, that she was going to sail the Pacific on a forty-two-foot yacht with a stranger. 'I'd learned to expect anything from April, but this sounded dodgy and dangerous. What was she thinking?'

Shirley Anne quietly retired from public life in 2023. She was too polite to pinpoint it, but then April was closing in on pension age and the thought of her skipping about out on the high seas was disturbing. Shirley, a triumph from her early days (co-starring with Albert Finney in *Saturday Night and Sunday Morning* (1960), Laurence Olivier in *The Entertainer* (1960) and with Steve McQueen and Robert Wagner in *The War Lover* (1962)) enlisted the help of their friend Anita Finch, daughter of actor Peter Finch, whom April had known since 1960.

'Anita and I were staying in Los Angeles at the time and constantly in touch with April who'd pitched herself up in San Diego. The freeway traffic was always nose-to-tail but we'd be delighted to see her and often make the trip down the coast. She was going on about being introduced by friends to a German guy who wanted to sail to Tahiti and needed a sailing companion. It sounded okay and then she told me she'd had dinner with the guy, and he was "sort of a Nazi" which didn't sound at all promising. I'd known April for a long time, and I knew it was likely to be a useless cause, but I enlisted Avril and we drove off to try and stop her doing what sounded like something very risky – certainly foolhardy.'

Shirley, over lunch near her home in Pimlico, London, suddenly burst out laughing: 'You know, of course, that we didn't have a chance in stopping her. April marched on to a different band to the rest of us. Fearless. Her determination always impressed me and sometimes frightened me. She was brave, maybe too brave at times but after the life she'd lived, no mountain was too big to climb.'

Or ocean to sail. It was only a few years after her voyage that April told me of her grand adventure. We were in a yacht club bar in San Diego for lunch – fish and chips, much salt – and there she went full nautical showing me maps and charts of the Pacific, marking out places of peril and where other sailors had perished. She loved it. For half a sixpence, she'd have sailed away again. Despite a rape attempt and fears of being a cannibal-inclined sailor's lunch.

I was determined to sail across the Pacific; it has been my dream for years. So what if my partner in this enterprise was a little strange? What could possibly happen to me? I was strong, tough and nearly sixty years old. My friends Manfred and Ginny introduced me to Ronald who was planning to make this wonderful Pacific trip. He had a limp, a hair transplant he kept smoothing down, was short and box-shaped, and older than me.

We talked over dinner and from the first moment I began to have my doubts. 'Had I ever eaten human steak?' 'Had I ever killed anyone?' 'Did I think I could commit murder?'

He went on and on, all in this heavy German accent. The fact was that I really wanted to sail the ocean. I thought I could cope with Ronald and his rather odd behaviour and attitude to life. He was not a ray of sunshine but I was in love with an idea. We had several lunches and dinners and he invited me to sail with him as far as Cabo San Lucas on the tip of Baja California. I was a little disappointed about that, but agreed. Next it was all off. Ronald had met the woman of his dreams and not only was she going to sail with him she was also going to have sex with him. That was fine too. Nothing to do with me.

I told him, 'Ronald, I'm so pleased for you. Have a good voyage.'

Two days later, he called me in a panic. His dream woman had gone. She was mad. She was crazy. Would I sail with him? First stop the Marquesas in the south Pacific?

No Cabo San Lucas?

'I'm going straight from Nuku Hiva.'

French Polynesia! Yippee! In forty-eight hours. My job was no problem. I was working in a hotel gift shop and bored. Ronald paid two months of my rent in advance, my wages as it were, and I offered my apartment rent-free to a friend on condition of keeping my cat Lily safe. Shirley Anne Field and Anita [Finch] gave up trying to stop me going off across a giant ocean on a small yacht with a man I barely knew and drove down from Los Angeles to see me off. They understood I truly needed to make the voyage, I was following my dream. I took our sailing papers to the harbour master and when I told him my first port of call was Nuku Hiva, he said, 'How incredibly exotic.' For a moment, I thought he was talking about me.

Shirley and Anita and her husband, Val, waved farewell and Manfred was there and let the mooring ropes go and we slipped into the main channel of San Diego Bay. It was a Sunday and the channel was crowded but it wasn't long before we were on our own – a little under three thousand miles to go. On our first day out, Ronnie pulled out a photograph of himself in the Hitler Youth. There he was, as bold as brass, with a swastika on his arm. He was very proud of it. Too proud. I've suddenly became very uneasy. Human steak? Was that going to be me? He knew I'd grown up in England during the war and here he was flaunting this photograph, boasting about the Hitler Youth. I told him to put it away and not to speak about it again. I was furious, thinking of Liverpool being bombed every night, of all the horrors of the war. I knew it was not going to be a comfortable voyage, either mentally or physically.

Now, believe me, I am not a spiritual person in the sense of second sight or mediums of all things mystical. I can't predict what I'm going to have for tea. Yet at sea out in the Pacific I had the most extreme experience. I had just got out of my bunk and I had this overwhelming feeling of someone standing over me. I thought it was Ronald and I spun around and there was nothing there. But there was a smell of something so very familiar – of a friend who had died at sea years before. I felt his presence. He'd always said he'd sail to Tahiti from the Mediterranean. He wasn't there all the time but there was this feeling of goodness around me and that wasn't anything to do with Nazi Ronald. It felt so comforting, for Ronald kept falling asleep at the wheel and I was up and down every twenty minutes making sure we were on course and not about to hit the *Titanic* or something just as large.

Ronald went on and on about sex and clearly wanted me to get in his bunk with him. One night he tried to get with me and I shouted him away. Another time he was much more aggressive, tried to rape me, but I was much faster, for his bad leg slowed him up. It was agonising to be with him for his mood changed quicker than the weather.

We'd sailed past the Marquesas, Nuku Hiva, Tuamotu, Manihi and were on our way to Rangiroa, the second largest atoll in the world. It's smack in the middle of totally shark-infested waters. When we got there the water was rough, but Ronald insisted he would take me to dinner at the yacht club for my sixtieth birthday. I protested that the dinghy would capsize but we went. The owner of the restaurant presented me with a birthday bottle of champagne. We had that, we had wine and then cocktails at the bar. Then it was time to get back to the yacht. The owner said the water was even worse now and we shouldn't attempt it, they had a room. You couldn't tell Ronald anything.

As we're approaching the yacht in these enormous waves he suddenly announced, 'I've lost my wallet with my passport and credit cards.'

I screamed, 'Why would you take a passport and credit cards to an atoll in the middle of the Pacific Ocean?'

With that, he whammed me in the face with his fist. He did it six times. It caused some kind of concussion and I couldn't see out of my left eye. Ronald scrambled onto the yacht. It's hard enough getting onto a yacht at the best of times but with these enormous seas and half-blind I missed the line. I fell into the water. I clambered back into the dinghy but in a moment, it turned over and I was in the water again. The yacht then bumped me and knocked me almost to the bottom of the sea. It was so clear and I could see the sharks. We'd watched them feeding at the entrance to the lagoon the day before. It's not true that you go down three times and then drown. I went down six times, tumbling in the water and almost drowned. It was like being in a washing machine. Ronald was watching all this. He looked quite mad.

Finally – he knew lots of people were aware I was on his boat – he let down the ladder. Somehow, I pulled myself up. I thought my ribs were broken but they were only badly bruised but that was pain enough. Ronald said, 'You're so silly ...'

I stopped him and warned him that if he touched me again, I would find some way to get ashore and have him arrested. I couldn't get out of my bunk for three days; every movement was agony. I was injured in the middle of the Pacific. I had little option but to be on guard and sail on.

When the weather got better, we took off for Tahiti. I was very wary of Ronald, but was helped by the comforting, ghostly presence of my old friend. He was there every day; I could smell him. When we got to Tahiti, however, his presence completely disappeared. I know it makes me sound like some mad old bat, but I can only say that is what I felt. We were on Tahiti for two weeks waiting for Ronald's credit cards to arrive and, when they did – as part of our business arrangement – he bought my plane ticket back to Los Angeles. As far as anyone knew Ronald vanished off the face of the Earth.

Manfred and Ginny were marvellous to me when I got back but it took a few weeks to get over my yacht voyage across the Pacific. I'd always wanted to do it – and I'd done it – but, oh my, it was an ordeal at times. Strangely, there was tranquility too, not like before.

At fifteen, George Jamieson sought salvation at sea. A regular customer on his delivery rounds from St John's Market was connected with the Cunard line and helped him find a place on a training ship, the *Vindicatrix*. Ada Jamieson didn't fuss about her son taking off to Bristol for six weeks training in preparation for life as a merchant seaman. April remembered counting the minutes until vanishing out the door to Liverpool Lime Street station. But also being patient.

Even then, darling, I had proper manners and I didn't want to be rude, to be thought to be rushing.

There were two driving forces, escape from home, and a forcible resolution to be a man, a tremendous act of will rejecting the overwhelming conviction to be and to live as a woman. Many years later she abhorred her own 'betrayal', dismissing the argument that, being so young, she couldn't be expected to deal with a gender puzzle which, decades on, provokes society. Publicly, she always made light of that cruel time, saying the blessing during these teenaged years was avoiding pimples. Quietly, she said it was terrifying, the expectation of developing one way, and the mystery of something altogether different.

Many people who reinvent themselves, by class or economic or academic improvement, *better themselves*, in a term from April's early years, often obliterate their past, their antecedents, yet April gloried in being from Liverpool and being from the rough end of the city. Never a pronoun fascist, she also never 'killed' George banning his name from her conversation or his life from her memory. Late in the evening, she'd talk of him in the third person and, in a surreal way, continue to be concerned for the boy who suffered everything but spots.

The seamanship training, literally learning the ropes, and tying herself in knots, navigating by the stars, involved living in close quarters with other boys and their shared ambition to be proper sailors fostered good companionship. The camaraderie led to more shipping contacts and the soon to be seventeen-year-old George's life as a sailor began in the early part of 1952 which, a little short of seventy years later, she told me marked the fledgling start of her epic life journey. The end of denial.

I went off, ran off to sea, to be something I was not and, in the process, discovered who I had to be. It was revelatory.

Yet threatening, and almost cost her life. On board the S.S. *Pacific Fortune*, which had taken to the high seas out of the Manchester Ship Canal, George was bunked up in a cabin with other young lads who had ambitions of a girl in every port. The sex banter was unhelpful, the work menial, scrubbing decks and dogsbody for the mess, serving food, washing dishes, cleaning, but the locations delivered exotic.

> I was trying to prove how masculine I was. Instead of getting into the catering department which I should have done, which would have been much easier, I decided to go for the rough part and be a sailor where you do all the dangerous jobs, hanging over the side of the ship painting it in the middle of the ocean and getting ready to bring the ship into port, spick and span.

They sailed to the Caribbean, through the Panama Canal and up the Pacific Coast to Los Angeles and San Francisco. The close living quarters induced an increasingly sequestered atmosphere, George acutely aware of his budding breasts.

With my body developing in the way that it was, I wouldn't shower. The others kept asking me why I didn't strip off to wash. It made me queasy.

Being a sailor was job enough. There weren't enough moments in any day, time alone was as rationed as the rum, and at sea George seemed to be first up, on parade as it were, and last to bed. The young seamen were naturally easygoing and helpful if need be. The older shipmates included some lairy characters and there were fights and attacks when they returned from drink-sodden shore leave.

They came in blind drunk, and they wanted to have a bit of fun. I was a hapless, hopeless, and truly innocent teenager. And I didn't know what I was. But they really liked the look of me. Clearly, they were after sex. I think I might have gone to bed with a man had he asked me to. It probably would have been more like fiddling around. In truth, it would have been homosexual sex, but not in my mind. I was going through this, knowing I should be one thing. I always say that if I'd gone to those men and told them I was having problems, those men would have been superb. They would have stood by me. They were mostly Scots, Jocks, so proud and marvellous. I didn't ask for help – how could I? What would I have said – 'I want to be a woman?'

The further the S.S. *Pacific Fortune* sailed, the more April was all at sea. Her mental health was in turmoil, her eyes startle as she recalls it, and she felt her head bloated, filled with air like a balloon, the pressure soaring as she expected to suddenly explode. Some nights she got no sleep, and her shipmates noticed the zombie-like behaviour of what they didn't know was a breathless soul, exhausted of running away. Food became something to remember, and eating was often too much of an effort. Like life itself.

On shore in San Pedro, the Port of Los Angeles, she found a California governed by the Eisenhower-for-President-supporting Earl Warren (he would head the Warren Commission into the 1963 assassination of President John F. Kennedy), where the moral guidelines were as neat and sharp as a military crew cut. This was the land where men were men, something that amused April when she met a *very lovely and very gay* Marlboro Man some years later, and George Reeves was the original television *Superman*. April said when she first saw Reeves walk into a telephone box and change in a moment from Clark Kent to the Man of Steel she fantasised about doing the same and flying off into the heavens, the ultimate escape as she saw it, but was trapped in an altogether different box. It was a long time ago and attitudes were as black-and-white as the television programmes.

Somehow, in the wide sidewalks of San Pedro, up the streets and away from the water, the lost teenager George found a doctor's surgery on West 6th Street and had the dollars to pay for a consultation. April admitted to being foolhardy, not having a clue what to say or what to expect, and admitted the medic could have been Doctor Who from what she could recall, as her mind was in such turmoil.

He appears to have been more patient than we might have expected for emerging post-war California. He did suggest the desire to be a woman was a madness. For that, in doctor default, while rejecting payment, he prescribed pills (*It wasn't aspirin, darling*), helpful sleeping tablets but also anti-depressants of which April could not remember the dose or make or much else other than there were plenty of them. The California doctor also suggested psychiatry on return to the UK. But April said she didn't know a psychiatrist from a physiotherapist. She knew and understood pills. If you took enough of them, you died. That was a plan and, quite clinically, April could recount her determination, as she put it, of doing away with herself and saving the world a great deal of trouble.

Later, she accepted that the world is generally disinterested in most of us or our actions. April always insisted trying to kill herself was not a cry for help but a resolute escape plan. It was, she said, in that moment, the only solution. She decided to commit suicide aboard ship. Powering down a combination of pills with glasses of water she went woozy and waited to die. On discovering her, the ship's crew called a priest but only to give her a talking-to as she recovered at a hospital in next door Long Beach.

Her ship had sailed, the S.S. *Fortune* had left port and, after weeks cared for in a sailors' charitable mission, she became well enough to be a tourist, taking the bus the twenty-five miles up the coast to Hollywood where George the schoolboy had written he always wanted to be a star.

This respite in the sunshine ended and with the shipping line meeting the costs, 'fragile Jamieson' followed the S.S. *Fortune* by air and sea and a train to Liverpool and returned to work in the increasingly diverse St John's Market, to be nervously reunited with disinterested Ada and, more flamboyantly, with childhood friend Tommy Robbins. Socialising was a hazard.

The night life was being beaten up and murdered.

Three

Liver Birds

'A Frenchman named Chamfort, who should
have known better, once said that chance was
the nickname for Providence.'
The Mask of Dimitrios, Eric Ambler, 1939

In everyone's life there's a moment when fate is a companion.
How else do the most remarkable things happen? The
still relentlessly confused George Jamieson, disguising his
developing body with overcoats and oversized shirts and
sweaters, bundling himself up to hide from the world, spent
most evenings jumping into a bottle of something and pulling
the cork in afterwards. These post-war forays around town
in the clubs when the pubs closed, afforded encounters with
those on the edge, the gay community, consenting adults or
not, an illegal group until 1967, and men dressing as women
and someone who, like eighteen-year-old George, desperately
wanted to be a woman. What were the chances of two scousers
from the back streets of the city being transsexual pioneers?
And childhood friends?

It was on the riverside, at the gathering spot which Liverpool's
Pier Head had become, that George Jamieson, a confusion on
two legs with longish, luxuriant dark hair, extra-large jacket
and baggy trousers, no makeup, and proud, long eyelashes,
saw and finally recognised a gloriously dressed and elaborately

made up Tommy Robbins. The smiley-faced schoolboy was a star of the Pier Head, the landmark fronting the Royal Liver and Cunard buildings, transformed as the ebullient *Little Gloria* which was a misnomer regarding the voice, a hallelujah of orchestral vowels.

April recalled being gladdened and repelled by the reunion, happy to be with a fellow traveller but disquieted by the enormity of the journey they were on. Also, she recalled, by the grotesque aspect of Little Gloria, as April saw it, a caricature of a woman – was this all there was? She didn't mind applying makeup (*always the eyebrows, darling*) but determined to never appear as a woman, in drag, unless she could truly be one. So, what was the point? They might just as well jump off a cliff. Or in the Mersey which rushed alongside them. It was, she recalled, the utter futility of it all, of her life, her circumstances and her absolute depression at seeing no way out, that made her do just that late one evening.

Her inelegant leap into the water got publicity and, like everything, she kept her press cutting from the *Liverpool Echo*, which excitedly reported about the young man saved from the River Mersey by a passerby who yanked the choking, hapless lad to safety by his long hair. It also got George a bed in the Ormskirk Mental Hospital, in a dull white-painted specialist ward shared with more troubled souls who before their morning and evening medications were given to raging at themselves and the world. George was on suicide watch; the lights stayed on around the clock, doors were locked and windows barred, there was nothing sharp, there were crayons to write with, paper cups and dishes, and there was seemingly no one to care.

They put me in the loony bin for being unhappy.

April said her release was very much a parole arrangement. Ada Jamieson signed the formal paperwork which allowed George to live at home but legally committed him to at least twenty-four months of outpatient treatment in the psychiatric ward of the then 'forward-looking' Walton Hospital,

Derbyshire. The tricks of the 1950s mind doctors, the men in white coats, were all tried. Surprisingly, more scientific versions than some twenty-first-century conversion therapy which leans more toward exorcism than understanding. Still, it was crude. April squirmed remembering being pumped with male hormones and questions about wanting to be female. The doctors, she said, appeared to think she was a homosexual with a fetish; no matter how much she attempted to explain – and it was difficult enough explaining to herself – how she had to be a true woman or die, the medics would circle back to her *homosexual attractions*. That she didn't have any wasn't the answer they wanted and exasperated them. They tried sodium thiopental, which swiftly treats acute anxiety – for many years it was the pre-injection drug before a lethal injection in American death penalty cases – and supposedly made patients tell the truth. It made no difference, and April is smiling as she tells it because her story never changed. It wasn't her truth but the whole truth.

They were so arrogant to believe they could 'cure' me when they hadn't a clue that I, along with so many others as it turned out, wasn't a misfit but victim of a gender anomaly. I want to be a woman, I repeated. They said I was mad.

But sane enough to be moved to a public ward where, what later seemed to April to be gothic torture equipment, was rolled alongside a fearful George's bed. It was the start of electro-convulsive therapy (ECT). Today it is administered with muscle relaxants and anaesthetic to literally relieve the shock. In 1953, they believed in a full blast to 'cure' schizophrenia and epilepsy and 'mental disorders'. Young George, they diagnosed, needed shaking up. And badly was, strapped to the bed, the ECT was administered with no relaxants or anaesthetic, electric current going between two electrodes on his head, causing a seizure. The thinking was that, as the patient instantly lost consciousness, there was no need for the modifying drugs. ECT methods had only been used in the UK for a dozen years when April suffered her treatment, repeated three time a week for several months. She said that every time she felt *a flash* to her system, like being punched by Mike Tyson she was out of it for some hours. She said there was some ego glee about the ECT technicians and the doctors, they were moving with the times, trailblazers. The result for their patient was a constantly aching head and agitated, kicking legs throughout the night.

> They thought they had a genius cure; they were splitting the atom. I still wanted to be a woman. That was the very first time when I was strapped to a bed and having electric shock treatment that I was able to talk about feeling I *was* a woman. It wasn't what they wanted to hear. When the doctors in the loony bin told me, 'Go away and be gay,' I said, 'I'm not a homosexual. I need to be a woman.'

George Jamieson left Derbyshire, ambiguous identity intact, and returned to Liverpool and the perils of Pauline, Little Gloria, Hazel, Raquel and Talulah, wanting to be 'straight' among this clan of increasingly more outrageous friends. It was difficult, she said, especially as then she did not want to be *different* – she wanted to be a woman but, unlike her new crowd, wasn't prepared to pose as one. Dressing up as a woman wasn't ever going to be enough. Not in public, anyway, but she told me she would 'borrow' dresses from the market stalls and try them on, anxious to know how April as a woman would look; she said she relaxed in those private fantasy moments, got lost in her dreams but suddenly, without thought, would snap back to depressing reality.

Approached all the time, she had no interest in homosexual activity either in a relationship or behind the market stalls. She was attracted to some men, but as a woman; an equation with some difficulty in solving.

Not even Einstein could figure that out, darling.

The maestro of energy, mass and the speed of light, $E=mc^2$, might have tried, if she'd asked him. April insisted their meeting of minds happened in 1953 in an Italian café in Soho a few weeks after she'd abandoned Liverpool for what she saw as the freedom of London. In what is now her legendary story, Einstein was sipping coffee and April, soaring on Benzedrine and Smirnoff, recognised him. He was bemused by her androgynous appearance and, chemically emboldened, April asked for his autograph – half a dozen copies. And got them.

In all her stories of the fatuous and fabulous people she met, she always seemed most pleased with Albert Einstein and Marlene Dietrich. Maybe because they both said that with her eyelashes she looked like Madama Butterfly. Recognising, on a rainy afternoon on Dean Street, the hunched figure of the seventy-four-year-old scientist, was a fondly recalled and regularly heralded, and prized coup. That day she rushed off west to the Earl's Court flat she was camping out at, to tell all to her friend and fellow Liverpudlian, Ronnie. He'd convinced April to make the move to London, her *decree nisi* with her mother and Liverpool, and a world of weak tea, spilled coffee, and watery scrambled eggs when they landed dogsbody jobs at Lyons Corner House.

> Ronnie was a platonic friend. I loved him. He was gay but incredibly conservative. He dressed conservatively, mentally he was conservative, but he was very funny and tremendously kind to me. We became great pals. I don't want to sound like that awful butler chap of Princess Diana, but Ronnie was my rock. I met all these gay people and Ronnie and I sort of fell in with them.

Their HQ, for a time, was a flat at the southeast end of Redcliffe Gardens where it meets Fulham Road, central for gatherings of their friends scattered around grimy Earl's Court and the warren of streets crisscrossing Chelsea and Fulham.

> We were thrown out of there because of the noise. It was hysterical. You never knew when your things were going

to be stolen. Ronnie truly was someone to hang on to. He was solid, someone to confide in, to trust, which was most difficult to find. I don't think I would have had the courage for London without him.

Or a future, as it turned out. April always took a moment when talking about this nomadic time of her life, citing the need for, and gently mocking the ubiquitous American 'comfort break'. It was a sliding-doors moment for permanent change followed. Little Gloria, a.k.a. Tommy Robbins, who spent two spells in the merchant navy, arrived in London and a similar crowd gathered around him and April. Little Gloria wasn't one for working and operated a shoplifting routine – one bottle of booze for the party, the other to sell for cash – and moving stolen cheques. Tommy was more Gloria now, dressing fulltime as a woman and became a 'working girl' around Bayswater Road. There's one incident recorded by the Metropolitan Police of Gloria being arrested for prostitution and 'impersonating a woman'. Prescience wasn't considered mitigation.

April watched Little Gloria's progress with alarm, unaware then that Gloria's sense of being was as devoted as her own. They were a little like nonidentical twins in their pursuit of true being and happiness, uplifted by the delusion of the woman inside them magically coming to life. It bred a certain selfishness, as after a bereavement it seems hideously unfair that the world can keep turning, behaving as normal, without your loved one. April was careful, always careful, with money and adored spending other people's. She called me *Champagne Charlie* after I arrived one evening with a case for her birthday, and she expected me to always live up to that name. She was also a tremendous hard worker and put in the hours at Lyons Corner House.

Ronnie and I worked seven days a week, and we were a team clearing tables and worked all hours and if they wanted us to work overtime, oh, yes, we'd work overtime. We would work like fury – the Benzedrine, darling – racing around, cleaning and handing out free cups of tea to those we thought in need. Everybody was always smiling in the wee hours. The Benzedrine inhalers ['Bennies' became prescription-only later in 1965] kept us flying high.

It was by train that she and Ronnie headed home for Christmas 1953, happily singing '(How Much is That) Doggie in the Window?', a UK No. 1 hit recorded by Liverpudlian Lita Roza, as they rattled along toward Lime Street.

Sitting with me in her garden in the south of France, she sang a couple of verses to focus her memory. She said she was regressing to the happy train journey, the run-up to her arrival home.

All my life, and I know where this comes from, I've adored giving gifts. Things to create memories. I was eleven years old before I got my first present off my mother, which was a pair of grey socks. She said, 'I have a birthday present for you.' We never got Christmas presents or birthday presents. My father never gave me anything but tall tales. I was at school that day and I couldn't concentrate – Mother had got me a birthday present! 'Oh, my gosh, my mother has got me a present.' I was so over the moon. I thought it would be marvellous. When school finished, I was home like the wind. My mother handed me a brown paper packet with a pair of grey socks. I thought, 'I will never in my life ever give anybody that kind of present.'

Going back that Christmas, I determined to take presents for all my family starting with a huge bunch of chocolates for Mother. I was careful about what I was wearing, and I think it must have been slightly bold, because the jacket had to be a boy's jacket but the colours

– it was blue with little flecks of red in it – were extravagant. We got off the train at Liverpool Lime Street and jumped on the tram car and it was quite a way from there.

I got home and I knocked on the door and they said, 'Oh you're home for Christmas, are you?'

I said, 'Yes.' I said, 'Oh, Mother, look what I've got you?'

She said, 'I'll put them in my bottom drawer.' Same old thing, nothing had changed, nothing at all. My brothers I bought, I can't remember what I bought, but nice things. She didn't offer me a cup of tea. Nothing.

I said, 'Mother, you have to open your gift ...'

She said, 'No, I'll put it in the bottom ...'

I said, 'Mother, you can't do that.' In the end I said, 'Mother, it's chocolate. Very, very expensive chocolate.'

She said, 'I'll put them in the bottom drawer.'

It's about nine o'clock in the evening and I'm starving. I haven't been offered anything to eat or drink and I'd made myself tea. I couldn't find a biscuit – I should have hoovered up Mother's bloody chocolates.

Then my younger brother Ivor said to me, 'Get yourself ready, we're going to go to midnight mass.'

I said to him, 'Since when did you become a Catholic? You've never gone to church in your life.' He said he was going to mass, and I said, 'I'm not. I'm finished with the Roman Catholic church. Absolutely finished.' Well, he hit me in the face so hard I thought I'd lost all my teeth.

Ivor, when we were younger, I kicked him up the bum so hard I'm sure he lifted off the ground. He couldn't walk for three days. He was always kicking me. He was a tough little thing, and I was very fragile. He was always kicking me, and we wore clogs of course.

I saw my mother and I said to her, 'Mother, what's Ivor going on about midnight mass?'

She said, 'You're going to midnight mass.'

I said, 'You two, you're Protestants. You're not even a Catholic. What are you talking about?' I said, 'I don't want anything to do with the Roman Catholic church.'

She said, 'You are going to do as you are told and you're going to go to mass.'

I said, 'No, I am not.' So, my brother hit me again. I turned round and I said to him, 'You hit me one more time and I will kill you!'

Finally, my mother hit me and said, 'Get out of my house and never come back again.'

I didn't. I left all the presents, picked up my little suitcase and I went. I was so desperately unhappy. I didn't even think about taking the tram car. I walked all the way to Ronnie's house, which must have been about five or six miles. You know, the moment I knocked on the door, Ronnie said, 'I know what's happened. Come on in, you can spend Christmas with us.' I slept on the sofa.

Then the moment Christmas was over, I said to Ronnie, 'I've finished with my family, there's just no hope. I'm going back to London now and I'm going to spend New Year on the town and then I'm going straight to work, back to Lyons.' My age? Seventeen? Eighteen? It didn't matter. I was all grown up.

We went back to London and one day I'm sitting there having a coffee at a table and this very glamorous girl talked to me and said, 'How would you like to work in an office? How much do you get paid here?', and I told her. She said, 'I am going to have another word with my boss about you.' She went off and then came back and said, 'Would you like to work in a theatrical office?'

I said, 'What, without an interview?' I asked what I was going to be doing. I didn't know anything about the theatre.

She said, 'Well, mostly you would be running the actors from one agent to another, you'll be helping me with press.'

With the divorce decree with her family all but absolute, this was a new sort of family where even the fake sincerity was warming. The J. Roland theatrical agency on London's Charing Cross Road had a new employee for whom a lifetime of mixing with celebrity began with meetings with the bountiful Diana Dors, emerging film star and Britain's antidote to Hollywood platinum. April recalled initially being rather censorious about Diana Dors and her Cadillac embossed with double-D initials and matching cleavage, but the actress was much more welcoming and down to earth than appearances allowed. She'd appeared in *Lady Godiva Rides Again* (1951), with other names April would encounter – Kay Kendall, Joan Collins in her film debut and the usual comic suspects of the 1950s – Alastair Sim, George Cole, Stanley Holloway, Sid James and Dennis Price. Given her personal identity turbulence, it was remarkable how April easily joined such a glittery constituency. It was a confidence bred, she said, of building her life from scratch after being disowned by her family. She said the Rank starlets she met showed bravado but inside they were as terrified of rejection, of not being accepted for this or that role. Which wasn't dissimilar to her place in life. From them she learned how to act a part.

Dors met a scheming rogue called Dennis Hamilton and five weeks later married him at Westminster's Caxton Hall on 3 July 1951. Hamilton was a control freak and she was a little wary of making new friends, but she became fond of April and in 1973 recalled their meetings: 'When we met, everybody always stared at April. She was intriguing, a mystery – Kim and I had no inkling of what was going on inside her.' 'Kim' was Michael 'Dandy Kim' Caborn-Waterfield, a longtime close friend of Diana Dors and an incorrigible playboy about town.

Over lunch in 2004 he told me, 'I saw April around the theatricals and I think then she was calling herself "Toni", a world, a lifetime away from the *grand dame* she'd become. I thought she was a beautiful-looking boy and as such not of interest to me. I should have paid more attention – in 1972 I married the former wife of her one-time boyfriend, a chap who wanted to marry her. Now that is one for the tea kettle, one to stew over. In the 1950s London was a village where everyone knew everyone else and partied around the clock. Benzedrine is what kept so many of the crowd going until dawn. I understand now how brave she was to put herself forward, for we're all curious, and even in a crazy time she instantly captured attention.'

In the grand theatre of gender everybody looked at April. April saw only Diana Fluck from Swindon being Diana Dors, *blonde bombshell* film star. Almost everyone she met appeared to be working at being someone else.

> She was very glamorous and fun. Suddenly, life became quite interesting. You were able to forget a little bit about your unhappiness. It was so lovely to spend time with movie stars like her and Marlene Dietrich.

Oh, yes, that'll be the legendary Marlene Dietrich. Through her theatrical agency work, April met a producer called Duncan Melvin who, with his friend Major Donald Neville-Willing, looked after Dietrich when she was in Britain. Neville-Willing – in theatrical circles known as 'Ever-Willing' – was camp and a model for the outrageous character Denis Quilley played in Peter Nichols' *Privates On Parade* on stage and the film in 1983.

Neville-Willing was also an Entertainments National Service Association (ENSA) producer responsible for bringing the nightclub Café de Paris, on Coventry Street, Piccadilly, back to life after the war. Famously, when it originally opened in 1924, Louise Brooks, who performed there, made dance history by introducing the Charleston to London. The heir to the throne was a regular, as were the Aga Khan, Marlene Dietrich and Cole Porter. Many patrons danced with the man who danced with the girl who danced with the Prince of Wales before he abdicated to become the Duke of Windsor. On

8 March 1941, two blitz bombs fell into the basement ballroom. They dropped down a ventilation shaft and exploded in front of the stage, killing more than thirty people and severely injuring eighty others. Following this carnage, Neville-Willing made it his mission to resurrect the club, which he did in 1948, as one of the grand theatre spots in London.

Dietrich and Noël Coward returned and showcased their cabaret acts and Neville-Willing lured new names such as Frank Sinatra, Grace Kelly and the emerging British comedian Tony Hancock. Ever-Willing knew everybody and it was to the Press crowd at the Café de Paris that April, who'd spent five hours getting 'dressed' for the moment, handed out the publicity material before Dietrich's arrival on 21 June 1954.

> Marlene appeared and there was amazement. She was incredibly beautiful. She was quite a character and she was totally fascinated by me. I could feel this woman, who wrapped herself in a great big white fur coat, staring at me.

Half a century later, as an afternoon interlude as she told me this story in France, April played a selection from a CD pressing from the recording made that night. We heard Noël Coward introducing Dietrich and April's favourites – Edith Piaf's signature song, 'La Vie en Rose', 'The Boys in the Back Room' and, with April crooning, 'Falling in Love Again'. Life in the pink, indeed.

It was claret-shaded in 1954 in London when Ronnie moved on and April was hot-bedding from flat to flat with all around her desperately trying to pay the rent, find the shillings to feed the insatiable gas meter. There were crazy days and dangerous ones flirting with the law and trying to keep ahead in a transient life. She escaped to the Channel Islands to work in a clifftop hotel opposite the sixty-two-foot-high lighthouse at La Corbière, which sits on a tidal island out at sea, surrounded by dark and historically shipwrecking rocks. At low tide, April walked the causeway, which is equipped with an alarm to warn visitors when the water is dangerously rising, out to the lighthouse.

It was part of her enjoyment at La Corbière, such fun that she invited some of her London friends to join her. It sounds a madcap and at times hysteria-driven adventure with this zany crowd taking great advantage and plundering the hotel at every moment. April would have none of that.

I got off to a wonderful start when I met Mr and Mrs Grimshaw who owned the hotel. She was a very pretty woman who said, 'Well, you'll be living in the hotel on your own because there's only one free room. Is that all right?' I said, 'Oh, that's fine.' They were just the nicest couple in the world, and they adored me. Of course, the moment they'd leave at night, all my pals would be waiting and we would be partying all night. I had to do the bar and everything. They just kept giving me more and more money. It was marvellous. I made friends with all the lighthouse people and took drinks over to them and I'd never want to leave.

They'd say, 'You'd better get back now the tide is coming in.' There were so many times we were almost swept away. I worked for the whole summer and then Mrs Grimshaw left him for another man. And he was such a nice man. We went back to London and of course it was the same old rigmarole.

With one crucial complication. Maybe the wine, the sunshine and Dietrich's 'Falling in Love Again' combined to make her more emotional that day but she revealed the identity and the depth of her passion for the one man she wanted to marry. It wasn't often you saw April's eyes gallop away, but she was very much in a what-might-have-been mood, of eluded happenstance.

The one I'd wanted to marry, you see, was the one I'd been in love with from the age of nineteen, Tony Thimber, a Jewish boy. We had an affair that lasted more than twenty-two years. Through two of his wives. He was one of the two men I loved, the only one I wanted to marry. He was my first love and I adored him. I was madly in love with him and when he met me, he thought I was a girl. George Jamieson was dead, and I was calling myself Toni. When he found out I wasn't, he wouldn't speak to me for weeks and weeks and weeks. Then one night, I was running the hotel in La Corbière hotel, and there he is at the bar. Wow. He said, 'I don't know what it is, but I can't get you out of my mind.' Then we became lovers in a strange way and I fell madly in love.

It was a strange thing because he wouldn't touch me anywhere. It was just a very strange relationship. A relationship? Oh, yes, but he wouldn't touch me. He would hardly kiss me. Emotionally, when you're in love with someone you accept anything. It's a strange thing, love. There's only two people I've ever loved. I was in awe of another man but not in love. Tony was well ... I would have walked off a cliff for him. It was strange because he would disappear all the time, so I'd see him for a week or so and then he'd be gone. He would never tell me where he'd go and when I was in London once I heard that he had broken his back. I went to hospital where he was at, Golders Green or somewhere like that, and he was furious with me. He said, 'You will have to leave right now; my family are coming. You must get out right now.' He threw me out of the hospital right there and then. He said, 'I don't want my family seeing you.'

I did bump into his sister in 1982 and asked how he was, and she told me, 'Oh, you two, when you're eighty-two, you'll still be jumping in and out of bed together.'

He did pop in and out of my life as you'll see. Would he have married me after Casablanca? The operation was absolutely for my happiness. I didn't think that maybe once I had the operation, he might marry me. No. The operation had nothing to do with it. That was for me, for my life, no one else's.

She swore that by then, although she had no map, she was on the road to Casablanca. With Tony – *what a wonderful silliness, Toni and Tony* – constantly in her thoughts she returned to London and luckily found a place to stay through a friend who worked at the Windmill Theatre on Great Windmill Street, twenty yards and a couple of steps up Shaftesbury Avenue from Piccadilly Circus. April would watch the early afternoon crowd from 2.30 p.m. gathering for the first presentation – performance is way too active a word – of the delights of the Windmill Girls. The identikit girls, with faces layered from the same makeup pot, displayed nude bodies which had not wilted on wartime rations. They were built for comfort. And motion, but that was against the law. The Lord Chamberlain, Lord Cromer, had acknowledged the argument that statues which depicted nudity could not be called obscene and prosecuted. Therefore, the Windmill could present their ladies in motionless poses. Wonderfully absurd, as so often, the law: if something moves – it's rude.

The audiences paid to view the glamorous girls arranged with some care in exotic *tableaux vivants*, living statues; this was artistic material and the shows were themed. The mermaids were obvious, the Annie Oakley *tableaux* of the wild west firecracker and friends most inventive.

I asked my friend, 'What happens if their tits wobble?'
   'Jiggle!' she said.
   'But what happens if their tits move? How does anyone know?'

'The police are there 'til' closing time. They get a good front seat and a nice drink by midnight. There's never been any problems.'

As ever, April saw life was a compromise. We were in a taxi going to lunch in South Kensington and stop-starting along Gloucester Road, when she pointed out the branch of Waitrose which brought back memories of Liverpool's St John's Market and her bicycle delivery days; it was where she'd worked slicing bacon, thin rashers, wearing what she said was a cute and delicate apron which she'd taken as part of her minimalist wardrobe. She earned enough to move from the Windmill girl's basement to a flat Little Gloria had found for her four minutes from Earl's Court Tube, a far cry from Muriel Spark's Kensington but room for her one small suitcase of possessions. The block of flats was a menagerie of mayhem, a world of larger-than-life characters who knew a potential benefactor's bank balance details as accurately as their inside leg measurement.

To this life on the edges flocked a galaxy of sly operators, the most intriguing grifters and hustlers, bandits and tricksters, mavericks and crooks, rotters and rogues, drag artists and scam artists, the chiselers and clip artists, the desperate good-time boys and girls, happy with ten bob and a thank-you, and the sophisticates expecting rather more for similar services and promising better hygiene and conversation.

I kept pulling the curtain down but, oh, it snapped up again and the band played on. But, like musical chairs, when the music stopped ...

Circumstances, as in lack of funds and demanding landlords, prompted a return to the Channel Islands and for the summer of 1956 April again found herself running a hotel, employing all her friends once more.

At the end of the season, because I had done such a good job, they gave me a good bonus. I thought, Now I'm going to have a holiday, and I went to the south of France. I had these friends there and they said, 'You must go and work at the Le Carrousel nightclub in Paris, where it's legendary for female impersonators.' I told them that I could never be like that. This was the winter of 1957 and they ended up driving me back to Paris and taking me to the Le Carrousel where my jaw dropped. This was why they brought me to Paris. To see for myself. At first, I couldn't believe my eyes. No, it couldn't be – these men were women, these women were men … no, it couldn't be. It was inside out.

Live at the Café de Paris, Marlene Dietrich.

Teenaged George Jamieson.

April centre stage at Le Carrousel.

Le Carrousel players in mufti.

Bambi, who April regarded as a true friend.

Pre-op April with her French 'mum' – Bambi's mother.

Coccinelle, the Grand Dame of Le Carrousel.

Bambi at the beach.

April styled for the flower power sixties.

The cover of Sarah Churchill's poetry collection, *The Empty Spaces*.

April and Arthur Corbett in the *Sunday Pictorial*.

A note on the back of a photograph referring to the opening of
April's new restaurant.

Menu

Gazpacho
Tomato and Basil Croutons

Steamed Salmon with Pesto
New Potatoes

Manchego Viejo, Arrigoni Taleggio,
Goat Gouda, Cignicora
with poppy and sesame thins

To drink
Alessandro Gallici Prosecco Doe
Bellinis

Archidamo. Re di Sparta
Primitivo di Manduria 2011

Andy Warhol's signature on the menu of April's restaurant.

PART TWO

Adam and Eve

'To be, or not to be, that is the question.'

**_Hamlet_, act III, scene
1, William Shakespeare, 1599**

Four

Sixth Sense

'It was the best of times, it was the worst of times, it was the age of wisdom, it was the age of foolishness ...'
A Tale of Two Cities, Charles Dickens, 1859

April Ashley arrived in Paris as the Fourth Republic was disintegrating and about to transform into the Fifth and the control of the beak-nosed General Charles De Gaulle, soldier, statesman and patriot, who believed himself the only person with a chance of saving France from economic catastrophe. April admired his self-esteem and formality which jarred somewhat with the new age of 'all-about-me', fashionable existentialism.

Yet, for all the Albert Camus and Jean-Paul Sartre chatter, the intellectual idea of the oneness of the individual in their own universe, April was an avid reader of the then-broad-sheet *Daily Mail*, attracted by the high satire cartoon strip *Flook*, drawn by the taciturn Wally Fawkes, whom she met at a party hosted by Donald Neville-Willing. Flook's special ability was to change into anything or anybody he might want to be and play a part in events like the late Queen's coronation. April bragged she was ahead of sixties' philosopher Marshall McLuhan in believing the medium is the message. On stage at Le Carrousel, in full makeup and gown, she fervently broadcast what she intended to be. She was single minded.

Live or die, darling.

Her needs were not unique but how she dealt with them was. By the time de Gaulle assumed the presidency in 1959, April shared his assurance, albeit initially nervous on stage. The politics of France, like the politics of Le Carrousel, were challenging but she'd harshly learned diplomacy in life and in debate along the open-air sidewalk cafés where she was dressing as a woman and calling herself Toni and then elaborating to Toni April.

Transition places a person on a lifetime tightrope; it's a living legacy, at every stage anxious, wary, scared of being one thing and not the other, burdened by the overwhelming desire to be someone else and the everyday challenge of being regarded as ridiculous while doing some such thing as casually walking to the corner shop to buy a bottle of milk.

Trapped in one body, targeted in another, the impact of what you are living with, while navigated by others, is inordinately on you. Indeed, who are you? Listening to April and others who leaped across the gender border, it sounds like living on a crumbling bridge. Which way to run?

For April, and seamlessly, the camaraderie of Le Carrousel provided a protective cocoon, and ongoing distractions, which evolved from 1926 when the club opened as a cabaret theatre called Chez Josephine at 40 rue Pierre Fontaine, near the Moulin Rouge. The name was an early salutation to the legendary black entertainer Josephine Baker, given by the club's founder, Sicilian Guiseppe Pepito Abatino, who was her manager and lover. Three decades later, Baker, who arrived in Paris aged nineteen, as April did, was still regarded as the epitome of stage extravagance.

The legend fascinated the newcomer: Josephine Baker shook up Paris with her erotic and all but nude dancing at the Folies Bergère, entertainment which that other star of the jazz age, Scott Fitzgerald, would hold as 'some not too plebeian, yet not too artistic fun'. There were other more exasperated reviews in

1927 of Baker's revue, *Un Vent de Folie*, when she danced in a tiny skirt comprising a string of artificial bananas and a beaded necklace. Her act involved a 'pet' cheetah called Chiquita who, fangs flashing, contributed added frisson by escaping into the orchestra pit. It couldn't overshadow the exotic Josephine Baker who became a heroic wartime intelligence agent working with de Gaulle's Free French. Hemingway was a fan, Picasso painted her, Jean Cocteau promoted her and April, on hearing all the stories, was desperate to meet her. Which turned out not to be a difficulty. Trickier, was convincing Monsieur Marcel Lasquin, in 1958 the show manager of Le Carrousel, of her qualifications for twelve pounds a week employment.

> He didn't believe I was a boy! I said, 'Well, I am a half and …' He wanted to see my passport. I got my passport out and he studied it and said, 'Can you sing?'
> I said, 'No.'
> He said, 'Do you dance?'
> I said, 'No.'
> He said, 'What *can* you do?'
> I said, 'Nothing.'
> He stared me up and down and said, 'You've got a job.'

Being a boy was essential to the job description: from 1936 Le Carrousel was a club showcasing cabaret by female impersonators. When April made her entrance, she never simply arrived anywhere – several of the performers were talking about or intent on becoming much more than impersonators.

Before the club became known for transgender acts in the late fifties and into the sixties, most entertainers were *transformistes*, performers who dressed as men off-stage and had no interest in transition. Yet, at Le Carrousel they aimed to provide glamour and sexual tease rather than the English music-hall, nonsensical, *cod drag* artists who strayed close to outrage for audience belly laughs. Aren't-they-or-are-they and lavish servings of razzle-dazzle proved much more marketable. Le Carrousel, governed by strict fire regulations, most reluctantly turned away custom every night.

> When I would come out, people would say, 'Ah, my God, no it can't be ...' The audience were amazed, even the regulars and there were many of them. You didn't buy a ticket, you bought a bottle of champagne or some drinks. It was more expensive than the Moulin Rouge. It was much more expensive than any of the big theatres because it was so avant-garde. People couldn't believe what they saw, they were saying that it couldn't possibly be true. 'They *must* be women.' All the big French stars came and the rest – where else could you tickle the bum of Rex Harrison and Elvis? Or get a miser like Bob Hope to buy a drink?

Audiences would have been more astonished if they'd been allowed a glimpse behind the scenes where hysteria often screamed over a purloined fake eyelash or a missing diamanté-encrusted thong. April laughed along with her stories but swore that she often expected murder in the dressing room, tucked away, like the performers' external genitalia, out of sight from the audience.

The claustrophobic dressing area, split in two with glaring downlight, spotlighted mirrors, crowded with rails of gowns and the talent shrieking like parrots and playing competitive contact sport for back to-back, wobbly stools between velvet chairs with antimacassars, was its own theatre, away from the flamboyant floor show which played most nights to a full house of more than one hundred sitting at stupidly small tables and on uncomfortable seats as though doing penance for their pleasure.

Often in Hollywood movies, they titillate audiences with the camera creeping along backstage as showgirls in collective stages of undress display an eyeful of breast or the glimpse of a bum, but this was altogether different. Here for, as April described them, the *chicks with dicks*, the big dressing-room scene was the relief of freedom as off came their wigs and the paraphernalia constricting them.

One guy had the most enormous whanger. He'd chase us around the dressing room waving it at us.

That would be Les Lee, John Falk Tomlinson, from Quebec and an eminent *transformiste,* a graduate of the San Francisco drag club Finocchio's, he arrived in Paris in 1954 and never left, dying there, aged eighty-one, in 2010, much to April's sadness. He was her unofficial mentor as he'd been to many of the 'girls' and, with his fluent French from Montreal, he helped with contracts and negotiations with Monsieur Lasquin, a French-Algerian often preoccupied by the ongoing Algerian War. Lasquin was acutely aware of politics, and secrets were never far from Le Carrousel.

For whatever their seemingly illogical reasoning, the Paris police shut the club down for three months in 1954 after France was ignominiously defeated by Vietnamese troops at Dien Bien Phu in the First Indochina War. The manager didn't want a repeat with the Algerian National Liberation Front so active in 1958 Paris. His fears were translated by Les Lee on April's arrival, but her focus was on closer to home, practical matters – convincingly becoming a woman on the club's small stage. Silicone and oestrogen treatments provided extravagant embonpoint for some performers, some outrageously so, but not for April, whose enhanced décolletage was modest, but below decks was an altogether different consideration.

With my penis being what it was, concealing it wasn't a bother. Les Lee's huge thing had to be tucked between his legs and they had special straps made for him. All I had to do was wear a tight girdle. They said I looked a dream in a backless dress; what I did was use ordinary plaster and just tape myself down. In a skintight dress, you couldn't wear underwear, or it would show, and the tape did the necessary. I was, again, marvellously lucky to get to work there because it showed you all the different shades of the drag queens, the female impersonators and the would-be transsexuals. That, of course, was more helpful than anything.

And puzzling: one performer who didn't want to transition had incredibly generous implants and was content. It was a complex world. April had no interest in being a man with breasts stuck on but now in Paris she was Toni April: tall, elfin in that her body was lean and athletic, and those who knew her then say she had a grace of movement. She intentionally modelled this 'look' on Audrey Hepburn, who she said had the elegance to which she aspired.

I was exquisite, with slim shoulders and wonderful legs and incredible skin. My bosom was the perfect size considering how tall I am – just a mouthful, I would say.

Hepburn would play Eliza Doolittle for Hollywood in *My Fair Lady*, 1964, but April got there first at Le Carrousel, presciently playing the flower girl from the wrong side of the tracks who blossoms, thanks to the specialist Professor Higgins, into a beautifully spoken and sought-after social sensation. She said her elaborate twirls from rags to silks were a bit daft but worked as an antidote to the rather jaded and more burlesque routines.

Socialising with April, there was always the moment when you thought some poor sod would curtsy to her. Her grand manner had that effect, and her fellow performers called her *M'lady*. Which is what hairdresser Robert Bodin cried out when he reunited with April in the south of France in 2011. In a scene from Merchant Ivory, with sunshine, swimming pool, parasols and a coiffured April arriving on his terrace, he cried out again and again, *M'lady, M'lady*. April played to her audience. As Bodin, the former stylist at Joffo's Salon for the performers at Le Carrousel, gathered his guests around the lunch table, April, champagne flute raised, gazed at them and announced: *You may sit*. In unison, they did. Robert Bodin enthused in fragmented English, 'She is like the queen of England.' Subdued, he said later, 'I met her when she arrived in Paris and she was most beautiful person I'd seen in my life, more beautiful than all the stars in Hollywood. And I told her so in 1958.'

This public change into, as far as any casual encounter could reveal, a woman, was simply that she believed she could truly achieve her wish to be one. She was having weekly oestrogen injections, which gave her indigestion and flatulence but more helpfully boosted her bone strength, and as her body reacted so did her mind – to the story of Christine Jorgensen, aka the American GI George William Jorgensen.

The world was alerted to this crossing of the sexual borders by a squealing headline in the *New York Daily News* on 1 December 1952. It was blatantly straightforward, just the facts, ma'am: Ex-GI BECOMES BLONDE BEAUTY. The *News* reported that George was now Christine Jorgensen and the first person to undergo a 'sex change'. In their enthusiasm for an American first, they got it wrong: the Institut für Sexualwissenschaft (Institute for Sexual Science) was at this edge of humankind first. Magnus Hirschfeld was the pioneer doctor running the institute in Berlin from 1919 to 1933 but, being Jewish and gay, he was suddenly in the wrong place at very much the wrong time. The institute was a mix of academia and practicality, doing research into and treating sexually transmitted diseases, infertility, nymphomania and impotence, and pushing against the borders of sex, questioning *Hamlet*-style the role and being of a man and a woman.

Dr Hirschfeld's case files burgeoned and, if not a Dr Feelgood working instant miracles, he made his confused and perplexed patients and his devotees feel better about themselves. When he arrived in Berlin in 1929 the author Christopher Isherwood – whose autobiographical novel *Goodbye to Berlin* (1939) became a play, a musical and the film *Cabaret* (1972) – rented a small, dark room from Dr Hirschfeld in the sprawling villa in Tiergarten which was home of the Institute for Sexual Science, close to the Bellevue Palace and the Brandenburg Gate. Isherwood had an acute eye, a master of observational journalism. He witnessed sexual history, very much *Babylon Berlin*, as the relaxed and liberal policy of the Weimar Republic allowed researchers to surmount the battlements of orthodox study and thinking. His landlord was infamous for his cavalier investigations into and on behalf of sexual minorities. It was almost half a century after events that Isherwood felt able to reveal and discuss his intimacies at the institute in *Christopher And His Kind* (1976). He writes about a private club close to the institute where he dresses in a tight sailor outfit and is delighted to be mistaken for a prostitute. At the institute it is every game in town as he describes the goings-on, involving *whips and chains and torture instruments designed for the practitioners of pleasure-pain; high-heeled, intricately decorated boots for the fetishists; lacy female undies which had been worn by ferociously masculine Prussian officers beneath their uniforms.*

For Dr Hirschfeld it was all about learning, about knowledge. Despite Nazi advocates on his doorstep, he publicly supported votes for women and, more daringly in the political atmosphere, decriminalising homosexual relations between men. Most of the records of his work were lost in 1933, when Nazi hooligans plundered and then destroyed the institute[1] and burned their books and records in front of the Berlin Opera House. What is recorded and known is that Rudolph Richter (later Dora Richter) was a longtime patient of Dr Hirschfeld. Richter, the oldest of six children born to a Bohemian farming

---

1 Where the building used to stand is a small, graffitied plaque, which notes the institute was established with a grant from the Prussian government: 'The institute was the first facility for sexological research and learning and was a place for medical care and refuge for everyone who faced societal discrimination for their sexuality.'

family, displayed a 'tendency to act and carry on in a feminine way'. As a six-year-old he tried to remove his penis with a tourniquet. He became a baker, a soldier and repeatedly moved town, dressing when off-duty as a girl, finally finding some peace at Dr Hirschfeld's practice in Berlin. He had his testicles removed in 1922, aged twenty-nine, before his penis went with surgery a decade later to allow the construction of a vagina, making her the first transgender woman on record to undergo vaginoplasty. From then, Richter worked as a domestic servant at the Institute for Sexual Research and was affectionately known as 'Dorchen'. Psychiatrist Felix Abraham, who worked with Dr Hirschfeld, published a paper about Richter's gender-confirming surgeries as a case study in *Zeitschrift für Sexualwissenschaft und Sexualpolitik* (*Journal of Sexology and Sex Politics*): 'Her castration had the effect – albeit not very extensive – of making her body become fuller, restricting her beard growth, making visible the first signs of breast development, and giving the pelvic fat pad a more feminine shape.' She was a cook in what became the Hotel Bristol in Berlin but in 1933 was caught up in an attack by Nazi supporters and was never heard of again, presumed dead.

Before Hitler's thugs got to work, Magnus Hirschfeld supervised four surgeries which transformed the Danish painter Einar Wegener into Lilli Elbe, the 'Danish Girl'. The full hospital records held in Dresden were destroyed during a wartime British bombing raid, but other paperwork gives details: in 1930, the first surgery removed the testicles, the next implanted an ovary onto her abdominal musculature and then took away the penis and the scrotum. The last surgery – in 1931, to transplant a uterus and make a vaginal canal – the second vaginoplasty following the surgery on Dora Richter, went tragically wrong. Her body rejected the transplanted uterus and infection brought on convulsions and, three months later, on 13 September 1931, she died when her heart gave out. Her story was posthumously published in Britain two years later titled,

Man Into Woman: An Authentic Record of a Change of Sex. Lilli Elbe's transition inspired *The Danish Girl*, 2015, which brazenly starred Eddie Redmayne in the title role causing upset in the transgender community, which the actor later noted, discussing the importance of consideration in transgender casting.

By chance – or providence? – the film, which won Redmayne his second Oscar nomination, brought April Ashley full circle and back into the past. The amiable young actor wanted to pick her brain. 'What was important for me was that this was a period piece, so it was about meeting people of different generations. When I told my dad I was going to meet her, he goes, "You know, I think I actually danced with her."'

Ah, that would be businessman Richard Redmayne. At lunch, April explained to him about not trying to 'do' a female voice, to seek a higher register, but to employ his own voice and control the softness and tone. He gave her his father's thanks for 'all the lovely dances' they had together at the London nightclub Tramp. April, Redmayne said, was most helpful and extremely jovial; it reminded her of London life in the sixties and the axiom that if you were there, you don't remember it.

I was terribly amused. I thought, God, I must have been pissed because I never liked to dance with anybody. His father must have been as good-looking as he is. I liked hanging onto the bar.

It was a little more than a dozen years earlier, after we'd had lunch (*just a little of the black truffle, darling, perfect with the Veuve Clicquot Rosé*) at the Hotel Le Negresco in Nice, that April and I took a walk from the Riveria landmark along the Promenade des Anglais to Gloria Mansions. The spot is a shrine to Dr Magnus Hirschfeld, now lauded as an original transsexual visionary. After escaping Germany in 1933 he made his home in the apartment building with its glorious open view of the Mediterranean. He was sixty-seven years old on the day he died there, 14 May 1935. On our visit, April did a little curtsy. Dr Hirschfeld was part of her heritage, for one change led to another, like Lilli Elbe to Christine Jorgensen, George Jamieson to April Ashley.

Darling, someone had to shine a light.

The Christine Jorgensen story was a spotlight for April.

Yet, the stage – the launchpad proper – was Le Carrousel and April's friendship and sometimes bitchy rivalry, she was stubborn when she wanted to be – with fellow performers Coccinelle and Bambi, who also craved womanhood. The difficult road to Morocco beckoned.

Five

Knife Edge

'Are You Lonesome Tonight?'
Elvis Presley, 1960, by Roy Turk, Lou Handyman, 1926

Kindness can forgive the historical error by the *New York Daily News*, for public knowledge of modern transsexualism rather did begin with George William becoming Christine Jorgensen; the first, as it were, mainstream male-to-female person, and a worldwide celebrity. Gender identity became a question, much to the bemusement of an America not yet talking about putting a man on the moon.

With hindsight, it's telling how far ahead of the sexual revolution April and her friends from Le Carrousel were, and how determined. When they read about Christine Jorgensen it felt like reading their own manifesto. George Jorgensen longed to 'relate to men as a woman, not as another man'. Growing up he disdained the uniform of being male, what he *had* to wear and sports he *had* to enjoy. He was attracted to other boys and, later, to men whom he had sex with, but he felt stained by the homosexual experiences. He wanted to be a woman and his quest began. Born in the Bronx, New York, aged nineteen he was drafted into the US army toward the end of the Second World War which, of course, gave the *Daily News* their 'ex-GI' headline.

Dismayed by his army experience, he became even more transfixed with transition and after demob he began taking oestrogen in ethinylestradiol (EE) pills. He'd heard that Scandinavian doctors were treating patients like him and was en route in Copenhagen visiting family when he met Dr Christian Hamburger, a hormone specialist, an endocrinologist and devotee of Dr Magnus Hirschfeld. Fate, again. And why, after surgery, he called himself Christine.

Strangely, there is more mystery around the essentials of Christine Jorgensen's surgery than that of the *Danish girl* in Berlin. As a transgender spokesperson and public figure, she influenced others seeking to change their sex and names on their birth certificates, but intimate details of her own 'transition' are vague. Dr Hamburger treated her with female hormones and, over a twelve-month period, concluding in 1952, performed castration, a penectomy and plastic surgery to establish 'womanhood'. Of course, it was a story too good to question too far. The medical team never explicitly said they changed Jorgensen's sex but, with the help of robust American tabloid journalism, 'sex change' in the public imagination was interpreted as just that. Indeed, as Helen Joyce remarks in her forensic, best-selling book *Trans: When Ideology Meets Reality* (Oneworld, 2021), the Scandinavian surgeons had left her 'with external genitalia only'. In 1954, there was further surgery in New Jersey and 'a shallow neo-vagina was constructed using skin from her thighs'.

Jorgensen did not publicly explain her rearranged anatomy or the surgery outcome, offering in 1958, 'Everyone is both sexes in varying degrees. I am more of a woman than a man. Of course, I can never have children, but this does not mean that I cannot have natural sexual intercourse – I am very much in the position right now of a woman who has a hysterectomy.' As April would be, Christine Jorgensen was a phenomenon: Hollywood called and there were myriad deals for films, theatre and 'my story' newspaper serialisations, alongside invites to all the important social and media parties. Christine Jorgensen embraced all this but never said how much of it she bought into; did they want her company for her talent or for curiosity? Did difference equal celebrity?

April likened the often exasperating inquisitiveness to the nineteenth-century crowds who paid to see the deformed Joseph Merrick, *the Elephant Man*, lured by supposed entertainment, like a dubious circus act. She herself was consigned to a dark oubliette and, of course, more curious than most to find an escape route. She was also thrilled to read about Roberta (formerly Robert) Cowell, a Second World War Spitfire pilot, racing driver, and all-round Tom Clancy character, who in 1948 became Britain's first known trans-woman to have gender-affirming surgery. He'd undergone increasing oestrogen treatment while living as a man and then – take a breath – met a man who'd been a woman who offered to turn him into a woman.

In those immediate post-war years in Britain, we can imagine the reaction of medical orthodoxy confronted by a wartime action hero desperate to be a woman. You don't step on Superman's cape. Yet, in 1946, the London physician Laurence Michael Dillon, formerly Laura Maud Dillon, was one of the first to get a phalloplasty – a constructed penis – in sex reassignment surgery from female to male, in an operation performed by plastic surgeon pioneer Sir Harold Gillies. That same year Dillon published *Self: A Study in Endocrinology and Ethics*, which argued that everyone should have the right to change gender. Robert Cowell devoured the book and became friends with Dr Dillon, who, in very private surgery, performed an inguinal orchiectomy (removal of both testicles – a surgery regarded as intentional maiming and illegal in Britain). This done, Cowell visited a senior gynaecologist in Harley Street, London, who decided Robert/Roberta was intersex, which allowed the issuing of a new birth certificate as a female. There's been confusion that Roberta Cowell was not a 'true' transsexual in that the genitals, in an 'act of God', were confused at birth. But it was human hands, belonging to Dr Dillon, which secretly made the rearrangements that gained the birth certificate. In 1951, the New Zealand born Harold Gillies completed the work in an early sex reassignment surgery, from male to female, deploying flap surgery[2].

Roberta Cowell, who liked to be called 'Betty', was recorded as saying after her surgery that with her love of cars and high speed it would be 'bloody difficult' to find a more daredevil, masculine person. Her body, not her personality, changed.

Such detailed accounts were not readily apparent or available to April in Paris but even the vaguest thought of what might be possible called for another glass of champagne and excited conversation. Coccinelle behaved more star-like and above it all, irritating the other two, but not a day would end without the notion being mentioned or debated. Always watchful, always frugal with her own money, April watched the francs and gathered American dollars at every opportunity, preparing for the ineluctable and to break cover, to stop hiding inside herself.

It was the joy of not being alone, a solitary being, and not so much discovering but reading in print there was an escape route, a trapdoor. I'd made a deal with myself – if I couldn't be a woman, a proper woman, by the age of twenty-five, then that would be that. There would be no 'cries for help' or silliness, I would bring the curtain down and close the show, end my life. At Le Carrousel, knowing surgery was possible – it had been done – made a future possible for me. Yes, darling, I thought of little else. What else would I think of from the moment I opened my eyes? And until I closed them again? I'd tried to get away from myself but no luck. I wasn't frightened or apprehensive

2 In reconstructive flap surgery, tissue is moved from a donor to the recipient with an intact blood supply and does not depend on growth of new blood vessels to help the wound to heal.

about any operation. Death? I wasn't that keen but, if there was no alternative, I was committed to it.

Although I'd disowned God, the Catholic teaching was embedded and I felt guilty at the thought but nevertheless assured I would end my life. I couldn't go on living as a man, if I could not live the life of a proper woman. It wasn't a 'moment' I was having – goodness, society wasn't endorsing or 'caring' or 'understanding' such thoughts in my time. We were on our own and then we were learning about Jorgensen and hope.

Tantalised by possibility, April and her friend Bambi and on/off rival Coccinelle, the applauded and sumptuously siliconed big star of Le Carrousel during April's tenure, presented as women full-time.

Coccinelle – Coxy to April (*'une coccinelle'* being the French for 'ladybird') – kept a collection of minks and men and was what the respected and all-but-sainted Brazilian plastic surgeon Ivo Pitanguy told me he and his colleagues called a 'retread', as in, never satisfied by their results, they keep returning for more work. Her nose had all but vanished, having been sculpted so often. Still, April closely followed it. Born Jacques Charles Dufresnoy on 23 August 1931, Coxy was that little bit older than April and, like her, had several missteps before debuting as a showgirl in 1953 at Chez Madame Arthur. The club was owned by Marcel Ouizman and the cabaret so popular there were half a dozen shows from 11 p.m. through to dawn.

In October 1947, *Monsieur Marcel*, to everyone, led a friendly takeover of Le Carrousel at 40, rue du Colisée, near the Champs-Élysées. The club being close to the Palais de L'Élysée began a noisy scandal but that was initial and helpful advertising.

Officially, it was illegal. Forty years earlier, in 1907, the *prefect* of police, Louis Lépine, solemnly portrayed by Marc Barbé in the 2022–23 television series *Paris Police 1900* and *Paris Police 1905*, in an interesting and very Gallic way legislated against transvestism other than on Sunday, Monday, Mardi Gras and Thursday of mid-Lent, and banned drag shows at dances and places with available booze. Decades later, like their London colleagues at the Windmill, the French police enjoyed free drinks and the show, as did Maria Callas, Josephine Baker and Marlene Dietrich, who had written police permission to go backstage to congratulate the artists. The club attracted playwright Tennessee Williams, fresh from the success of *A Streetcar Named Desire*, for what he called 'the beautiful male whores'. For most, the ongoing attraction was the *transformistes,* themselves a mix of those pretending and those wanting to be, and others improvising as they rolled along. There was a token male impersonator, Mickey Merer and the same show – a *tableaux* which concluded with ensemble singing, feathers and, sometimes, talcum powder puffed out of amusing spots, which ran all year. If you'd seen one show you'd seen 'em all.

April and Coccinelle would compete about their famous 1950s encounters, meeting such opposites as Dietrich and Debbie Reynolds or fans Claudette Colbert and Ginger Rogers, Judy Garland, Edith Piaf, Sacha Distel with Brigitte Bardot on his arm, and together they added up that Bob Hope had been to at least twenty shows.

I couldn't possibly comment.

April and Bambi were more amused than interested in their stage-door admirers acknowledging the world is crowded with those for whom the unusual is all that matters. And, of course, the curious. They had a legion of fans.

I was pre-op, having oestrogen shots, but Elvis wanted to go to bed with me. He was stationed in Germany at the time but came to Paris every weekend. He liked virgins, but nevertheless went through nearly every one of the Bluebell dancers. He made a beeline for me but, sadly, he was a little too premature in my life. I wasn't altogether prepared, as it were, to properly entertain his intentions. I felt obliged to point out, '*Mais, monsieur, nous avons une petite inconvenance*,' and Colonel Tom Parker, his manager, stopped him. Elvis still sent me champagne every night he was there. He liked deflowering girls.

Salvador Dalí came to see me at Le Carrousel every night for six weeks. He specifically wanted to see me; he was excited by me. Put simply, Dalí, the Great Masturbator, liked chicks with dicks, and the masturbation of and by them. (There's got to be a name for it – she-males? – for it's so terribly popular. There are thousands of internet sites about it.) Dalí gave me lots of presents and wanted to paint me naked as Hermaphroditos, the son of Hermes and Aphrodite. In mythology, he was joined in body with Salmacis the nymph. It was before my operation and the whole idea was anathema to me. I said not. I said, 'No, never, never, never.' And he begged me and begged me.

I was appalled at the thought. I didn't know if I was one or not. Hermaphrodites have both sets of organs; they're incredibly rare but do exist. As far as I was concerned, in my mind, I was a woman. My penis did not exist – the purpose of a change was to make that fact, as well as my psychological certainty. Dalí persisted with me, turning up all the time with chocolates and champagne. I introduced him to Peki d'Oslo – later very, very successful as Amanda Lear – who I'd taken under my wing. It was 1959, so Peki was only seventeen and she claimed she met him later. It was Peki whom Dalí came to know well. She was his muse. I don't know what went on between them sexually – probably more mutual marketing than mutual masturbation, I think – but they were close for fifteen years. In her 1985 book *My Life With Dalí*, she wrote, 'Dalí is a genius who likes ambiguity and he tends to talk to women as if they were men.' More than interesting, given our circumstances. Of course, the men who came to Le Carrousel knew we were men dressed as women – it was the most famous drag club in the world. Later, I heard, Dalí would show cohorts photographs of Peki/Amanda or point to her swimming naked in his phallic swimming pool and take great joy in revealing, 'She's a man.' Ian Gibson, in his fabulous book *The Shameful Life of Salvador Dalí [1997]*, quotes Nanita Kalaschnikoff who knew them both: 'Amanda's transsexuality was part of her attraction for Dalí. He loved collecting oddities.'

Something April so desperately wanted to escape from being. As did Bambi, who began her quest to be a woman at Madame Arthur's in 1953. Algerian Marie-Pierre Pruvot was eighteen months older than April and was as convincing in a swimsuit. It was a Pied Piper moment when she and April strutted along the beach in Juan-les-Pins. April gave me a photograph of her and Bambi sunbathing on the beach and explained that what they are staring over at are a crowd of young men applauding them.

I won the most beautiful legs competition in the south of France. Pre-op.

They were in the south of France in the summer of 1959 to appear at the Le Carrousel outpost in Juan-les-Pins and it was at one of the shows that April met, importantly, the British actress Margaret Lockwood, famous as the star of *The Wicked Lady* (1945) and for her literal trademark, a beauty spot high on her left cheek. The actress and her daughter Julia became more than close friends; they became the allies April needed. They were part of the conversation she and Bambi had about becoming 'real' women. April was anxious to do that, Bambi often impetuous, dragging her friend to visit questionable doctors, but for a time there was the steady counsel of Margaret Lockwood, one of the best-known faces in Britain, a remarkable person.

Bambi and I being the same age, had become best friends and we went everywhere together and, wherever we went, we looked for doctors. That summer we found an Italian one in Nice, and he frightened the hell out of me. He hadn't a clue but there was never a thought to stop searching.

Everyone around them could see their yearning, despite April deploying her instinctive insouciance. Kiki Moustic, a rather lovely sounding star of Le Carrousel, was constantly helpful. April said Kiki, who left his drag in the dressing room and went home to his wife and two children, looked, off-stage and carrying his ever-present briefcase, like a bank manager, a taller Captain Mainwaring from *Dad's Army*. Female impersonation was simply a job in entertainment, not a stop on a far more permanent journey. Kiki helped April with the mundane, finding cheaper accommodation, the better to save, and with encouragement. The renowned hair stylist Robert Bodin was also practical by driving April over the French border and into Belgium simply so she could return with a newly dated stamp on her passport allowing her to stay in Paris for another three months. It was all catch as you can.

April was taking steady doses of hormones as she searched for doctors who were disciples of Magnus Hirschfeld. In Paris, she sought out help visiting 'clinics' in most of the arrondissements but these establishments were even more fearful than the life she was living, crammed into areas where it was easy to imagine Dr Frankenstein in the phonebook. Or a phantom from Gaston Leroux's imagination at her shoulder. She said it was that spooky, and scary.

Yet, when we talked of her time pre-operation in Paris it seemed clear that being in France made dealing with her gender conundrum more comfortable, certainly easier than home in Liverpool. It didn't make it less complex, even French grammar complicated things with *le vagin* (masculine) and *la verge,* one of the many words for 'penis' (feminine). And, always, the French superiority, as in Flaubert's '*le premier peuple de l'univers*', which she constantly encountered in Coccinelle, who had become intently secretive about her travels.

Usually, Coccinelle would be boasting of visiting here and there, being wined and dined by the great and the good and not-so-good. She was, for April, incredibly quiet. Until the afternoon when she suddenly appeared at Le Carrousel with a grin as wide as the Champs-Élysées. 'Look!' she shrieked and wickedly rolled onto the floor and opened her legs. April shook her head and peered down. And there it was, what all agreed was a superb vagina, a work of genius. Ten out of ten, full marks. Handmade.

I felt I should be giving her vagina, her Zee Zee, a standing ovation.

April now knew for certain there was someone who could make her the woman she always wanted to be. Yet, her newly reformed girlfriend, grinning and gleefully flashing on the floor, played games and said she was bound by confidentiality. No matter how empathetically April encouraged, Coccinelle would not say who her surgeon was.

It was no deterrent: she and April's future were entwined, April said it was in the stars, and Coccinelle was one of the brightest in France. She had a fabulous story to tell.

In time, she did, providing more first-person surgical detail than April – although forthcoming of the horrifying aftermath, she was quite prudish around such intimacy – ever did. That ultimate bit too much like butchery, too traumatic for even morphine-blurred recall. Coccinelle was not so reluctant. Like many great stories, it began in a bar.

Six

The Mysterious Dr Burou

'My girls are the crème de la crème.'
The Prime of Miss Jean Brodie, Muriel Spark, 1961

Coccinelle was pumped up with silicone and female hormones but unfulfilled until she preceded April to the Clinique du Parc on rue Lapébie in Casablanca in October 1958. She contained her news, convalescing in Morocco for many months, before revealing all in the Le Carrousel dressing room to the amazement of April.

I'll never get over it. She threw herself on the floor stark naked, she opened her legs and there it was. All that praying ...

Which did not deliver the immediate and vital information that April craved. She started prying around the Le Carrousel dressing room like Miss Marple, searching for any clue to the identity of this mystery, miracle-making doctor. It was nearly three decades later when Coccinelle published *Coccinelle par Coccinelle* (Editions Filipacchi, Paris, 1987) but what was lost in time for many years was 'her story' which ran in Hollywood's notorious *Confidential* magazine in 1962. By *Confidential* standards the revelations were wholesome, their meat and potatoes were the extravagant and uncensored peccadilloes of movie stars, but even for a readership jaded by sensation the details were revelatory. They were disdained by some American readers as 'impossible', while Coccinelle was the first transgender woman to become an entertainment star in France. *Confidential* magazine was shut down by a combination of lawsuits and good taste, but copies are filed for the public record in Los Angeles.

Coccinelle's first-person story is told with an illustration of her breasts spilling out of her evening dress and photographs of her with Bardot and Debbie Reynolds and actor Van Johnson. There's also one with her husband, the journalist Francis Bonnet, whom she married on 20 March 1962 at St John Church, Montmarte. Like April's story and life, transition is pivotal, but not everything, and within Coccinelle's telling to *Confidential* is a sad love story reflecting that change doesn't always deliver all you want.

This is the start of an edited version of what appeared, *Confidential*-style in 1962, which nevertheless, I believe, helps us to understand the people, the time, their fears and the dilemmas, April's world at Le Carrousel, and what followed.

In the Casablanca clinic in October 1958, a friend surgeon made possible for me to cross the sex barrier. By a revolutionary technique, perfected by experiments with monkeys, he performed a delicate operation that suppressed the only remaining traces of my original manhood. It opened the way for me to live like a normal woman, normal in all respects except one – I could never have children. But of course, there is always the possibility of adoption. As for the rest, I really am a woman, a liberated woman. For years, my whole being unconsciously sought that solution. Born a boy, I began to hate everything masculine with my first toddling steps. It was revulsion rather than a perversion – a revulsion of nature's terrible error of giving me the heart, brain and nervous system, feeling and desires of a woman along with the organs of a man. Little by little, I became conscious of my problem while I was an apprentice hairdresser, and later a page boy. I found a palliative but not a solution by becoming a female impersonator or transvestite. I made a name for myself in Paris, and on the road. Was starred by Le Carrousel, a specialist nightclub where boys, camou-flaged as artfully as possible, perform as girls.

After incredible tragic-comic goings on with the French army, I'd finally been discharged. I was free to earn my living, surround myself with friends. I shared my Paris apartment and hotel rooms on tour with a fellow artist, Robert. Our relationship had become darkened by my special burden, that error of Nature. It was up to me to do something I felt but what? Then luck came to my aid. Perhaps it was more than luck. There is another word which I hesitate to use as it might sound sacrilegious. I was at Casablanca with the roadshow starring at the *Negresco* cabaret where friends and acquaintances often came to chat with me in the bar. One evening, a young girl approached my table, greeting me. I glanced up: tall, well-built, elegant, she had shoulder-length braids of red hair. I returned her greeting politely. But wondered: Who is she? She looks familiar but where have I seen her before? In our profession, we meet so many people all the time. It's impossible to remember them all. The young lady sensed my puzzlement.

'Don't you recognise me?' she asked.

I made faint, polite sounds but she persisted. 'Then you've forgotten the lad at Nice, the electrician?'

I didn't get the connection. I looked at her closely. No, not possible. She couldn't be that boy dressed up. After all my years as a transvestite I can usually spot an imposter a mile away. A friend called her and she disappeared into the supper crowd. But she came back another time and we talked more. She refreshed my memory.

I'd worked at Maxim's, a cabaret at Nice located over the Whisky à Gogo, a drinking spot with continuous music in the background controlled by an electrician, a hi-fi specialist. The electrician that year was a very pleasant young man who seemed interested in our show. He came backstage one day to see me asking if there was any possibility of working with Le Carrousel troupe. I told him that after all, it wasn't up to me, and he should see the manager. That was the last I'd heard of the young man and here, face-to-face with me in Casablanca, was the very same person. The pretty redhead girl was none other than the electrician.

'How come?' I asked.

'I've had an operation.'

I jumped. I asked a million questions. She was terribly reserved at first, almost annoyed. She was very timid. But after a few more drinks, I dared to return to the subject. Come into my dressing room and let me see, I implored. She refused, blushing. I insisted. Finally, she gave in and came backstage. In spite of her embarrassment, she lifted her skirt, slipped off her panties. One glance was enough. Unless I was dreaming, she was a girl. Back at the hotel later, I couldn't sleep a wink.

Afterwards, I made a point of inviting her to my table and our friendship grew. She called for me in her car to go to the beach and we headed for a deserted inlet on the Moroccan coast. There, I confess my doubts to her. I begged her to let me see again, graciously she consented. I looked, scrutinised, examined, even touched her. No, no doubt was possible. She *was* a woman in every sense of the word.

Jenny – it was her name – showed me obligingly her anatomy transformed: her beautiful female sex, her breasts harmoniously developed … I was dazzled, I hardly dared believe it. So, everything about what I have always dreamed, everything could become reality. My head whirled, I bombarded her with questions. She told me her story, a story rather like mine, except that she'd never worked in travesty [as a female impersonator]. A native of Casablanca, she'd heard people talk about a clinic there, a private maternity and gynaecological hospital where a brilliant surgeon or doctor called Dr Burou performed miracles. Interested in sexual anomalies, the doctor developed a theory by laboratory tests through trial and error: he finally succeeded in changing a male monkey into a female. Jenny called on Dr Burou who was extremely reluctant at first but finally agreed to risk the operation, but disclaimed all responsibility in advance. He could guarantee nothing. This was his first-ever attempt at such surgery. But before my eyes was the conclusive evidence of the success. There and then I decided, I too, would be operated on.

My redheaded friend went with me to see the surgeon. The doctor examined me, weighed up the possibilities. Finally, he accepted in principle but insisted that before taking any such drastic step, I must seriously consider every aspect of the problem, including the possibility of accident in such an audacious intervention. We talked price. It was expensive, of course, far beyond my means. There were also long-term contracts I had to fulfil for the Le Carrousel, so we set a tentative date for eight months later.

Back in Paris, I pondered the pros and cons. Conscientiously, I discussed it with my friends. In general, everyone understood my motives, but they insisted on the moral and physical risks I'd be running. I talked at length with Robert – after all, I hoped to spend my life with him. I wrote to Dr Burou confirming our date. The time came and I took off for Casablanca. I arrived at the clinic as expected, I went to sleep in a small room sparkling in its fresh coat of white paint. Several hours later, I woke up suffering horribly, but I was a woman.

Dr Burou worked at the Clinique du Parc until he tragically died in 1989 when outside Mohammedia harbour on the west coast of Morocco, his boat ran out of fuel and stranded, he drowned, his body not found for five days. By all accounts, he was kindly and certainly April found him so, breaking down in tears when she shared the sorrow of his death, aged seventy-nine, with his son Alain. She was tearful as she mentioned this again so many years later, in October 2021.

I told him that his father saved my life, made me one of the happiest people in the world the day he operated on me. There's still joy when I think about what he did for me. I shall never forget him. He was a miracle worker.

To the medical community, the Gauloise-chain-smoking Dr Burou was also a maverick. After trouble about abortions at a gynaecological clinic in Algeria in 1940 he moved to wartime Casablanca, serving in the Fourth French-Moroccan Mountain Division and was part of the liberation of Alsace. After the war, he created his three-floor Clinique du Parc, open for abortions as well as maternity services.

On the top floor he established two blue-tiled and modern operating theatres, and it was in the one by the stairway where he first 'turned man into woman'. That first patient, of course, was Coccinelle's Jenny, the former electrician, who had been turned away by many specialist doctors and gynaecologists. It was experimental; his first such surgery, and he performed the successful operation for free. Yet, his costs were high and from then on payment was required – an average three thousand pounds, in American Express traveller's cheques. In the beginning, a biblical moment for some, outrageous to others, Dr Burou constructed a vagina using a live graft taken from the penile skin; he was unaware of previous experimentation and vaginoplasty. He created his own technique of duplicating the female pelvic area on male patients, certainly, as it were, looking the part. No more of that suffering of repeated surgery from the Berlin days when the penis and scrotum were junked and skin from the patient's thigh used to construct the vagina. Dr Burou's vaginoplasty kept stable the skin and nerves of the penis and scrotum to replicate a vagina and labia. Everything is completed in one surgery: the penis and testicles are moved but remain attached to the patient's body for the tissue to remain 'live' and be moulded to create a vagina, the work of a sculptor-surgeon.

There is a deadline, as the surgery must be complete before the tissue becomes useless. With castration and a penectomy done, the perineum (the sensitive skin between genitals and backside) is cut and an opening conjured between the prostate, bladder and rectum. The penis skin is inverted into the newly created hole, the vagina. The remaining scrotal and genital tissue is then used to complete this new vagina and create labia. But the artificial opening will work to close up and the solution is regular sex with a man or, literally, plugging the hole. Nature abhors a vacuum. 'We do our best to put nature's mistakes right. Every human being has the right to try and find happiness,' said Dr Burou in 1970, as his name and fascinating specialty skills were circulating worldwide.

Coccinelle led the way for April, but the details only came later in *Confidential* magazine, the first, if until now all but forgotten testimony, of her transition at a time when the world thought such meddling with nature was science-fiction at best, bestial, freakier art at worst. She also revealed Dr Burou's 'secret' skills:

When Dr Burou approached the floodlighted operating table, he had before him an operating field carefully delineated by compresses: roughly speaking, the lower abdomen. The intervention had been meticulously prepared beforehand. Laboratory examinations, analysis, X-rays from every angle. The doctor had scrutinised them with careful attention. He had talked to me at length, I told him about my life, the various physical and moral reactions that constituted my exceptional case. Because of professional ethics, he first had to convince himself the operation was useful and necessary.

So now, an assistant handed him the first instrument. Taking the male organ, he slit it lengthwise and removed the unnecessary parts, isolating the urethra. He placed it where it would have been if nature hadn't erred. Forming an opening he anchored it, then cut off the useless remains of the canal. Next, taking the organ he slit open, he sewed it up, and turned it, as one turns a sock or gloved finger, inside out.

He placed the resulting cylinder where it would exist in a normal female attached to the wall with catgut, which would eventually disappear. To avoid any accident or deformation, he inserted a metal plug the shape of a candle. During the next two weeks it would be gradually rotated along with an injection of oil to prevent the metal from sticking to the skin. This way the graft would take perfectly.

The rest of the operation was like ordinary plastic surgery. With the male gland skin, he normalised the external area of the operating field. He created folds, minor and major, which blind nature had thoughtlessly forgotten, and which later developed normal sensitivity. (In fact, everything became normal in about a month.) Now the operation was finished except for the usual antiseptic and pain killing precautions. I was wheeled back to my room.

It was a horrible awakening for me. I was feverish, obliged to lie flat on my back without budging an inch so as not to displace the metal plugs during the first few days. If I'd had the strength, I think I'd have jumped out the window. My pain felt like those of a woman about to give birth. Slowly, the agony lessened. There were still a few bad moments, when the surgeon and his assistant examined me, injected oil and turned the metal plug.

Then one day they took the plug out. I felt liberated. After came the removal of certain stitches, about which I felt dreadful in advance, but which lasted only a second. Finally, convalescence.

That is the story of my operation, my body has done the rest.

Take, for instance, my chest. I had followed an intensive female hormone treatment, resulting in beautiful breasts, but they had been maintained by booster shots. Since my operation there has been no further need for medication. Dr Burou had predicted as much; 'You won't secrete any more male hormones, you no longer have male glands and your female hormones – your whole life proves how strong they already were – will become dominant. Your breasts should stay firm and round.'

And he was right. My organism has become entirely feminine. The latent lubricating glands have taken over and function normally. As do all the thousands of tiny nerve ends and blood vessels which permit natural sensitivity. I must even admit that one or two days a month I feel weary, heavy, congested. No other symptoms, of course, as I can't have children. But it proves that Dr Burou's knife only corrected a technical, organic error of nature, re-established a normal equilibrium in my body. He completed medically the metamorphosis that I'd begun all on my own by instinct as soon as I was old enough to think.

Back in Paris, I told Robert all about the operation. He listened. On a certain evening I knew my convalescence was over, no more pains. My tissues completely healed. The terribly important moment was at hand. After four years of living with Robert in a somewhat equivocal situation, suddenly I felt like a young girl about to be married. The lights went off, I was frightened. It was truly my nuptial night. Somehow, with one corner of my brain I couldn't help but noting Robert's unexpected roughness, or was he perhaps uneasy?

'What is the matter, Robert?'

Brutally, he replied. 'Frankly, I'm no longer interested. Girls? There are millions of them on the Earth.'

My world collapsed. This was the result of all that I'd desired, done and suffered. I became desperate. I began to act like some of the girls of whom I'd always disapproved. I no longer resisted some of the handsome lads who importuned me before without success. Perhaps I exaggerate, but I lost count in my despair. I survived on a galaxy of suppers and road tours before officially finishing with Robert, who sullenly left my house.

Am I on the wrong road?

Have I taken the wrong turning?

Then one day Kikki Moustic introduced one of her friends, a tall, good-looking lad with wavy hair and regular features; sweet and kind, and rather timid, a lad who hadn't yet found himself and, little by little, this pleasant lad became an important part of my life. His name was Francis. It was easy to go out with Francis, he let me be myself. He let me expand, he was never jealous. He was always there. Once I arrived with Francis at the Broche d'Or in Paris and I was very Brigitte Bardot in a superb, low cut frock and waist-length blonde hair. There was complete silence, and a whisper went from table to table: 'Is it her?'

Playing the part, I ordered my dinner and, ten minutes later, the real Brigitte Bardot – escorted by Sacha Distel – walked in. She looked at me, startled for a minute and then she burst out laughing. After all, next to her, I was but a pale copy. Brigitte's always been nice to me, but I can't say as much for some of her relatives. All the big stars have helped me. One of the kindest is marvellous Marlene Dietrich.

I made her acquaintance at my favourite restaurant. And we see each other often since I've become free. It might have been a question of getting going on the road with her. At the Carrousel all the big stars turn up. There was never a problem of being photographed with them. Some even became my friends. That's the way I got to know Anita Egbert before she had such big success in *La Dolce Vita* [1960]. She was a bit crazy. Not speaking to her husband one day and madly in love with him the next.

It was a time of Americans in Paris and the baseball star Joe DiMaggio, Marilyn Monroe's ex-husband, turned up. I was in my Marilyn phase, and I think he was quite amused. I was offered a contract to appear in Australia and I included gentle Francis Bonnet as my secretary. In 1959, Australia was still marked by 'Made in England' puritanism. A striptease hadn't yet been seen on the boards. A few shows had nude girls but, to stay within the law, they stood still on a revolving stage, not speaking not smiling, above all, not making the slightest gesture. When my impresario Lee Gordon learned my Paris number included a striptease, he concocted a Machiavellian scheme. He announced the coming engagement to the proper authorities and described the numbers of the show; at the mere sound of *striptease* the authorities screamed.

Then Gordon loosed his secret weapon. 'It's not a woman. It's a man. You can verify that in his passport.' The poor Sydney officials, what could they do? So little Coccinelle flew in from Paris to open the new chapter in Australian showbusiness. My famous striptease was performed on a bed, surrounded by my chorus girls. My closing number was a frenzy Charleston in a short dress with fringe, swinging wildly. I also wore a yard long feather boa and a very 1925 wig. I went on twice nightly at seven and eleven. Except on Sundays.

The hours being more reasonable than Europe, I could lead an almost normal life in Sydney. So after the first few days at the palatial Rex hotel, I rented a furnished apartment for Francis and me. I lived *à la bourgeoisie*, doing the cooking and washing like almost any wife, and I had time to appreciate Francis and his kindness, patience and affection. Right from the start, there were advantages that hadn't existed with Robert. First, and most important, I really was a woman for Francis. He hadn't known me as anything else. On that score, there wasn't the least shadow in our relationship. Also, officially he was my secretary. He had no activity of his own. There couldn't be that terrible jealousy which so often exists between show people and still astonishes me; no scenes such as Robert had made because he couldn't stand my being a star when he wasn't. Also, let's admit it, I'm a bit of a martinet.

April happily endorsed that. She never truly forgave Coccinelle for holding out on the name of Dr Burou. Talking about the cat-and-mouse game (*pussy and mouse, darling*) over the doctor's name and location in the favourite San Diego bar, she stared at the ceiling and played at recalling her memory. Coccinelle, who died in 2006, aged seventy-five, was aged sixty-six years old at that moment. A meow.

If I'm correct, she's still getting her tits out at every opportunity.

Seven

The Razor's Edge

'I called upon the British consul in the morning. It occurred
to me that I might die in the course of changing my sex and
I wanted him to let people know. He did not seem surprised.
Always best, he said, to be on the safe side.'

Jan Morris, *Conundrum*, Faber & Faber, 1974

April made promises before she flew, on 10 May 1960 from
Paris Orly to Casablanca, and kept them all. Apprehensive, she
said what disturbed her most was the thought of arriving at the
Clinique du Parc and being rejected for what to her was a life-
saving surgery.

Delayed by Coccinelle being a nuisance about the identity
of her 'miracle worker', she finally got the details from the
kindly Kiki Moustic and wrote a carefully thought-out letter
to Dr Burou. After a positive reply she told Le Carrousel
she was off to Africa for 'the change'. She got support and
warnings, with Monsieur Marcel saying she'd ruin her life,
but April said it was all irrelevant, it was do or die. Was she
brave? No more, she thought, than the boy on the burning
deck. She'd been given no choice. In later years, especially when she was being particularly rather grand, in such
moments, I always thought of her as Lady Bracknell taking
the Grand Tour. April portrayed her time in Casablanca as
if from a Somerset Maugham novel. Although bursting with

self-knowledge, she indulged in a fanciful romantic drama in search of oneself.

Yes, there's the kasbah and the Atlantic Ocean but this was the prime European city of Morocco, of shopping malls and white-painted commercial buildings – the *Casablanca* of Bogart and Bergman was filmed on the back lot of Warner Brothers in Burbank, California. Indeed, Dr Burou's functional clinic wouldn't have been out of place in Beverly Hills: clean, efficient, and with a respect for *all* patients. Any romance was in the consideration of Dr Burou, more raffish than his city, who was the first medic in Morocco to offer in vitro fertilisation (IVF). And had done so, if necessary, without the consent of the husband, so as not to offend his manhood, fragile ego or any other possible sensitivities. It was the results that mattered.

April looked across the leather consulting room couch and into Dr Burou's magnetic eyes, a shade of gunmetal, she thought, as he ran through a ticklist of medical and psychological questions. She hadn't slept – who would? – before the interview which began with a physical, a check to establish what was where and whether April had undergone previous work. Dr Burou was aware of the trail being trekked, from redhead Jenny the former electrician who contacted Coccinelle, and, with April, the ongoing link to Le Carrousel. They truly were pioneers. The doctor told *Paris Match* magazine in 1974: 'I started this speciality almost by accident, because a pretty woman came to see me. It was a man, I only knew it afterwards, a sound engineer in Casablanca, twenty-three years old, dressed as a woman, with a lovely chest which he had obtained thanks to hormone shots. He felt his body was an accident, and I made her a real woman.'

With his innovative, one-stage surgery – what all the proper medical magazines call 'anteriorly pedicled penile skin flap inversion vaginoplasty' – *Dr Burou gives great Zee Zee.*

After the event, April could be marvellously flippant, but whenever confronted by those seeking help and advice, she never held back on the *cruel pain* in the aftermath of the operation. One evening in 2003, in her apartment up in the hills above Nice, our talk was interrupted by a gentle knocking on the door. It was a young man who wanted to be a girl who had traced April's whereabouts. It wasn't that easy to get to by car, a good hour's drive. He'd walked and run, he said, anxious to see her. He was not distressed. He wanted a blessing. April was caring and careful, as she was with the countless and confused people who asked her for help, guiding him toward official medical help and, patiently, telling again the story of Casablanca, before a couple of hours later we paid a taxi to take him down the mountain and home. Had she sugar-coated the experience for him? Absolutely not. She understood the drive and desire and the never-ending need of someone who is rejecting their own body. Except that she called it life or death a thousand times. She also agreed with Dr Burou that so much was psychological: 'I do not transform men into women. I transform male genitals into genitals that have a feminine aspect. All the rest is in the patient's head.' The doctor guarded his surgical technique for some years after April's operation, only revealing details and making the latter declaration at a 1974 medical conference at Stanford University, California.

April's life change on 12 May 1960 missed her 29 April birthday and self-imposed deadline of becoming a woman by age twenty-five. She was born at a time unprepared for her and, generally, insensitive to her needs. Which, April always said, were simple enough – she wanted to be happy. Being reborn was painful – physically and psychologically – and for all the happiness it did bring her there was much heartache and humiliation involved. The oestrogen injections helped develop bosom and hips. The process was excruciating and the side effects – dizziness, nausea and swelling – persisted. Now, clutching a velvet evening bag containing savings of two thousand pounds, she heard the fifty-year-old Dr Burou invite her over this sexual frontier.

The pinnacle of happiness and a joy beyond words.

The agony followed. Madame Jeanne 'Nanou' Burou had attempted to soften the antiseptic clinic with paintings of flowers in a patient's room. April was African violets and, once inside the functional, pre-op room, a little cell-like with single bed and toilet and a balcony view of a Moorish building over the road, attended to the bureaucracy of becoming a woman. She again heard the pros and cons of such drastic surgery from Dr Burou, nodding get-on-with-it as he explained in his challenged English and she signed consent forms relinquishing the clinic of all liability should she die. The nurses were kind and, after an injection she slept, knocked out by the drugs. She thought she dreamed of camels in the desert and running after them wearing a dishdasha.

Despite the *Adhan*, the call to prayer, she only woke when given a little shake by a nurse who arrived before 7 a.m. with a trolley and shaving kit. April asked for the razor and shaved her own pubic hair. Somehow, she said, the shaving soap smelled like Camay, but admitted she was still hazy from the powerful pre-op injection.

Two nurses gently lifted her onto the hospital trolley and wheeled her to the operating theatre. In a phrase she would dine out on for the rest of her life, the last words she heard were from Dr Burou:

Au revoir, monsieur.

★★★★

All her boyfriends say Dr Burou did perfect work.

I knew the pinnacle of happiness, a joy beyond words.

She was one of the first and enjoyed being a woman for more than sixty years. Of course, there were the perils, in less than enlightened 1960, a time when 'messing with nature' was absolutely regarded as the work of mad doctors and Mary Shelley's imagination. She took the name April, after her birth month, and Ashley after Ashley Wilkes in *Gone with The Wind*. Tomorrow *was* another day. When she came around after the surgery, her mind tiptoeing through the anaesthetic, she first recognised a smiling Dr Burou. Who offers another future dinner table bon mot.

Bonjour, mademoiselle.

It was a clever and kind, if subdued, welcome. The fanfare followed, including the appellation '*the most famous transsexual of the century*'.

On that hospital bed, bandaged and drugged, April could only find a small smile at her welcome. There was discomfort but not yet the pain which would begin to crush her, as if captive in a medieval torture chamber. Over the years her vocabulary struggled to give a fluent account of her suffering. There were no words. And no sufficient painkillers for fear of strong doses becoming addictive.

This was major and traumatic surgery and April suffered for her happiness. She struggled and sweated like a drug addict in withdrawal, bloodied and bruised and her rebooted body doing topsy-turvy twists, inducing tormented screams. Always, when questioned about her *need* to be a woman, and about the faddish nature of modern transgender 'trends', April would recall the agony before the ecstasy confidently explaining it's not an adventure undertaken on an impulse, like a day at the seaside.

There was more to suffer. The nurses were constantly in attention, alert to the need for hygiene while the labia and vagina healed. The artificial vagina wants to close, to fill the vacuum and, as Coccinelle explained, the need for the oiling of her metal plugs. This plug, a vaginal speculum, was placed inside April when her surgery was complete. Twice a day for twenty minutes a time it was manipulated, April told to breathe slowly and cough to allow the speculum to move in and out smoothly.

I always wanted to win an Academy Award, so I called it Oscar.

Internal bleeding continued for weeks, akin to post-natal motherhood, and April learned to use tampons to soak up the blood. The body doesn't stop wanting to heal, so the new vagina must be dilated often. Regular and penetrative sex with a man will also keep the opening operational and as large as intended. The sexual pleasure, the anticipated orgasms – all a matter of the healing, the tissue transfer, the nerve ends and the individual. There is no warranty; this is one job where satisfaction can't be guaranteed.

I am a transsexual. I was born a man, but I was a woman inside my brain and my body. I became a woman, but I am a transsexual. That's important.

Of course, April was lucky in that she was a beautiful boy. Her form and features and her early age surgery were a bonus, but she still endured nasty disbelief, with strangers poking her breasts to see if they were real, others reaching to pull off her eyelashes, a move she sidestepped, turning to flutter them at passing cars. April was single-minded, in that her life was now as a woman, she'd become herself as well as a founder member of a then small and exclusive club, a time when LGBTQ+ was an unimagined conjuration of support codes. Getting about was painful, her happiness most glorious. The bits of her body she'd despised were gone but still courage was needed to face the world. To dip a toe in the water, so to speak.

Julia Lockwood, five years younger than April, arrived to be with her, bringing mature conversation and advice. April said that she talked to Julia, as she did with Bambi, as if they were in scenes from the series *Sex in the City*. It was eternal gossip and plans. Yesterday was, well, *yesterday.*

Julia Lockwood sounds most grown-up, capable, being present when April was being cleaned and re-bandaged and manipulated, a helping arm for a walk along the corridors, an ear for the hope and fears, and a recipient of a classic gin-dry April-ism. They'd gone for a drive from the clinic and stopped at the beach hotel's swimming pool. The heat was oppressive, and Julia leaped into the water while April, warned not to immerse herself, sat at the side paddling her feet. Finally, it was all too hot and too much and she lifted herself into the water, to Julia's horror. April, as the water rose to her neck, saw the shock on her face. She glanced down.

It's all right, darling, it's waterproof.

We were sitting in her flat in Fulham, London, in early autumn 2021 when, from her sick bed she told the story to a couple of visitors. More than sixty years on her body was again giving her pain, but she smiled at the end of the telling – you knew she was seeing that moment – and said she'd rarely been happier. The fulfilment meant everything. Watching her, she was reliving one of those days when you're certain the sky is higher than it should be. There's an enchantment in the air. That day by the Moroccan swimming pool there was nothing but hope.

Her face, full makeup for her guests that day, now lined and cut a little with the discomfort of dying, was sketched with a little Bugs Bunny smile, her teeth over her lower lip.

I put up with bullshit all my life. After my operation I felt so strong and triumphant. I had all the arrogance of youth. If I'd known what I know now I wouldn't have been so sure of myself ... the lows I've experienced are the same proportions of the tremendous highs.

The renowned travel writer Jan Morris, formerly James Morris who, as the correspondent for *The Times* was with the British team which completed the first ascent of Mount Everest in 1953, was operated on by Dr Burou in 1972. At a dinner in Oxford in 2005, we talked about Casablanca. It was only for a few minutes, for the subject that evening was politicians and spies, but April was a common cause. Jan's *Conundrum* spells out her experience but that evening there was joy in her eyes as she recalled her 'moment of freedom'.

Did she try to contact April or any other Casablanca graduates?

'Everyone was anonymous there and everyone was happy as individuals. The point for most of us was starting again, having another life. We all left Casablanca as someone else. Dr B [Jan Morris never fully identified Dr Burou in her book] was a saviour.'

The prolific and accomplished author, who began transition with drugs in 1964, went to Morocco because surgeons in the UK and Europe would only treat him if he and his wife Elizabeth, they married in 1949 and had five children, divorced. That was too much.

By 1972, Dr Burou's name was circulating more widely and he did at least two surgeries a day. He had many requests, some remarkable: 'I often get appeals from patients to operate on their teenaged sons. I tell them to wait until the boy comes of age, because the operation is final and irreversible and you can't risk making a mistake.' He said that by 1974 he had operated on a French Roman Catholic priest who was aged fifty, an Italian professor, several doctors, writers and artists and many prostitutes and transvestite performers. With the publication of *Conundrum* that same year, even only identified as 'Dr B', he became, in the vernacular of the day, 'Mr Sex Change'.

Jan Morris caught his essence in her first book written under her new name:

I did not know his address, but when I arrived in Casablanca I looked him up in the telephone book and was told to come round to his clinic next afternoon. He was exceedingly handsome. He was small, dark, rather intense of feature, and was dressed as if for some kind of beach activity. He wore a dark blue, open-necked shirt, sports trousers and games shoes and he was very bronzed. He welcomed me with a bemused smile, as though his mind were in St Tropez. What could he do for me, he asked? I told him I thought he probably knew very well. 'Ah, I think that's so. You wish the operation. Very well, let us see you.' He examined my organs. He plumped my breasts – *'très, très bons'*. He asked if I was an athlete. 'Very well,' he said, 'come in this evening, and we shall see what we can do. You know my fee? Ah, well, perhaps you will discuss it with my receptionist – *bien, au revoir,* until this evening!'

In 1970, because of a news event in April's life, a headline hysteria, *Sunday Mirror* journalist Paul Hughes accompanied my friend, the photographer Eddie Sanderson, to the Casablanca clinic. Their lavish report and images spread over two pages reflected the fascination and fear at the very notion of the changing of sex. Eddie Sanderson says the clinic was quieter, neater and more professional than many he'd visited. The focus very much on maternity with screaming babies and lots of happy mothers. Still, it was a cocoon of a Brave New World. Madame Burou talked at length to Paul Hughes and explained, 'We have at least two applications a day for the sex change operation. They come from all over the world. This week we have done three operations. Last week we did four. All over the world there are these people who feel so tragic because they are mentally and psychologically women but have the characteristics of a male body.' She elaborated, and it sounded like a boast, but it was the heart of the matter: 'A couple of months after the operation here, our young women could have examination by doctors in their home countries who would probably not notice they had ever been men.'

Which is what April very much believed, no need ever more to live in subjunctive mood. She sent letters to her friends at Le Carrousel, to Les Lee and Bambi and to Little Gloria in London, and also to Tony, the boy she said was one of the two she always wanted to marry. For her, the fumbling romance with Tony was a milestone, something to be officially sanctioned and in her thinking they were the love of each other's lives. Tony was not so convinced. When she wrote to him about the operation, how their union could all be joy, he replied with, ironically, a Dear John letter. He'd married. Coccinelle's lover Robert abandoned her after surgery and April's Tony moved on. For the moment. Few forgot April.

Luckily, by then April had returned to Paris, escorted by Julia Lockwood, and was with familiar faces, people who understood and cushioned her dismay and disappointment. After the surgery, her person was a whirlwind of thoughts and hormones. She'd kept her promise to herself and become a woman, not a *born* woman but surgically created: a transsexual. She understood this in 1960, and looming, heading toward seven decades later, the controversy over status continues, festooned with arguments and rage about legal and moral rights. In the world of Wittgenstein what would the great philosopher make of such a dramatic change of identity? By doing so do you stop being the person you were? Cease to exist? Is unconditional love possible? Who are you? Initially, in Paris, April's concern was more basic – sleeping with her American friend from Le Carrousel, a lean, muscled dancer whom she knew as Skippy. They'd been, according to him, *mates*, a word she disdained, but he was relaxing and fun and quite stunning.

A handsome beast, darling.

He was her other promise. He'd seen her off at Orly airport and coaxed an agreement that he could be the first to have sex with her.

It was Bastille Day and we were dancing until four in the morning. He took my hand and said, 'You're coming home with me tonight.'

I was terrified out of my life, but we made love, and it was astonishing. I didn't think it would work and afterwards I started crying, I was so happy. He said, 'What are you crying for?' And he threw open the window – over the rooftops of Paris – and you looked down at the rue Pigalle covered in bunting and all the cars were tooting their horns and he said, 'There you are, the whole of Paris is celebrating the loss of your virginity.'

April never tired of telling this. On her sick bed she pointed to her balcony and out to a bleak London day and asked her friends, as she talked about that night with Skippy, to imagine blazing rockets shooting to the sky with the Eiffel Tower glowing with approval in the background. That, to her, was how it was.

All because I'd had it away, darling.

What you want to know is, how was it for Skippy? Was it different to making love with someone born a woman? April, for all the brazen demeanour, was prim about this intimacy. She said that Skippy told her their lovemaking was no different to his previous sexual experiences. Or, throughout the years, had anyone else said different. She agreed, they might have said different things to others but everybody she knew was such a gossip, she surely would have heard. Most of her lovers knew her background, some did not. There was no fuss about it either way. She said that she never bothered telling one night stands her secret and they found nothing different about her. What they did think, she said, is that they'd hit the jackpot.

She was hesitant when our conversation focused around the mechanics of her gender reassignment, how her bits worked. It wasn't prurience but interest and, of course, a curiosity on behalf of the millions of people who were engaged with her so ahead-of-its-time story. She said she'd never exchanged notes with other women about how their bits worked so why dwell on hers. She always insisted, with clever April avoidance, that the 'money shot' was always a champagne moment. Importantly, she was happy. Sex, she said, was a revelation, and that first experience had been everything.

A painful delight, darling.

To keep things functional – and less painful – she carried on practising as well as performing at Le Carrousel, which had fading allure for her. Now that she was officially *Miss April Ashley* – changed by deed poll for a baker's dozen of pound notes – she was certain she'd broken a bad spell and left her past in a foreign country and opted to live as such; the George Jamieson paperwork would be an almost whole lifetime complication with officialdom everywhere. She got used to hassle. And hassling.

Miss Ashley calling.

PART THREE

Social Butterfly

'I've been everywhere and done everything. I've eaten caviar at Cannes, sausage rolls at the dogs. I've played baccarat at Biarritz and darts with the rural dean. What is there left for me but marriage?'

The Lady Vanishes, Iris Matilda Henderson (Margaret Lockwood), 1938

Eight

Darkest Hour

'Destiny's waiting for tea, so hurry along,
it won't wait for you.'
'Lake of Gardonne', *The Poems of Sarah Churchill*,
Leslie Frewin, 1966

It was time for April to play her favourite Hollywood character: Scarlett O'Hara. Everyone wanted her attention. She was stunning and at times stopped the music in the London she returned to, a city equally in years of transformation. It was wealthy and poor in turns of the corner, divided by us and them, a metropolis healing from the scars of war and also struggling to find itself. April fitted right in.

Dandy Kim Caborn-Waterfield said he'd seen April around town, but it was only in early 1961 when he enjoyed a drink at Les Ambassadeurs with her and Shirley Anne Field that his wonderment began. Immersed in having a good time, in clubland and society nightlife, he thought no more but he was a conduit for introductions. Les Ambassadeurs attracted an eclectic custom, a place prowled by playboys and film producers and decorated by the talent they were chasing. Rank starlets and ambitious models set their sights on the real and the would-be movie moguls. April rather preferred a title. She admitted that her *the duchess* persona had led her into the hands of those with indulgent privilege. Happily, there were lots of loveable chancers like Dandy Kim about too.

Low on funds, she'd rented a tiny flat in Harrington Gardens in South Kensington but relied on kindness for much of her day-to-day living. Arguably, she was an early 'influencer', in that people liked having her around to show off their life-style. April was always smiling, happy and up for fun. Writer Veronica Howell reflected in 2021 on what was on display: 'As a young adult the released joie de vivre, her changed self made her a welcome good-time-girl at any party and she crossed class and social boundaries as an early celebrity funded by largesse – champagne sent to her table, gifts of clothes and jewels, rides in private jets to swinging places.' But, as April always said, no one truly ever knew, or could be expected to understand, how furiously this particular swan was paddling under the water and the heart-fluttering anxiety of keeping Miss Ashley's secret submerged.

At Les Ambassadeurs, of course, we agreed, the glamorously dressed crowd were so busy on their quest of being wonderful, they didn't trifle with her antecedents. Les Ambassadeurs and the Milroy club ('Mil' from owner Jean-Jean Millstein, 'roy' from bandleader Harry Roy), established as the 'nighttime headquarters of society', quickly became part of April's social geography. Towering at 6 feet 4 inches, Millstein became John Mills, but never lost his mangled diction. His early partner, like him from Kraków, Poland, was Siegi Sessler. There was much talk about how they got their seed money, for both became serious players in London nightlife. April liked the tale that they'd been intelligence agents in the war and con-tinued connections as east-west relations chilled in a neatly carved post-war Europe. Others told April they had aristo-cratic connections.

Millstein/Mills most certainly romanced Rosemarie Kanzler, but that was when she was Swiss builder's daughter Leni Revelli and long before, after five husbands, she became one of the world's richest women. Any romantic notions about the money were that – romantic. Mills and Siegi Sessler were both in catering during the war, in charge of meat for troops. They made a fortune on the black market. They had the commodity that everyone wanted, everyone needed. Secret information? No, bootleg sausages.

When April began going to the club, it was located at the bottom of Park Lane, at Hamilton Place, overlooking Hyde Park. Mills had split with his partner and his background investors were managed by a lawyer with offices by the Connaught hotel. On the top floor he'd placed the Milroy, with society favourite Paul Adam replacing Harry Roy as, in many ways, the leader of the band. For himself, Mills created a small apartment one more floor up, to which he added a movie room, where he could screen films for special guests – especially visiting Hollywood stars like Bob Hope, who always denied stalking April. The club was a spectacular introduction for April to a group of whom many were as lost and finding their way as she was. Oh, she had fun. With aristocratic elocution and wit of a scouser she was a sharp foil in this world of too much cuff and too little chin. She adored all the history, the tapestry of her surroundings, anxious to know who was who and what was what and most were eager to tell her.

No. 5 Hamilton Place, built in 1810, stands on the site of one of King Henry VIII's hunting lodges and was purchased by Leopold de Rothschild in 1878. Rothschild waved money at the building and it is very much fin de siècle Louis XV. The Barbetti staircase remains a marvel of woodcarving and has led many guests to dizzy heights of enjoyment. April's future friend and admirer, the First World War veteran and accomplished scientist and inventor Captain Leonard Frank Plugge and his wife, Mrs Gertrude Ann Muckleston, took over Hamilton Place when he sat as MP for Chatham. Plugge was a connoisseur of beautiful women and would engage an assortment of them to cater to his every need, his only prerequisite being that they were completely naked while doing so. 'Dirty Lenny' is how Kim Waterfield knew him: 'He kept a couple of mistresses in Dolphin Square and had what in the Deep South of America they call "weird ways".'

When Dirty Lenny sold Hamilton Place with its magnificent garden to John Mills in 1950, he was a central member of the rich, titled and aspiring Princess Margaret Set. It was Les Ambassadeurs to which April's new fast-living crowd went, almost every evening, in almost every circumstance. April would spend hours doing her makeup, picking a gown and almost as long making her entrance. She floated in. But there were rules. The American-Polish film producer Gene Gutowski was a habitué, recalling in 2012, 'There was dancing to the orchestra of Paul Adam [tagged 'Princess Margaret's favourite bandleader']. Dark suits were obligatory, as were black shoes. I was once turned away at the door for wearing a dark blue blazer: "This is not Miami, Mr Gutowski," the man at the front door admonished me.'

April never had a problem looking the part. She was credited, even before Casablanca, with an *instinctual style and understanding of the artifice of glamour.* She was also hilarious and kind company. Julia Lockwood adored her. In Paris, the young actress had introduced her to Sarah Churchill, the wartime leader's daughter and someone who'd be an elder – by more than twenty years – soul sister. She tutored April in being part of a difficult world. Darkened by the shadow of Winston Churchill's fame and achievements, his eldest daughter rebelled by running away to the theatre with Vic Oliver, a fabulously famous actor-comedian she met when he was topping the bill at the Adelphi theatre in London.

Giving her father a V-sign – but not for 'victory' – she married Oliver amid much media fanfare in New York in 1936. By the time she took April's arm she was divorced and widowed. Her second husband was Anthony Beauchamp, the celebrity photographer of April's favourites Vivien Leigh and

Audrey Hepburn. Beauchamp had killed himself in 1957 with a drugs overdose at their flat in Hyde Park Gardens in London. April, grateful for the social guidance, felt protective of her new friend. She also looked after herself as a fashion and photographic model, natural employment for a graceful beauty with connections, a job she often found as bitchy as the Le Carrousel dressing room.

She didn't advertise her transition but model agencies who learned where she'd worked in Paris put up shutters. She learned then that 'friends' from the past were jealous of her progress in finding herself and well-remunerated employment. She says she should have known better, she'd seen much cruelty at work in her life. April did what April always did – soared on against the wind. She became one of what in later decades were called supermodels, a group of go-to faces and bodies, perfect for showing off new fashion, lingerie and highlighting accessories. She worked semi-naked, all filmed by clever camerawork and delicate propriety, for soap and deodorant brands. An asked-for underwear model for *Vogue,* she was photographed by the glossy magazine's star Brian Duffy, who also regularly requested Jean Shrimpton for his shoots. It was a step up all sorts of ladders and if you look at the images, April sweeping toward the camera, photographed by David Bailey, or in chic Chanel and elaborate hats, posing and posturing for the already legendary Terence Donovan and the upcoming and naughty-faced Terry O'Neill, she looks confident, competent and relaxed.

Because I was so tall, all the photographers were on my side. They were always incredibly nice to me.

April's busy work was with Roter Models, who staged live showcases for their latest fashions, and it was very much a hectic, tantrum-and-tiaras time with the girls and designers all going full pelt. April made good lifetime friends, and one of them, Pauline Moore, appeared at her memorial service in Liverpool in June 2022. Like everyone there she was sad but upbeat. April was never ever anything other than someone to be celebrated. She'd got through the barrage of life. April often talked of her delight at Pauline's reaction when she finally told her of Casablanca: 'That's lovely.' Pauline explained, 'I was a fashion model when I met her in 1960. Unbeknown to me, obviously, she must have just completed the operation which, of course, none of us realised. And she joined Roter Models which was a fashion house in the heart of the rag trade. It was a special time for her because she wasn't being judged in any way. Nobody knew her secret. I didn't, and we spent a lot of time together. She didn't talk about what had happened to her – at that point, she couldn't. Because my parents' pub was only in Duke Street, St James's, she came back there quite a lot. We used to go on little pub crawls around South Kensington and Knightsbridge and it was a marvellous time.

'And I'm glad she had that special time because once the news came out, everything was very different. And people spoke to her and looked at her in a different way. At least the time we had at Roter Models she was able to be herself. I think how lucky I was to have actually spent that time with her in the 1960s because there's never been a period like that, Mary Quant and King's Road which was full of strange people; it was wonderful, a great period of time. April was happy and she was very entertaining. She had a very difficult life but I think she certainly made the best of it in every way. What else can you do with anything? She went on to help a lot of people which was wonderful. She turned it around and put it all – her life and her troubles – to good use.'

April had ambition and boyfriends. She'd hooked up again with 'love of her life' Tony but being 'the other woman' was dismal. Far more fun was going on the razzle with her new set, including friends like the actor Peter Finch and the eccentric bunch that constantly surrounded her.

The toffs and tarts of life, darling.

That round-the-clock social mayhem eased the way as she reluctantly left the married Tony behind.

Tony's family knew all that time about the whole thing. His second wife – she's a big, Australian girl, I used to go and play with the children in the park – said to me: 'I thought I would hate you because I know everything about you. I have to admit I like you.'

Most everyone did yet, despite all the social action, April acknowledged this was a lonely time. She had no home proper. Julia Lockwood, who she'd camped down with on first arriving in London, and Sarah Churchill were devoted to their acting careers. Sarah Churchill, who'd played, to April's delight, the Dietrich role in a 1950 US production of *Witness for the Prosecution*, was also seeing Thomas 'Henry' Touchet-Jesson, Lord Audley. Any conversations about this period in her life led April to such elaborate bouts of aristocratic name-dropping it was helpful to consult *Burke's Peerage*. She made it sound that, at least after 6 p.m., she rarely met anyone without a title. There was always a story.

Her modelling colleague Bronwen Pugh was married to Lord Bill Astor – *Viscount Astor, darling*. Between trysts with Mandy Rice-Davies in the London flat she shared with Christine Keeler, Astor hosted the supposedly great and the good, including a Russian spy and war minister John Profumo at his Cliveden estate in Berkshire. When in 1963 the security-sex scandal began to dismantle prime minister Harold Macmillan's government, the last grandee Conservative administration, April became a sought-after refuge for on-the-run Christine Keeler.

Here happenstance is once again astounding, and there's another puzzle: what magic magnetism caught April, circling her with people who knew people who would matter in her life? By accident, she'd again met Duncan Melvin who, with his friend Major Donald Neville-Willing, mentored her in the theatrical agency days, and was invited to a Sunday afternoon gathering. As if a lead domino fell, the friendships and liaisons dominating the perils and pleasures for the rest of her fascinating life began.

The afternoon was a grand affair filled with, to her, familiar and famous names but which time has gently forgotten. April mingled and found herself furiously being fed champagne and flirted with by a fan for once about her own age, a tall, jolly chap called Tim Willoughby, the grandson of Nancy Astor, mother of Bill, and Britain's first female MP. It was only when he escorted her to his Wilton Row home near Belgrave Square, stopping in Belgrave Mews to receive insults and refreshments from cantankerous landlord Paddy Kennedy at the Star pub, she learned his full and somewhat aphrodisiac title. Blood rushed to her head.

And elsewhere, darling.

Lord Timothy Willoughby de Eresby was an adventurer and heir to a fortune. The friends he'd introduced to her at the Star were luminaries, gamblers, chancers and masters of London's criminal underworld. Belgravia was a long way from Pitt Street. April offered a Michelin guide of London's restaurants, a list of elite nightclubs and country houses they visited, a phonebook of names for which there was always space in the gossip columns of Charles Greville, *Daily Mail*, and William Hickey, *Daily Express*. For them, April was another attractive traveller with the latest round of society Beautiful People. She said she adored Tim Willoughby but didn't want to marry him. They slept together but there are imponderable platonic episodes in their time together, interrupted by his travels or mood swings. April could be diplomatically vague. Others have suggested he was sexually ambivalent. April was happy to drift along: this was a new world, and it was exciting, if exacting with the constant fear of the revelation of her life before becoming the most sought after Miss Ashley.

We were in her flat in the south of France, it was forty years and more on from the stories she was telling, her memories clearly still fresh, and she pointed to the door of the fridge which was decorated with a nostalgia of photographs. Her long finger sought out a particular one. It was of the six maids of honour at the Queen's coronation in 1953, of which Tim Willoughby's sister Jane, the daughter of Lord Ancaster of Drummond Castle and Grimsthorpe, was one. She's alongside Lady Jane Vane-Tempest-Stewart, sister of Lady Annabel Birley, later Annabel Goldsmith for whom the nightclub Annabel's in the basement of the Clermont Club in Berkeley Square was named.

I knew them both, but Jane Willoughby and I were friends. I used to see her almost every day in London.

She also met characters – flamboyant and ambitious people striving, as she was, to find a place in this quickly changing world. None more so than Tim Willoughby, who was always up for a punt at the gaming tables or in some madcap scheme. Along with Bernard van Cutsem and Simon Fraser, he was a guarantor for the rent of 44 Berkeley Square where the amoral John Aspinall established the Clermont Club. April was uneasy around Aspinall – a man only comfortable in his own zoo – liked Mark Birley and James Goldsmith, but was affronted by Ian Fleming, the James Bond author tempted by all things exotic, who frisked her head to toe with his eyes. Lord 'Lucky' Lucan, who was Aspinall's stooge at the Clermont Club, was polite but distant and engaged better with Tim Willoughby than with her. The two often gambled together at illegal chemin de fer games, which Aspinall hosted at friends' homes, including Tim Willoughby's in Wilton Row; the usually losing players included David Stirling, founder of the Special Air Service (SAS), Sarah Churchill's brother-in-law Christopher Soames, Lord Derby, the Duke of Devonshire, Lord Bob Boothby and, if the house was luckier than usual, the Fiat empire's Gianni Agnelli, the uncrowned king of Italy.

April loved the story of Tim and Jane Willoughby being arrested when police raided one of Aspinall's illegal chemmy games at 1 Hyde Park Square, echoes of Little Gloria's charge sheet. It was, we agreed, something out of the Keystone Kops when on 10 January 1958 stone-faced uniformed policemen broke up the evening and charged all involved. It was an event considered unremarkable at the time, but it would change the face of gambling in Britain and rapidly turn London into the gambling capital of the world, as the court case forced gaming law legislation. All Aspinall's fault for holding the game on 'the wrong side of the park', thought April, although she said Tim Willoughby enjoyed the 'great lark' of being bundled into a police van with Mrs Birley and the others. Lady Jane found it more uncomfortable. Tim Willoughby shrugged with mild amusement, but Aspinall's mother Lady Osborne, grandmother of George Osborne, the future chancellor of the exchequer, known as 'Lady O' and hostess for the evening, her game pie had been highly praise, was horrified at it all. She watched as her son was formally charged with 'common gaming house' offences.

When it was Lady O's turn to face the lawman, she seemed to swell in her body and took on a great presence and boomed at the hapless arresting officer, 'This is absurd. All these people are friends of ours. And none of them is common. Young man, there was nothing common here until you walked in.'

Nevertheless, London's good, great-and-not-so-great were driven the short distance to Paddington nick. April recalled hearing the story.

It was all quite civilised. The police are awful snobs, so they treated these people with the right accents in a very nice way, cups of tea and that sort of thing. Of course, half of them were pissed and found it all a great joke. Not so funny for Jane – the next night she went to the club and it was past closing time but, of course, ordered a drink. The next thing the police ran in and she got arrested again. For drinking after hours. It was quite something to be arrested twice in forty-eight hours.

By the time April arrived on Tim Willoughby's arm the gambling laws had changed, and the action had moved into casinos, but the gamblers wore the same hopeful faces. She said she found herself more relaxed around another gambler, the painter Lucien Freud, to whom Jane Willoughby was devoted. So much so that she did his laundry for more than forty years. The group were regulars at the Star, which even if a little obscured by the arch framing the northern entrance to Belgrave Mews West, attracted – was a magnet – for an eclectic cast of characters, many of whom thought luck was a skill. Maybe an art form. Rather like life. They mixed with the taciturn and tea-drinking Billy Hill, the boss of London's underworld, soon-to-be Great Train Robber Bruce Reynolds, who planned the raid in the upstairs bar, and an April favourite, the Eton-educated, Sandhurst graduate and newly divorced Maharaja of Baroda, Sir Pratap Singh Gaekwad, one of the richest men in the world, who she called *Boss*. When he was at Eton he'd been approached by a master and reprimanded for not attending church.

'But why would I?' asked Boss.

'To pray to God,' boomed the pompous master.

'Sir, in my country, I am God.' He didn't act the part at the Star. He was always happy to buy a round, ordering in his soft, agreeable English-Indian accent, which endeared him even more to the crowd. The wartime hero double-agent Eddie Chapman, another drinking friend of April's, reckoned Boss was the nicest 'foreign person' he ever met.

For April, this was one of her most happy periods. She was carefree. Content. No one she met appeared to give a hoot where she'd come from. Their only interest was that she wasn't boring and was intent on enjoying a good time. Which was pretty much, if at times a little harsher, her own philosophy.

Tim was marvellous. He was glamorous and exciting. We would do the craziest things. He never gave a damn about anyone. One day he rang me up and he said, 'Can I take you out for dinner?'

I said, 'Oh, yes.' I'd always say, 'How shall we dress?' because you never knew where you were going for dinner. Whether you were going to end up at a ball somewhere.

He said, 'Oh, nothing special. Something elegant and ...'

I wore a little Dior suit and we arrived at this house and I said, 'Tim. You bastard. They've all got tiaras on. Whose house is this?' It was the Earl and Countess of Thirsk and all these women were in ballgowns. It was a ball we were going to.

I get to the top of the staircase and I meet Lady Thirsk and I said, 'I'm terribly sorry Lady Thirsk, I wasn't told it was a ball.'

Later, it was one of those lovely, mad moments at the end of dinner. There's about sixty or seventy people sitting down to dinner and then all the ladies withdraw, which they did in those days. Lady Thirsk saw me and she said: 'April. Don't you want to join the ladies?'

I said, 'No, thank you, Lady Thirsk, I'm having so much fun with the boys I'll stay here.' Shocked was Tim but he said, 'That's why I adore you.'

We used to go to the Mirabelle all the time and he'd say, 'Caviar and champagne, please,' and the waiter would come with the caviar. It was always in a big silver bowl, within a bowl and ice and the pot and they would give you a dollop or two. Tim would say: 'Leave it.' The whole bloody bowl.

Then one day we're both sitting there, and he said, 'Oh, look, there's my father over there.'

I said, 'Which one is your father?'

He pointed out this man and said, 'That's my father.'

I said, 'My God, what shall we do?'

He said, 'Nothing. Eat your caviar.' When we looked around, his father had gone.

He said I had to go down to Grimsthorpe but I chickened out of that. I've never forgiven myself. I chickened out at the last minute. I was so petrified of meeting these earls and countesses and he was furious. He said, 'I sent the butler down with the chauffeur to pick you up and you weren't on the proper train, and you didn't come … you will never be invited to Grimsthorpe or Castle Drummond ever again.' Later, he changed his mind but then drowned in 1963. He was a year younger than me, he'd have been twenty-seven. Tim always said to me, 'If you could have children, I would marry you tomorrow.' Jane inherited the title – and 75,000 acres – under some medieval succession rules.

That would be Nancy Jane Marie Heathcote-Drummond-Willoughby, 28th Baroness Willoughby de Eresby. April loved sending her letters and made a point of the postman checking the name and address.

Jane Willoughby, fearing an understandable lack in April's knowledge of her brother's temperament, tried to help her negotiate around his wilder and more wanton ways. On the other side, Lucien Freud liked to join in the action. In the first part of William Weaver's deservedly award-winning two-volume biography *The Lives of Lucian Freud: Youth 1922–1968* (Bloomsbury Publishing, 2019), the author offers:

Willoughby conducted himself as a neo-Regency buck; his dissipation so extravagant that, marvelling at it, Freud felt moved to compete. 'I used to go with Tim to Aspinall's on Thursday nights. "Let's go and play cards," I said, "I feel really lucky." Ludicrous behaviour; I always lost; I'd lost a hundred pounds or so before; anyway, I'd go halves with Tim.

'He said, "I'm feeling incredibly unlucky; oh, OK, I'll be lucky." We went to the Clermont Club and I, amazingly, won £980, a huge amount in the fifties (I remember Aspinall saying, "It's the first time I ever wrote a cheque for £980"), and gave Tim half, and bought the Rodin Crouching Woman, for two hundred or four hundred pounds, amazingly modest. I thought this is the life and went back a few weeks later. The only genuine players were Lord Derby and me, the others were house gamblers, phony.'

These were known as 'the good furniture', 'bait for the big money'. April synched, her initial apprehension adjusting to the cavalier kindness of most she met and puzzled at the obvious love between Freud and Lady Jane. She asked Tim if he thought they would marry but he never explained. William Weaver quotes the painter as saying:

I was asked quite a bit to Grimsthorpe. I liked Jane's father, a one-legged courtier. Jane's mother wouldn't sleep with him because of the leg missing ... they can't have disliked me that much ... Jane couldn't understand why I didn't want to get married. The situation of her houses and things – she takes trouble about tenants and farms etc. – and being a nominal dauphin: the element of duty to it, foreign to my nature. Obviously after Tim died, they were thinking of the line not dying out. I thought how odd that people think like that. Jane said, much later, 'I'm glad we didn't. It wouldn't have worked.' There would have been bad feeling.

Tim Willoughby vanished in the week beginning 5 August 1963. That summer April had visited a somewhat depressed Willoughby in Morocco and their plan was to catch up again in Spain. She never saw him again. Investigators made a piecemeal job of attempting to establish events. The consensus was he'd sailed in a small boat making for Corsica in inclement weather; in the days after his disappearance Jane Willoughby arranged vain flyovers across the area.

For April, the world seemed upside down: Stephen Ward, central to the Profumo scandal, killed himself on 3 August and on the eighth, drinking pal Bruce Reynolds led the Great Train Robbery.

William Weaver has Lucien Freud reflecting on the millions in used banknotes hijacked from the Glasgow-to-London mail train: 'It had a terrifically heartening effect.' Which was especially true for those rushed to the fields around the tracks, searching for fluttering fivers. He quotes Freud being astute on Tim Willoughby: 'One interesting thing in retrospect: Tim Willoughby was suicidal in a frivolous sort of way. He was begged not to go out in the boat.'

Like April, Tim Willoughby loved the sea and she was convinced it was his presence she felt when she was stuck in the Pacific decades later with Nazi Ronald.

> I was in total awe of Tim. I adored him but I wasn't in love with him. Tim was this incredibly handsome, swashbuckling man. To be that rich and so young and have an enormous title and to have fun with me was wonderful. Yet, awesome. Everywhere you go, you never have to wait for anything. 'Yes, my lord … No, my lord'. I adored him, but I could never say I was in love with him not like I was with Tony. I'd have walked off a cliff for Tony.

Which, metaphorically, she did with another heir to lavish aristocratic accoutrements. The Hon. Arthur Cameron Corbett, first son of rigid Presbyterian Lord Rowallan, the chief scout, formerly governor general of Tasmania, was born to inherit a castle, title and seven thousand east Ayrshire acres of Scotland.

He called himself Frank, he rarely was, when they first met on an arranged date at the Caprice restaurant in London's Mayfair. It transpired he was a transvestite and his wife did not understand him. April sympathised over daily champagne cocktails. Frank/Arthur was besotted but when April told him she was involved with the equally grand aristocrat Tim Willoughby he had a jealous tantrum, a proper wobbly. April said that was the warning she ignored. Her new suitor would not be deterred. He persisted as if on an Arthurian quest and demeaned his rival with detrimental comment. She, in turn, years on still irritated by the memory, had countered with an April aperçu.

I'd tell him: at least Tim's title is from the thirteenth century and not bought from Lloyd George like yours.

More slings and arrows were to follow.

Nine

Outrageous Fortune

'In Nature there are neither rewards or punishments,
only consequences.'
Robert Green Ingersoll, lecture, 1873

Arthur Corbett, at age forty-two, could be a charmer. While
over-serving April with champagne at the Caprice he'd pause
between gulps, light a cigarette, and murmur: 'You are going to
be the most beautiful Lady Rowallan that ever there was.' Her
eyelashes flutter in dismay but also her thoughts at the prospect
of properly becoming one of the regal ladies of the land.

When April decided she was being above herself, she'd
attempt retreat, targeting Arthur during one of his tireless and
shameless seductions.

Yes, Arthur, but where's the castle?

Far from Arthur's thoughts. A closet transvestite from childhood, he was fascinated by Le Carrousel and April's star turn
at the club. He'd seen her at the Caprice with Tim Willoughby
and, playing incognito as Frank, arranged the first meeting
through another drag aficionado. From their lunches, which
quickly moved from once a week to every day, she guessed
even before Frank confessed to being Arthur that his deepest
desires were outside regular parameters. Awarded the Croix
de Guerre for wartime heroism, he was a full-on, overachiev-
ing, A-personality male but the desire to dress up as a woman

was increasingly overwhelming. In Beak Street near Piccadilly Circus, the Old Etonian was a regular at a facility which accommodated his needs: he would dress as a woman, apply full makeup, and engage in mutual masturbation with one of the ever-changing team of young men.

April found him interesting but cloying and his confessions even if fascinating were disconcerting, but there's no question the thought of Rowallan Castle − *Kilmarnock, darling?* − no matter the location and torn seams of the place, was attractive. She'd happily acknowledge that throughout her life she was sure she'd be queen of somewhere. Lady Rowallan had a pleasant rhythm to it. Arthur's tolerance, all but unique for the day, when she explained about Casablanca during their his-and-her confessional conversations, endeared April.

I told him my secret. He didn't care at all. He was determined to have me, it became an obsession with him.

Being the centre of anyone's life is seductive and, given April's antecedents as an outcast, the appeal was enormous. The twist, of course, was that Arthur didn't want so much to be with her but to truly *be* her. His crucial comment, picked up over the years by both professional and amateur psychologists, was that the reality of April was more heart-stopping than any of his own spectacular and indulgent fantasies.

From 16 November 1960, the day he first gave April lunch at the Caprice, there were four people in Arthur Corbett's marriage: himself, his other self, April and his slender Scots wife Eleanor Boyle, who knew of his penchant for dressing as a woman. They'd married in 1945 and had four children. He borrowed her clothes yet Eleanor believed these other moments were infrequent. For Arthur, they were more and more recur-rent. He convinced himself that if he brought April full-time into his life, he would be content with her, presumably as his living fantasy, and keep his own trousers on.

Yet, even in full office uniform or dressed for formal occa-sions, the woman in Arthur would suddenly appear like a genie out the bottle and creating as much fuss. This character was also a gourmet of cruel insults. April, she's twenty-five, only months since Casablanca, gets the full blast of Arthur as Jekyll and Mr Hyde. The gentler Dr Jekyll, in time, outweighs the bestial Hyde, annoyingly overcompensating, but enough to keep a fragile April on side.

When I met him, I liked him so much, but the more I got to know him, the more I went off him, which was rather sad, because usually the more you get to know someone, the more you like them. I'd never met a schizophrenic before. I'd never met a transvestite before, even though I worked in a drag club. It was all a job. It was the schizophrenia because with Arthur – now I call her 'she who must be obeyed' after *Rumpole* on the television, because when she appeared, he would smoke with the cigarette up at arm's length, like a prop for Lauren Bacall in a film. The legs would be crossed in a very exaggerated way, the voice would become slightly higher pitched. He didn't know when it would happen. 'She' arrived daily. She was a very nasty woman. When the knees went very high in a very sober, sort of feminine way, I'd think, Oh my God, she's arrived. I'd say, 'Why don't you put a dress on and get it over and done with?'

She didn't like me at all. She was very jealous and very bitchy. Then when he was back to being Arthur, he would be jealous of anyone who would pay any attention to me. It was very difficult. Even at Le Carrousel you were shielded. You could be a nun. Unless it was someone very special like Josephine Baker you could not even sit with the customers. Mixing with them was a risk – if you got a suspension you were in real trouble because you didn't get paid for ten days and couldn't pay your bloody hotel bill. We all lived in hotels. We looked after each other; Bambi and I could sense trouble and be off. You had to really, really behave. Suddenly, having escaped those sorts of dangers, I find a transvestite schizophrenic. I'm only twenty-five and I haven't lived that well in my life. I was brought up in a very working-class atmosphere. I didn't know much about life, other people's peccadilloes, I had enough of my own concerns to worry about. And even though I'd travelled halfway around the world in the merchant navy, it was all with very rough men, who were lovely and nice but not sophisticated. Kinks for them were something wrong in the engine room. And I get Arthur.

It wasn't only Arthur who had eyes eagerly focused on April. With her photographs in magazines and the talk-of-the-town gossip, London was socially still a village revolving around Oxford Circus, improvement in status was never discreet.

Others saw April's Pygmalion-progress, including her school-days friend from Liverpool, Tommy Robinson a.k.a. Little Gloria who, in 1961, had abandoned prostitution for a legitimate waitressing job to get NHS help in changing gender at Charing Cross Hospital[3] on the Fulham Palace Road in London.

With her income depleted, Little Gloria was pleased to earn extra cash by telling the broadsheet Sunday newspaper, the *People*, that the model and social star April Ashley was once her Liverpool school friend George Jamieson. Veterans at the paper weren't convinced. They thought it was an absurd joke. Or a ploy to distract their resources. They were busy campaigning against the Messina brothers, who controlled vice across London. Now Little Gloria, suspiciously connected to the streets, wanted paying for some tale about a bloke becoming a

---

3   The Charing Cross Hospital was quietly ahead of its time in gender reassignments. Mary Edith Louise Weston, England's celebrated female shot putter, 1924–1930 and 1927's star javelin thrower, became Mark in 1936, following two surgeries by South African surgeon Lennox Broster; two months later he married Alberta Bray in Plymouth.

woman. Sex change? Ridiculous. But, and there's always a but if you're any good at the job, what if? Editor Stuart Campbell looked around the newsroom and his eyes narrowed on hard-bitten reporter Roy East, forty-six, as ever keen to conquer Fleet Street on a Sunday morning.

They unleashed him and some decades of consequences followed. April couldn't confirm it, but I'd put money on Roy East wearing suede shoes, de rigueur for the Sunday news-hounds, when he put his foot in the door of Flat 5, 46 Emperor's Gate, Kensington, to stop her closing it on him. He proudly announced himself and his newspaper which boasted a huge circulation only challenged by the direct opposition, the *News of the World*. Shaken by this unwelcome attention on a cold and icy winter evening in 1961, April blinked her eyes and thought furiously what to do. Instinctively, she shut the door. Or tried to. East pressed the door, she pushed from inside, his foot ventured further inside, she closed the door on it, and pain gave way to valour as he withdrew it at the same time, asking if she had once been a boy called George Jamieson. He'd been investigating her story. They had a verbal joust with East deploying the usual, 'Best to give us your side of the story' and April, having run out of defences, decided that might be best. She wasn't sure how much information they had but with Little Gloria as the source – she was paid five pounds – it was accurate. She said she vainly cajoled East to drop his inquiry but back at his office the headline for 19 November 1961 was THE EXTRAORDINARY CASE OF THE TOP MODEL APRIL ASHLEY: 'HER' SECRET IS OUT. There had been whispers before but this was a thunderclap. April enlisting Arthur Corbett's help heading off exposure only linked him into the story – made it *sexier*. And, of course, by subliminal endorsement, boosted the *People*'s publish-and-be-damned determination. Roy East opened in full flow:

> Her face is familiar to millions of women. It appears regu-larly on advertisements in fashion and beauty magazines.

It has graced *Vogue*. In the plush West End salons and fashion houses, twenty-six-year-old April Ashley is looked on as one of London's most attractive model girls. But last week one of Mayfair's best-kept secrets came out. April confessed to me ...

The top-model-who-was-born-a-boy scoop, which whistled around the world, was not so much a confession as a confirmation but any nuance – *the operation did not transform me, it completed me* – of the why of it was lost in this salacious and early Christmas present for the circulation department. Sales soared, so much so that the rest of Fleet Street was quickly and enthusiastically camped on a distraught April's doorstep. Nearly half a century later she said she could still picture the faces of her mob of would-be interrogators.

It wasn't a beauty contest.

Strangely, and maybe, the years had gone by and she was thoroughly sanguine about her life, she remembered the 'outing' as an opportunity, difficult to endure in the moment, but nevertheless a chance to live the rest of her life with total honesty. There was always the part of April enjoying the spot-light, any little attention: she'd be bereft in a world without Miss Ashley being noticed. She dressed every day for it. Once, when talking about the newspaper exposé, April was staying with me in a guest cottage in farmhouse grounds. This particular morning was wet and miserable and she said she'd come out with me to the shops.

With thunder clouds bunching above, I warned April of the impending storm and grabbed a seen-better-days Henri Lloyd waterproof. April appeared as if dressed for the opera, raised an eyebrow at my loud and aged coat and shrugged off thoughts of the rainstorm.

Water off a duck's back, darling.

And, indeed, we drove off and dodged the storm, and April made a grand entrance at the local Waitrose, where the staff and most shoppers looked at her. Ignorant of her identity, they instinctively knew she was somebody.

It's incredibly difficult to go and have to be a personality. It's fine when you've been through it. With Le Carrousel, I was quite famous in France. Once the show was over and the makeup was off and we'd go out to breakfast, and it was just a load of kids together. We escaped from the star roles. It was extraordinary how ordinary the conversations were. It was about, 'Oh God, tomorrow we've got to get back to work again. I wonder if I could get a day off?' We worked seven days a week. We did two or three shows a night. We worked until two o'clock in the morning. Stardom?

Suddenly, there it was in the press. Overnight, I had to become a personality, I was a celebrity so to speak. That was incredibly difficult. Everybody recognised you. Everybody wanted to meet you. That's how I met everybody. I was the freak. I didn't want to meet them. They wanted to meet me because I was current 'freak of the moment'. I think people react differently.

Even The Beatles had a chance to get used to the idea of what was coming. I was there. I'd been modelling. Now, there were hordes of reporters outside the house. I never denied who I was. People would say to me: 'Do you ever work in France?' I would say I did. 'Did you work at Le Carrousel?' I never tried to deny who I was. I never tried to pretend. I didn't expect to have every single job that I had cancelled overnight. Yes, yes, every one of them. Some photographers who I worked with were furious, but my agents knew. All my friends knew. A lot of people I worked with knew. Every time they wanted their underwear modelled, they chose me, because I was very tall and the lingerie looked so good on me. Every job was cancelled. I never saw them again. I had lots of jobs booked for months in advance and every one was cancelled. Every single one.

Then, they had an audition for Bournville Dark Chocolate and my agents said, 'April, they've asked for you to give a reading.' I was thinking that if only I could get that job. I was going out of my mind with worry about what I was going to do. I thought maybe it wasn't over. I thought maybe there was a little chance. Well, I did the reading, and it was wonderful. Hey, they wanted a beautiful woman with a dark voice to imagine the dark chocolate and they had me read it six times. They applauded and there was a table of about ten people looking at me. There were about two hundred girls there, I think. They said they would let me know.

I walked out and there was a wonderful, wonderful agent called Cathy Kenton and she came running down the stairs after me and she was crying and said, 'Oh April. My heart is broken. They loved you. They said you were magic. But they will not give you the job. It's not them, but Bournville Chocolate say they can't have their name associated with a sex change ... I'm sorry, my darling.'

She threw her arms around me, and she was crying. I decided to take my agent's advice and just give up. There's been many versions but that's what happened. All but overnight I was persona non grata in the fashion world and in England generally. I was never again able to get a job modelling in England. I was monster du jour.

It was a precursor of a more devastating judgement, one that would rule she did not exist at all. By outrageous fortune, for the moment, she had Arthur Corbett. Yet, if you reflect on this confusion of personalities, it was like striking a match at a Guy Fawkes party. The blue touch paper was smouldering. As was Arthur. He wanted to be 'with' April but not, she said, in a sexual sense. He wrote many letters to her pledging his affection and 'pleasure at the thought' of her becoming Lady Rowallan. It was this affection and durability – being there when her work-social network was shattering – which made April reliant on Arthur Corbett, a conflicted man misaligned with living in the mainstream. Corbett knew his father's stern and unflinching nature and that he was gambling with his five-million-pound inheritance but, for April, he was willing to risk all. In return, April was willing to take a chance too.

Her ardent suitor separated from his wife and began divorce proceedings but had also been busy buying a nightclub in Spain, a property close to the then horse-and-cart village of Marbella. While he negotiated the sale of the Jacaranda Club, April's secret was plastered all over the *People*. It didn't deter Arthur, who also arranged to take a nearby villa for his future Lady Rowallan, while in London April saw the life she'd worked so hard to achieve disassembling.

The decision she made, but didn't voice, was to take on the mantle of 'somebody' for protection – as 'nobody' she'd been tried by and convicted and ostracised for gambling her life to complete herself. The so-called Establishment, urged on by the fearful, hiding behind suburbia's net curtains, had stomped on her. Arthur, with his clacking false teeth, early pull-'em-out Scottish dentistry, could reward her with a title and literally surround her with battlements. As 'somebody', she would not be discarded to oblivion on the whim of a callous judge. We discussed this one evening in San Diego, in California, the most progressive of American states, and struggled to solve the puzzle of who could fairly judge April and other transsexuals' life decisions. How many were truly knowledgeable or impartial enough? How do you know what's in a person's head? The question remains pertinent.

In London that Christmas of 1961, April suffered the consequences of a knee-jerk verdict.

There was one young man. He asked me for a date. I said, 'OK. Come round to my flat and pick me up.' He came and I said to him, 'I'll just go and get my coat from the bedroom.' When I came out the sitting room was empty. He'd gone.

Suddenly the telephone rang and he said, 'I'm an awful shit. I've suddenly realised who you are. I can't be seen with you. I'm sorry.'

I said, 'Thank you for at least ringing.'

Most of them were very nice. The shopkeepers because they treat you like a celebrity. It's like going to a restaurant. You always got the best table but you guessed why you'd get the best table because everybody could see you. Vidal Sassoon immediately called and said, 'Come and have your hair done, it won't cost you anything.' I had my hair done for years and years and years. Never had to pay a penny. Marvellous. I looked so rich. Lovely jewellery, beautiful shoes. I always had Chanel shoes and to think I used to throw them away. They would be museum pieces now. I was in these ravishing clothes. I never wore jeans until I was about fifty. Designer jeans, darling.

It was frustrating because I would meet so many movie directors who would say to me, 'With that voice, that figure. Those legs … I am going to make you the biggest star in Hollywood.' I can't tell you how many times I was told that. By directors. The next day they wouldn't even speak to me. They'd been told in the meantime, and that happened an awful lot in Europe too. I'd go places with them and we always had the best seat. It's amazing how everybody stares at you all the time. They all think you're a movie star. The next day, they wouldn't speak to me.

What angered April, anger rather than the accustomed disappointment of being shunned by supposed friends or dropped by the advertising agencies, was her treatment by Hollywood in terms of the film appearance she made with her old friend from Paris, Bob Hope, who was clearly a devout fan of *Le Carrousel*; he saw the show at least twenty times and took April to breakfast after her appearance in Juan-Le-Pins. She recalled that when Hope filmed *Paris Holiday* in 1958 with his French comic counterpart Fernandel, the two stars posed for a publicity photograph with one of the 'girls' from Le Carrousel. They had their arms around each other. All three had erections.

Arthur often did too but I'd tell him to put it away.

Hope, and his regular film partner Bing Crosby, were making *The Road to Hong Kong*, released in 1962, at Shepperton Studios west of London, with their *Road* ... movies regular Dorothy Lamour and the promising Joan Collins. April, with much of model-world London, auditioned for cameo walk-on and speaking parts. She got a job and the road to fame was paved with an altogether different hope which was abruptly halted when the movie people discovered she was transsexual.

> They gave me a part and just before filming they found out who I was. They tried to sack me. The six girls that I was working with said, 'Well, if April goes, we go too.' Which I thought was the most marvellous gesture. They took my name off the credits, which was unkind. My agent Simone – she was Eurasian and always wore an orchid in her hair, she was the Queen Mother's favourite model – told me, 'April, leave England, you'll never get another job here.' She knew. When I applied for jobs, they said, 'We don't want people like you.' When Arthur asked if I wanted to go to Spain, I said, 'Why not?'

Ten

Viva España

'You can't always get away from yourself by moving from one place to another.'
The Sun Also Rises, Ernest Hemingway, 1926

Self-deprecation was an alien concept to April.

I've always known how to move on. When it's time to do something, it's time. When it's over it's over. Close the door.

I went off to Spain with Arthur and when I modelled, they paid me three times as much as they were paying me in England because I was me. They weren't familiar with tourists, even motor cars were fairly new in Spain. It was very strange. If you were beautiful, men would follow you and just look at you. I'd go into a bar and have every man in the bar wanting to buy me a drink. I always got the best seats, and I always got the best table, reserved for Miss April Ashley.

The flaw, the complication, was the determined Hon. Arthur Corbett. He demanded absolutely all of April's attention. His declaration, and one he'd made many times to his wife Eleanor, was that with her help, he could overcome his transvestite obsession. To him, April would fantastically become the epitome of his problem and the solution to it. She would be his saviour.

An inflatable Barbie doll was really what was needed.

Early in the relationship, she said he attempted quite forcibly to have sex with her, but she rebuffed him on both occasions. When his alter ego appeared 'she' wanted to be April, but 'he' was constantly jealous of anyone who even said a good morning to her. For three years, although he proposed to April every day, he never once made another a move on her. He never kissed her. As always, she was watchful, her fear antenna, attached since childhood, constantly on alert. With Arthur, the switch was sudden, each day like a kitchen sink drama by Stephen King.

It was mind-boggling, gave me chilling goosebumps, to see him sitting there and suddenly this man that you know suddenly becomes somebody else. He would say, 'My pendulum was swinging and I'm sorry.'

I said that it was very nice to be called a whore and a prostitute and be accused of sleeping with this one and that one. I said, 'It does make me very fond of you I must say. You wonder why I'm beginning to dislike you. Well, just ask *her.*' Sometimes he would go and buy me a little gift. Even that was a joke because he would buy me an expensive pair of earrings and I'd say to him, 'Why are you buying me tiny little things like this which I never wear? Why don't you save up and buy me something big?' No, he never treated me beautifully at Jacaranda Club. He was jealous because I'd always arrive with someone nice – like Harry, a writer I liked – simply seething jealous and not because I'd been to bed with them. I'd been out to dinner with them and I was bringing them back to the club because that's where everybody met up at the end of the evening. That's where people came to see me. When a man visited he was insanely jealous. By the same token, there were times when I'd been naughty.

I was always terribly, terribly discreet because of Arthur, but he'd called me a whore once too often. I said to him, 'You call me a whore, I'm going to be one.' I did have an affair with Harry, and everybody knew about that. His girlfriend one day came screaming into my house; he'd just jumped out of the window, I'd passed out. We'd spent more time drinking than having sex. She found me sleeping like an angel, burst into tears and said, 'Oh, I'd thought April was screwing my boyfriend and look at her, she looks like an angel.' I had an affair with him for many, many years.

Drink killed him years later. I was here in San Diego when I found out. That was hysterical too, because he dropped dead. He was the biggest drinker in the world and towards the end it made him look oriental, like a little Chinese man. Drink and sex. That will do it, the eyes would disappear, and he had wonderful eyes. He was incredibly handsome. He married this older woman, very rich. Her brother was an earl ... or maybe a duke? But certainly something. Then my friends rang me up and said, 'Do you know that Harry dropped dead the other day?' He was only sixty-one.

I said, 'My God, I'll have to ring Jane up immediately.' I rang his wife up. 'Jane, I am so sorry to hear about Harry.'

'You'll have to come round right away,' she said. 'Come and have some tea. I could do with being cheered up.'

'Jane,' I said, 'that would be rather difficult. I'm calling you from San Diego.'

'Oh dear. I thought you were here. We're off to Spain. I can't disappoint the children. Harry died, that's it. I can't disappoint the children. I'm taking them off to Spain.'

I said, 'Jane, I'm so sorry. Anyhow, much love to you.'

I put the phone down and started screaming with laughter. I suddenly recognised the children were about thirty or forty. The way she said it, you would think they were little kids. They weren't even his children. They were her children from her first marriage. But, Harry, happy days ... he did enjoy a drink. Great larks.

She did enjoy the escape, although her time in Spain with Arthur was frenetic with furious rows and tantrum walking-outs, by them both, Arthur constantly saying he was going to kill himself – always by drowning – and all to the backdrop of running the Jacaranda Club in what was then becoming a prime holiday destination for those with lots of time and money. The relationship was difficult, but they were in the right place at the right time, like a sudden change of wind saving a ship heading for the rocks. Arthur bought a home which April called 'Villa Antoinette'. He said it was for her but didn't deliver the deeds. One of April's huge talents was quickly acclimatising to her surroundings and circumstances and squeezing them to best advantage. The early 1960s Costa del Sol was a spectacular stage for her and the newish Marbella Club an attractive playground. She often said that if it hadn't been for Arthur, it would have been paradise. Sarah Churchill, although deeply into drink and hysterical binges – she was arrested several times and spent time on remand in Holloway prison, north London – was a constant friend. She'd married Henry Touchet-Jesson, becoming Lady Audley, in 1962 and he owned the Villa Santa Cecilia close to the Marbella Club which, protected by the Sierra Blanca mountains, enjoys the agreeable arithmetic of 325 days of sunshine a year.

April, naturally, met everyone. In the bar, Sarah recited her poems, written in longhand and typed up by Diana Mackintosh, the mother of theatrical billionaire Sir Cameron Mackintosh. April gave me a rare copy of her friend's *Empty Spaces* poetry collection inscribed as owned by a Paula Boothby. I raised an eyebrow.

Paula loved regifting, darling.

The club was founded and owned by Prince Alfonso von Hohenlohe-Langenburg and co-run with his cousin Count

Rudi von Schönburg. Count Rudi told me stories of the early days of the club and argued it was a blessed place. 'Marbella' was named by Queen Isabella for the beautiful sea it sits besides. Count Rudi recalled April being there and ticked off her name with those of the Duke and Duchess of Windsor, King Juan Carlos of Spain, Ava Gardner, Audrey Hepburn, Coccinelle-lookalike Bridget Bardot, Gina Lollobrigida, Liz Taylor, Aristotle Onassis and Maria Callas, Adnan Khashoggi, and hard-to-catch-the-name Monte Carlo tax exiles and Arabian and African royalty. He remembered sending condolences to Sarah Churchill in August 1963 when Lord Audley died. He also recalled occasions when the club's guests were slow to grasp the day, to have fun. April, he said, would connive with him and spike the water jugs with vodka. It always got the party going. He told me, 'God forgive me, but I sent Ava Gardner up into the hills on a group horse ride and to this day I don't know how she didn't fall off.' He also said that Arthur Corbett would hound him around the 450 acres of seaside property, searching for April. He raised an eyebrow and confessed he never said where she was. 'I never knew why he didn't follow the trail of champagne corks ...'

It was never clear to me whether April was sleeping with every young man with a suntan or simply flirting to get Arthur's goat. She'd tiptoe around, citing affairs of the heart. She took acting classes as well as diction instruction from Sarah Churchill, reading aloud from her poems. Her It-girl swoon was impressive, full-on Clara Bow. If there was ever anyone always ready for their close-up ...

Her big romantic name of the period had – of course he did – a title. April made much of a romantic interlude with the Duke del Infantado and she'd roll her eyes theatrically about this love match with the married duke and the ire of his aristocratic family: all the drama of the local bullfighting, the sizzle of the flamenco.

Operatic, darling. He fell madly in love with me and invited
me to Seville and I told Arthur I was going for a short time.
He didn't have a problem with it at all. He took me to the
airport and said, 'Why do you need half a dozen suitcases
and your great dane with you?'

I said, 'It's so hot in Seville one needs so many
changes.'

I suggested she must have been exhausted by the time she did
return and encountered Peter O'Toole and Omar Sharif in a
bar, between filming sequences of *Lawrence of Arabia* (1962).
Over the years on television talk shows around the world, April
enthused about her 'love' with the actors, what sounded as
pleasurable fumbling with O'Toole and full-on sex with Sharif
and in their lifetimes they both behaved as gentlemen; they
never said a word. The clever Peter O'Toole, when I asked him
about his friendship with April, said he'd been 'in character'
and couldn't comment on another person's affairs.

Somehow, somewhere along their difficult entwinement,
April and Arthur became engaged; he and Eleanor were officially divorced and April chose an engagement ring from
Asprey in Bond Street. Neither of them saw this as a landmark
moment but it was. April who had once been George was going
to marry Arthur, an event high on the Richter scale. When we
view the engagement retrospectively, with the knowledge of
today, who in 1962 could faithfully, absurdly, expect to be on
that jury and offer a verdict? At that time April sold her life
story to the *News of the World* for ten thousand pounds but found
the ensuing attention – her story ran for six headlining Sundays
– difficult. For someone who could make a gala of opening the
fridge, suddenly appearances in public became so threatening
she shied away from socialising. It gave her time to read her fan
letters. There were scores of them, tragic, sad, uplifting and all
appealing for April's guidance on how they too could 'change

sex'. The letters were the seeds of far-future activism and she replied to every one. She didn't feel like a champion. We agreed that was her St Augustine moment – *'Please, God, make me good but not just yet'* – for April was only a couple of years into her new being, a change which she did not want to dominate her life. Yes, she was a transsexual, but she was living as a woman, getting on with her life and what was between her legs wasn't an issue for her every moment of the day. She knew it's different for every person but for her 'normality' was a goal. We laughed at that for, as her life turned out, 'normality' didn't really align with her personality; she was larger than the life she chose. Which, in time, allowed her a platform to inspire millions of people, to show being different need not be a sin.

It was tough in the early days. She was young and still attempting to root herself in the world. And make her own living. A want-to-be P. T. Barnum rascal of a manager, he'd taken a big chunk of her *News of the World* cash, exploited her notoriety with a series of appearances around England, including a turn at the Astor club in Mayfair. She knew she was guilty before and after the fact of exploiting herself. Audiences didn't flock to see her sing and dance but to ogle the 'sex change freak'. She despised herself. She escaped to Spain.

Arthur remained on the prowl. He was often despondent about April but that never paused his business acumen and the Jacaranda club flourished. April entertained the guests and herself. Sarah Churchill was a constant drinking pal. One afternoon in late 2021, when April was running down memory lane, the Churchill name came up, the Churchill statue in Parliament Square had been defaced by protesters, and she laughed about her friend's misbehaviour a lifetime earlier. It was a little lecture on handling the inebriated.

Sarah went walkabout one afternoon from Dolphin Square and I was sent to find her. She was directing traffic on the Embankment, wearing only a négligée. The cars were racing around her and I had to carefully get into the middle of the road and speak to her. I didn't shout or berate her – there's no point when people have had too much to drink. Always wise to remember that, darling. I helped her with directing the traffic and I explained that it was getting chilly and she should come into the flat and put on something warm. She put her hand up and confronted the traffic which slowed and then stopped. We linked arms and went inside and had a nice gin and tonic.

Events gathered in April's life that summer of 1963 – it was in August that Tim Willoughby was lost at sea. She insisted she never loved Willoughby or wanted to marry him but said his loss was heartbreaking. He was so larger than life it seemed impossible that he should have lost his. She felt she'd lost a protector. Yes, she thought, possibly it was because of this tender moment, she agreed to end their long engagement and marry Arthur. In moments of insecurity, fear for the future, egotism prevails, and it seemed she convinced herself she could make it work.

He proposed to me every day and produced letters of his father dying of cancer of the throat. 'My father's this, my father's that and he wants me to break up with you ...'

I would say: 'Well, don't you? I don't love you. I wish you would stop it all.'

I stupidly was engaged to him in 1961 and I must have given him the ring back a hundred thousand times, but he would always put it back on my finger. I know exactly why because I felt guilty about him leaving Eleanor and the children and I felt guilty about his father dying of cancer [Lord Rowallan survived cancer of the palate and died in 1977]. He was always blackmailing me. I never thought about myself for a moment. He was always blackmailing me mentally about his father and said his father was getting ill because of us and if I were to marry him every-thing would settle down. He had great allies in Bill and Doreen Godwin, who were news correspondents for the whole of the Costa del Sol. They were great friends of his and they'd say: 'Oh April, you should marry him. He loves you so much.'

All my friends were saying, 'He loves you beyond words.'

I said, 'Yes, but isn't it funny that all those people that I meet through Arthur think I'm a bitch. Where do you think it comes from?'

People would hate me. I'd meet people and we'd instantly get along and they'd say they didn't expect to like me. I'd say to them, 'Well, what gave you that impression?'

It took me a long time to work it out, too. It was Arthur. He would do it in a very odd way. They always came away with the impression that I was some kind of awful bitch.

It was strange how people would say, 'You're not the bitch that I thought you would be.'

I would ask who they had been talking to and they would say it was only Arthur. And I thought he was so in love with me. It was sick, he had circled me for himself.

Suddenly, there was a young couple, Mike and Caroline Stocker, and she and I immediately fell in love with one another. They used to call us the Two Duchesses because when we'd have a few our noses would get higher and higher. We were at the bar and I was a bit tiddly and they were leaving the next day, not enough money to stay on. I said: 'As a little wedding gift, why don't you come and stay with me for a week?'

They stayed for three months and it was Caroline who finally told me, 'My family and Arthur's family are great friends and everything he always told me I always thought you must be the biggest bitch in the world.'

Arthur's romancing of April was a victory of attrition. A wedding date was set, 10 September 1963, and Fleet Street duly reported the news. Lord Rowallan, still receiving medical treatment, begged his son to reconsider. April's friends, including Sarah Churchill, looked on in some dismay but did not interfere. April thinks they thought her too mercenary, blatantly chasing a title. She wanted financial security.

Before we got married, he said I should have two thousand pounds a year spending money, which wasn't bad in the 1960s.

Whatever the motives, the uncertainty persisted. Arthur might dismay with his antics, but he was shrewd and intelligent when not being driven out of his senses by his fantasies and April acknowledged she often underestimated his intellectual practicality.

The wedding was set for the Register Office in Gibraltar, an easy hour or so drive from Marbella, and where Sarah Churchill and Lord Audley had married. The legal requirements were such that April's passport, which recorded her name change but no declaration of gender, was all that was needed for the blessing of their union. It was a close thing. Even as the car eased gears down the Villa Antoinette driveway before taking the road to Gibraltar, April told Arthur marriage was an awfully bad idea. She didn't love him; in fact, she didn't even particularly like him any more.

She launched a tirade: April was sick of 'she' appearing, of Arthur misbehaving. He hadn't paid her a single penny for three years' work. He paid her maid and the electricity, twelve pounds a month. What were they doing? It was a very bad idea. She didn't love him. 'Oh, darling, I love you enough for the two …'

I drank a bottle of whisky and got married.

There was time for boozing as they arrived twenty minutes late and the registrar had gone to lunch. However, the moment did arrive. Arthur wore a triumphant smile on his lips. April wore a lampshade affair of a hat.

I was so drunk. When we came out the whole of Gibraltar
was there and the only thing I can remember is that I got
married in a three-pound coat and a one-pound hat. It was
very pretty. I had this huge black picture hat. It all looked
very nice. There's a newsreel somewhere too, darling,
you should see it. It was a lovely hat.

She was wearing a sun hat in Spain decades later, revisiting her
old haunts and mellowed memories. The Marbella club had
changed but the aroma of Malaga remained and the sights of
the fish markets astonished: the fishmongers' stalls with shrimp
somersaulting on the trays of ice while their big brothers –
gambas, *langostinos*, *cigalas*, carabineros and *santiaguinos* – fight
for space with soles, turbots and cod, oysters, crab, mussels
and a catalogue of clams. There were short, silvery eels, blue-
backed sea bass and pink fans of skate. Most intriguing among
all this – the squid and the scallop shells, the langoustines,
lobsters and crayfish, *salmonetes*, sardines, sole, bream – are trays
of UFOs: Unidentified Frying Objects. Cut by just a drop of
creamy milk, the café cortado matches the oriental mood and
heavy perfume of the jasmine and oleander in the Andalusian
air. From the cafés, there's always an intrusion to the scented air
from the blended olive oil cooking the potato- and onion-rich
Spanish omelettes, sizzling spicy sausage, flavouring the bread
toasting on the grills. There's also a feast in the architecture –
which, like the majority of the glories of southern Spain, is the
legacy of the Muslims who arrived from north Africa in AD 711.
That conquest, which all but changed the course of European
history, lasted for nearly eight hundred years, and ended only
seven months before Columbus set sail for discovery.

Of course, some time after 1492, the bucket-and-spade
families had every right to their invasion in search of sun, sea
and sangria. Yet, as April pointed out, she was again a trail-
blazer, all but a founder member of this geographical anthem
to hedonism. Yet she talked then of the unexpected appeal of

the England which she believed had abandoned her, certainly typecast her as a curiosity. Home was home, and she felt a need for London and for Liverpool.

Clearly, she knew marriage to Arthur was a mistake. Possibly, if she'd loved him, she wouldn't have married him. She didn't think she'd been cynical, she wasn't sure if she'd believed marriage could or would resolve the anomalies of their relationship. Maybe repentance of her time with him was only possible when she made that mistake, crossed the line and faced the havoc of trying to get back over it. Disentangling herself from drama and conflict was the theme of her life, maybe the agony and ecstasy of the struggle was what made that life worth living. One for her friend Lucien Freud's grandad.

Eleven

Let It Be

'Falling in Love Again (Can't Help It)'
Song performed by Marlene Dietrich, *The Blue Angel*, 1930,
by Friedrich Hollaender

April and Arthur Corbett were properly together as a married couple for fourteen days.

I was never unfaithful to him while we were married.

Which rather counts as one of April's lesser achievements. She said it was her inbred Catholicism which brought on enormous guilt about her marriage to Arthur Corbett. Had she not renounced the church?

You never get over being a Catholic.

Which she proceeded to be in her taste of men, swapping bon mots with John Lennon, dodging Paul McCartney's bedtime offer, being so in awe of Winston Churchill she hid behind a sofa before being presented to him and encountering a history of names from the Madrid, Rome and particularly the London of the sixties. She swapped insults with that other gourmet of the put-down, Francis Bacon, played spoof for drinks with Lucien Freud, admired another painter, the up-and-coming David Hockney and wore frocks designed by his friend, the designer Ossie Clark. It was a shamelessly show-off world. A walk along the King's Road was like going to the circus with the acts and the costumes on display. Seldom has *you are what you wear* been as accurate as so many struggled to be cool, be with it. And that meant buying that week's latest fashion, a look which April never truly abandoned.

Somehow, supply met demand which, happily, wasn't too demanding on quality and longevity. The *now* message was in the name of the Mr Freedom boutique at the World's End tail of the King's Road. You could be as disposable as your clothes. Names and boutiques came and went, Dicky Dirts – shirts – and the Hungarian Star Shirtmaker, Mr Kipper and Tara Browne, an early King's Road mascot, immortalised, a legend in a lyric, following his 1966 death, aged twenty-one. The young aristocrat, heir to the Guinness fortune, became The Beatles' lucky man in Lennon–McCartney's 'Day in the Life'.

April, never gnomic, told me she could have slept with all the Beatles. Falling in love[4] was her pastime so she had to be selective. She illustrated this memory one evening over dinner at St Paul de Vence in Provence, when Beatles' music was gently playing along the street.

I regret not going to bed with Paul McCartney. It might have been nice. I turned Paul down. We were at the Aretusa club on the King's Road and I did a very naughty thing. He wanted to go to bed with me and kept asking. He was persistent. He always seemed to get the girls he wanted. Well, I decided he wasn't having me, much as he clearly wanted to, and one night I said, 'Get rid of the entourage.' And he did. While he was paying the bill, I went outside and got hold of a taxi. I knew every taxi in town at the time, and said to the driver, 'When I say, "Go",

---

4   An enduring April favourite, 'Falling In Love Again' was covered live by The Beatles featuring Paul McCartney on lead vocals; it's on the double LP *Live! At The Star-Club in Hamburg, Germany; 1962*, originally released in 1977.

go very quickly indeed.' We waited and Paul appeared. I said, 'Go' and we went.

Paul was running down the King's Road after me and shouted his frustrations after us. It was a hoot. I could have gone to bed with them all, all the rock stars. Every time I turned around, there was some famous face slobbering about me. I was very tall and very glamorous. I looked like a star and just about everybody was a starfucker. Even the stars themselves. A little bit incestuous, you might think. At one time, I was taken home most nights by Keith Moon. We would sit in the back of his Bentley or white Rolls-Royce, whichever one was on call, sipping huge whiskies. Keith's passions were drink and schoolgirls. One evening when he'd been at the whiskies, he said to me, 'It's about time you found me some young girls.'

'Oh, no, darling,' I replied. 'It's time you found me some nice young men. I'm working too hard.'

He looked over at me from deep in the seat of the car and said, 'Well, let's have another drink. A large one?'

He was adorable and such a wonderful drummer. Before Keith, drummers just drummed, if you know what I mean. It was excess again, but it was ironic that he died in 1978 of an overdose of pills that were intended to help his drink addiction.

I could have slept with the lot of them but being pursued so much can be tiresome.

That didn't stop her marching along the King's Road, with pit stops at the Chelsea Potter pub, from Sloane Square to World's End and once again meeting up with Christine Keeler who was central to the downfall of the Minister of War John Profumo. During the height of the scandal, Christine fled to Europe driving through France and into south-east Spain. Short of funds, she was searching for somewhere to stay and hide from the pursuing press and through Arthur Corbett found a villa close to the Villa Antoinette. Arthur couldn't understand how the lodgings were too expensive. April was more accustomed to penury: she pointed Christine toward Altea, a fishing village where there was a villa for thirty shillings a week. It was a sanctuary. Christine, laughing, told me, 'April said we should have something for our journey and I thought she was going to give us a pack of sandwiches. Instead, she produced a couple of bottles of champagne and insisted we drink one with her and take the other for the journey.'

When Fleet Street first descended, a burly team from the *Daily Express* leading the pack, April feigned no knowledge of a young woman being pilloried by the establishment. The newspaper teams decided to believe she was harbouring Christine on the Costa del Sol: the weather was nice and the reporters liked the location and laid siege to the Villa Antoinette. Day and night, reporters would appear and April admitted she enjoyed the attention in that it distracted her from coping with the conundrum of Arthur's oddities. April saw her own persecution reflected in the trials of Christine Keeler who flirted with and fell foul of the British aristocracy.

As the holiday property potential soared, the Hon. Arthur sold the Jacaranda club and grounds at a profit to a conglomerate planning an apartment complex. It put him in his wife's arms at the Villa Antoinette but the realisation of all his months of dreaming of consummating their union was disappointed by the reality of unsatisfactory fiddling and fumbling. Of erotic ecstasy there was none.

Lot's wife had more fun after she looked over her shoulder.

A couple of weeks after her marriage, April was in London and Arthur – after their brief, unsatisfactory honeymoon in town – was back in Spain. Yet, as she made her nightclub entrances and flaunted along the King's Road, she was officially the Hon. Mrs Arthur Corbett. As such, doors opened, as many in the being gentrified Chelsea and Notting Hill as

Belgravia and Mayfair. The friends were many, the income not so plentiful. April collected double-barrelled names – for every Smith or Brown there was always a hyphen and an elaborate surname, and endless appearances of duchesses and countesses in her conversation. They got the same value as Ben the bartender down the Chelsea Potter who always sneaked that extra drop of gin in her drinks. It was a world superficially smiling but one with layers of deceit, ripe with rotten betrayal and blatant hypocrisy. April learned to hide her dismay that some of these 'friends' contemptuously regarded her like an unflushed lavatory, and her surprise at so many social invitations. Being popular provided hosted lunches and dinners but it didn't pay the- day-to-day bills. April became involved with a generous and wealthy young man, Clive Raphael, her friends thought she'd found security *and* happiness.

Raphael, who was involved with Middle East 'business arrangements' (he died suspiciously when his light aircraft exploded over France in March 1971), was quick with his fists. It was textbook domestic violence, the punches and the bruises and the pleas for forgiveness and pledges of marriage and it 'never happening again'. April decided it never would and fled their affair. It provoked the ongoing problem of funds. In England her notoriety was such that she couldn't get a job as a salesgirl. She thought about working as a cleaner, and left it as a thought. To emphasise, she was legally the Hon. Mrs Arthur Corbett and correctly maintained, as she'd told Arthur often enough, that she married him for security. And here she was, extremely insecure, both financially and mentally, jittery with the unknown nagging, her perpetual watchfulness at times debilitating.

But as her world had changed, so had that around her. In London, offering escape from Arthur, once again Sarah Churchill was a proper friend. She'd been cast as Mathilde in a re-staging of *Fata Morgana* at the Ashcroft Theatre in Croydon, co-starring David Hemmings before he achieved global stardom in 1967 starring in Antonioni's *Blow-Up*. There was no role for April but in the spring of 1964 Sarah gave her a job as assistant stage manager. They agreed, and, remember, April's notoriety was such she couldn't get work, that April would use the name Jane Spencer. It was difficult to be incognito with all the younger players like Hemmings who enjoyed going on the toot with April. Tony Singleton was also in the cast and over lunch at his London home in July 2023 he was marvellously entertaining about this first encounter with April and, indeed, of their nearly six decades of friendship:

'I was cast with Sarah Churchill but the person who fascinated me was a very elegant girl stage manager called Jane Spencer. She was very beautiful and simply elegant and spoke a very perfect English with that slightly husky voice that Garbo, Dietrich and Bergman had. I think it was the third week of rehearsal, and someone came up to me and said she'd had a sex change.

'I remember saying: "Well, that was certainly very successful."

'At some point when she knew that we knew that she knew that we all knew. I asked her which she preferred me carrying on calling her Jane or April. She laughed and said, "Oh darling, just call me April," and I really felt our being friends would continue. I loved her sense of humour.'

Tony treasures his photograph of April being introduced to Sir Winston Churchill at the final matinee of *Fata Morgana* in April 1964. There's Sarah Churchill to her father's right and the young David Hemmings gently smiling toward April and director Ellen Pollock overseeing the introductions. April, rather overwhelmed at the thought of being presented to her hero, had tried to avoid the meeting by hiding behind a stage sofa but her friend Sarah insisted and there she is, her hand in his. With his wife, Clementine, he'd sat at the front of the audience, and after the performance took centre-stage himself with cigar and a glass of vintage cognac before being introduced to the cast and crew. April said he was very frail and she was right, it was only weeks until his final illness and months till his death in January 1965. For April it was a treasured moment, one maverick meets another.

Tony Singleton was impressed by her sophistication: 'Despite my having been in the navy I hadn't come across the Liverpool version of April. This was very much part of the London version, the sixties London version. April became so much part of that. London in the fifties and into the sixties, a whole new outlook was being created.

'There was a fresh music culture bubbling away, the 2i's coffee bar in Compton Street in Soho where Tommy Steel and Cliff Richard started out and where the word "teenagers" was invented. I did both mods and rockers which occasionally got me into trouble. A very young John Lennon and Mick Jagger were popping in to hear music at Chris Barber's club opposite the Windmill, discovering skiffle. Trumpeter Ken Colyer bringing trad jazz over from New Orleans. Juliet Greco with the French "cool" jazz ... even the Lyceum Ballroom for a foxtrot and an occasional tango. John Stevens starting out in Carnaby Street, Barbara Hulanicki's Biba in Kensington and Mary Quant in Chelsea. Twiggy, a fashion model ricocheting all over the place. With new painters David Hockney, Francis Bacon. Lucian Freud – yet all of us could paint the town, and we did. April most of all. I remember one time we were getting organised to hit the clubs, asking her why she was making such a heavy use of the hair lacquer and April said: *It's to make sure that when you wake up early in the morning, surrounded by press photographers and you just happen to be lying in the gutter you still look immaculate.*'

Tony revealed another of April's priority tips for when looking the part was very useful: *When you are thumbing a lift home at 4 a.m. and there doesn't happen to be a Rolls or a Bentley available, make sure to flag down an ambulance.*

'For a time, April came to live with me in Baker Street, and that's when I got to know the real April behind the glamour.

You can't really hide from someone over morning croissant and coffee with the occasional hangover from our last night's trip to the Ad-Lib Club. That was one of the most exclusive, fashionable London clubs in Leicester Square. Up on the top floor via a very, *very* small lift. It's where the, just exploding, Beatles, Paul and Ringo, George and John, first met April. Yes, that way around. John rather disdainfully called her "the Duchess" but he later came and apologised to her for being rather silly. Everybody wanted to meet April. Looking back, I realise practically everyone was winging it. Nobody quite knew what they were doing. Everybody was prepared to take risks with ideas, writers, painters, actors and suddenly among them was this stunning determined and witty woman, April Ashley, stepping into this exciting, hopeful, possible new world that was happening all over the place.'

Still, April, for all the boozy nights and theatrical fun, slipping lanes with present and future super talent, remained quite lonely. She never displayed her woes – she later admitted to me that the glitz was just that, glitz, fun but not emotionally rewarding.

She found solace in a tragic and sad romance with a kind and loving young man called Edward Maddock; tragic because Edward – the only man other than Tony she wanted to marry – died in a car crash while driving from St Tropez and sad because, at the height of April's romantic rapture, he declared he wanted their relationship to become exclusively platonic. This was some time after they spent a summer in Ibiza when there was no need for a full moon for howling in the night.

The island tempted an artistic crowd and for a time the king and queen of the place were Frederik and Nina van Pallandt, the successful singing couple Nina and Frederik. Some years later, over dinner with her and her second husband, the South African humourist Robert Kirby, at their home nineteen blocks from the Pacific in Santa Monica, California, Nina remembered the characters in her life: 'April walked around as though she was in paradise and I suppose she was. On the island you could forget about all the cares in the world, especially your own worries and concerns. We invited April to all our parties. She was such good fun and would talk to anyone. She was always asked to lunches. She was always first to offer to mix the drinks.'

I was a tremendous drunk.

When I talked to Nina – she and Frederik had separated and she'd had an affair with another island resident, Clifford Irving, who found his fame as the author of the hoax 'autobiography' of American billionaire Howard Hughes – she was making movies in Hollywood. In 2023, aged ninety, she was back living on Ibiza. April had tried to contact Nina a couple of years earlier but by then she'd rather closed her front door on the world.

They were Beautiful People, but the cute, sweet songs of Nina and Frederik didn't fit the reality of the couple. They were always kind to me and Frederik was a wonderful sailor. Once to everyone's dismay, including his wife's, he brought his yacht into harbour perfectly, with a spectacular manoeuvre in rotten weather. He was always what we might call today laidback. That was probably due to the drugs he was inhaling. He was as high as his sail at sea that day. Frederik was murdered in 1994. He was involved with a drugs cartel, transporting large amounts of cannabis in his own boat and clearly upset some people – with the tragic consequences. Nina was lovely and always nice to me. It was a joyous time in our lives, careless.

The free lunches helped April and Edward survive, as did the money he got through his family and the pawning, guiltily by April, of her wedding ring. Edward Maddock's brother, Peter, was a witness to April's time in the sun and spoke of it fondly in June 2022 when we were in Liverpool for a celebration of her life: 'I met her in the summer of 1966 in Ibiza. I was twenty-one and a law student and Ibiza in those days was a sleepy island with unpaved roads, donkeys in the streets, old widows dressed from head to foot in black. The vanguard of English actors and artists and musicians had migrated to the island near the early sixties and many people in London in 1966 decided to spend the summer there, and I was one of them. To get that summer into frame it was the year that The Beatles issued *Revolver* the album, flower power followed, and then it was *Sgt. Pepper's Lonely Hearts Club Band*. Ibiza town was the place where everybody met in the evening. And most young people gravitated to the terrace of a café called La Tierra. It was an old, derelict building that had once been a pork butcher's shop and indeed, there were still hooks on the wall above the bar.

'I was sat outside the café, and the Frenchman on the next table said very loudly, "Here comes a princess in bare feet." I looked up and a tall figure was gliding toward the café in – what would I call it? – a diaphanous kaftan. As she got closer, I saw that she was wearing an *enormous* Moroccan amber necklace, no makeup and, indeed, no shoes. She stood next to me for a while looking around the terrace for a table and then caught my eye. And I said: "Would you like to join me?" And thus began a friendship that lasted more than fifty years.

'April had surprising talents. She was, for example, a first-class navigator – a map reader who would leave Google Maps in the shade. At the end of that summer, we went a week driving back to London through Catalonia and along the old French N roads. And we never took a wrong turning. And I think this was the journey that cemented our friendship.'

April and Peter's brother Edward – *my Rosenkavalier* – lived off their wits and charm but were apart when he died in 1972. By then she was recovering and rebuilding her life from what, in the controversial world of debate over gender identity and its ideology and biological sex, the so-called 'penis wars' of the twenty-first century, was *the* trial of the previous one. For all the earlier humiliations in her life she'd blanked out, never told a soul, it was that dry cruelty of the English legal system which flayed April's core. It punished her by forcing her mind back to being George Jamieson – before Casablanca and her gender reassignment, what the headline writers of the day relished as a 'sex change'. But April never acknowledged her birth genitalia, she felt female. As such she wasn't, in her mind, a complete male. She was inside out. The Casablanca surgery completed her as a female by artificial means but, again in her mind, she wasn't a 'natural' woman.

It was, I suggested, like being abandoned in space, floating, and one can see the emotional horror of not being one or the other, a misfit, while only wanting to be recognised as the person you have fought and suffered to become.

That, she said, was overthinking, being clever. Or trying to be. The intimacy of the experience she felt unfathomable outwith the cognoscenti, those who'd lived the experience.

I thought the best way I could do it was by example. I wasn't about to live in a twilight world. I wanted to live in the real world and do what everybody else does. And have fun. I like being jolly.

And you never felt jollier than being with April.

Especially at the best of times. Yet, for a period it was the worst of times, with the law seeming at its most Dickensian. It's a system where you can be done down by a point of law or, perhaps, because a judge or jury doesn't like you. Or the look of you. It's judicial Monopoly where you don't go to jail on the turn of a card but on a caprice, some vague conjecture conjured like a genie from a bottle.

'Corbett v. Corbett (Ashley)' even sounds like a case with cobwebs in the rafters, echoes of Jarndyce v. Jarndyce. It has casual antecedents, a mundane spousal property dispute, but vast social consequences. The origins were to be found with April, all but struggling to find shillings for the gas meter in one of her in-between Fulham flats, when she thought she might cash in the Villa Antoinette. Hadn't Arthur gifted it to her, a dowry as part of his pursuit of marriage to nullify his inner demons? April wholeheartedly believed she helped establish the Jacaranda club as a profitable enterprise. She'd helped Arthur succeed in business.

Darling, they came to see me. They didn't come to see him.

The legal process was slow and she was encouraged to alternatively pursue marital maintenance. In return, and the back and forth had already run two years, Arthur's legal team countered in 1967 that his marriage to April was null and void. He didn't want to pay alimony.

Arthur, who is on record as saying he never regretted losing his five-million-pound inheritance by marrying April, argued the marriage was fraudulent because April on her wedding day 'was a person of the male sex ... [alternatively asking] for a decree of nullity on the ground that the marriage was never consummated owing to the incapacity or wilful refusal of the respondent to consummate it'. April returned fire in similar language, citing Arthur's inability and/or refusal to consummate the marriage. The detail in terms of premature ejaculation and Arthur's disquiet – as in hysteria – about it and problems with penetration, her internal abscesses, would be for the string of nine experts summoned on behalf of the unhappy couple floundering in a place where neither of them truly wanted to be.

Justice is rarely swift. Weeks and months dragged on before the matter reached the courts and possibly the continual pressure added its own stress on her love affair with Edward Maddock; the end of that affair was another heartache April had to endure when her 'trial' began.

Somewhat ironically and, true to form, illegally, Little Gloria had married the man of her choice without truth or immediate consequences. April's childhood friend from Liverpool, Tommy Robinson, a.k.a. Little Gloria from London, was now

Mrs Brian Greaves. In 1964, Little Gloria qualified for gender reassignment on the NHS at the Charing Cross Hospital. It became a career move. Delirious with her 'sex change', Gloria went into the lucrative business of being the sadistic Madam Stern[5], a high-earning dominatrix with plentiful clients, including King Charles's great-uncle Lord Mountbatten. Ms Stern dealt it out to famous actors and theatrical knights, a cross party of MPs and prominent members of the legal profession, some of whom would wear nothing but their wigs. She hosted them at an elaborately equipped basement dungeon in Clarendon Street, Belgravia, catering to submissive males seeking humiliation, flagellation, bondage and help with bottle- and breast-feeding, *Pit and the Pendulum* moments with torture equipment and other fetishes of choice. One evening, in 1967 while spending her profits in a Mayfair restaurant she met Brian Greaves and with Gloria employing a fake birth certificate, they married at Caxton Hall, Westminster, and were together until his death in 1989.

A 'marital' longevity eluding April, who throughout her life liked everything to be neatly confirmed and legally in order. For all her apparent carefree spirit – and suggestive of the need for order in a large family – she liked regimentation in her business and social arrangements. Tea was at teatime. God forbid she was on her second glass of champagne by the time you arrived for a catch-up.

Traffic tedious, darling?

---

5   Gloria, who died aged eighty-four in 2016, was convicted in 1982 of living off immoral earnings and jailed for eighteen months. Only men could be convicted for that offence. She was taken to Holloway prison in north London, a women's jail. In February 1983, three Appeal Court justices ruled that 'men who have a sex change' must remain male and Gloria's appeal against her conviction, saying that she was a woman, was dismissed. It was another glorious example of the inadequacy of society and the law dealing with anything which breaches their textbook parameters.

April's devotion to good manners was very much part of her Liverpool beginnings. She saw how being polite could be of benefit and the inherent kindness of the equality of man. And woman. She was about to witness from the front row stalls a reversal of fortune and the heavy hand and prejudice of the English class system. The scales of justice were in Arthur's favour from the off: 'legal sex' as a category was about to be invented because this future lord of the realm wanted to avoid the obligation to support the working-class woman he had taken as his wife. Certainly, old Etonian Arthur had begged April in letters to be his future Lady Rowallan and, after their Gibraltar marriage, wrote many times asking when she would return to Spain and be with him.

Bev Ayre, April's friend, and an executor of her estate, has bundles of letters written by Arthur which were presented in court and in May 2023 she offered, 'I think it's quite easy to realise why judgement went against her because after he wrote a lot of letters to her professing his love to her. And it appears that she had gone, she'd left Spain one day for a week, and never went back. He's writing to her constantly saying, "I really want my wife to come back." And she's writing back, "I'm just staying for another week." He's writing, "I believe you've got a job in this theatre", "I believe you're doing this", "When are you coming back?" April was living her life but at that time a woman being independent was frowned upon. With the attitude of the time, the male breadwinner, the letters didn't help her case.'

Ms April Ashley was most certainly not playing out the prescribed role. The letters did her no favours. Nor did Mr Justice Ormrod, Sir Roger Fray Greenwood Ormrod, Privy Council, a member of the informal 'old school' and formally educated at Shrewsbury School and Queen's College, Oxford, who had trained as a doctor and served in the Royal Army Medical Corps during the war. He was a judicial star in 1969 and, because of his medical knowledge, chosen to preside over

Corbett v. Corbett. He had strong views on the relationships of men and women, and about 'abroad'. In 1962 he granted an Englishwoman a divorce from her Belgian husband and warned: 'When a woman marries a man of thirty-one who has never done a day's work in his life, she must accept that she is marrying a considerable problem.' In 1967, he dismissed as 'ludicrous' a husband's plea for maintenance although he'd taken charge of all things domestic for his rich wife. He was the first British judge to order a blood test to establish paternity. He ruled in favour of a wife who said that sex once a week for her husband was enough. He had negative opinions about 'flamboyantly dressed' women and disdained fathers who gave up work to look after their children. His rule in divorce was the wife must keep the house and sufficient money as she would bring up the children. Yes, as noted Old School Ormrod, April said he didn't like her. Wouldn't look her in the eye.

He had other people look everywhere else.

It's very arguable that Lord Justice Ormrod's thinking – he was born in 1911 – was focused on defending the institution of marriage that is, of course, heterosexual marriage. The concept of same-sex marriage was an anathema.

The case was held in the days before the divorce laws relaxed and when one or other party had to have grounds for divorce. No fault divorce did not exist. This was the time when, with flashbulbs popping, seedy private detectives leaped out of wardrobes to find a case for divorce, catching one or other married partner in flagrante. A reason for divorce had to be presented in court. Arthur's lawyers went to town to prove April remained a man, a biological male, the marriage never happened. Another of Arthur's fantastic fantasies, perhaps? Throughout, the court called her Mrs Corbett.

April and her lawyers, members of the same often arrogant and dogmatic profession, and no great experts on gender and the reassignment of it, were putting the case that she was a woman and since the day of her surgery had lived and functioned as a female. Most obviously, since Casablanca, she could not fulfil the sexually dedicated role of a man. She was a woman. She could marry a man.

Lord Ormrod, as the world was rapidly changing, not many months after Neil Armstrong landed on the moon, when Little Gloria and others were 'changing sex' on the NHS – had to decide: what, legally, is a woman? Conversely, what is a man? What is the definition of male and female? A question perplexing elected and fearful-to-offend politicians and law-makers these many decades later. Politicians embarrassingly dithering on television about what percentage of women have a penis makes you miss April and her pithy putdowns more than ever. Like many politicians, Ormrod rather dodged the fundamental issue, and in doing so imperilled the lives of many across five continents. What began as a financial dispute about sunshine and sangria, a villa naturally decorated by pink-purple bougainvillaea and Chinese hibiscus, inadvertently made April Ashley a crucial landmark in social history, a character again condemned to a state of limbo, one tilting toward a foreboding future. Neither one of her favoured *Künstlerroman* or *Bildungsroman* protagonists. Maybe, *lost in space* is a better analogy.

Twelve

Into The Void

'There is nothing bad in undergoing change.'
Meditations, Marcus Aurelius

April dressed conservatively for her day in court, unwilling to brandish her femininity for fear of adverse newspaper comment of making too much of a good thing, but wrapped in a blue velvet coat that wet Tuesday, as the rain swept up Fleet Street and west along the Strand, it was only door-stepping photographers she had to deal with and they could not follow behind the gates of the high court.

As a family court matter, the details of the Corbett v. Corbett action could not be reported, only Lord Ormrod's judgement, and for the journalists covering the case that was frustratingly long in coming. Yet it allowed time for gathering background information and interviews to publish following the verdict.

My longtime friend John Hiscock worked for the Diers agency, which reported high court cases for all the UK newspapers, the BBC and ITV, and as such watched April and Arthur and their lawyer perform in court from the first hearing on 11 November 1969. Strangely, he told me in May 2023, the case 'wasn't very sexy'. It was day after day of medical testimony and terms difficult – and even in the 'swinging sixties' often deemed too offensive – to qualify as news fit to print.

But on the matter of law, it had voracious students and John recalled furious debate among lawyers at the Devereux pub in Devereux Court near the Middle Temple. The conversation was more biblical, more cockney Adam and Eve, when the law drank with the fourth estate at the George across the street from the high court and a couple of doors down at the Wig and Pen Club. April kept away from such gatherings and quenched her thirst at the Clachan in a small courtyard off Fleet Street near the Inns of Court. The Savoy was too public to sneak in for a wash and brush up but the discreet Howard hotel onlooking the Thames from Temple Place, was a sane sanctuary for a sandwich and a sip of something. April needed energy for her harrowing seventeen all-but-consecutive days in court running through to 9 December 1969.

A lifetime later, she could recall the weather if not the exact temperature of each day, days in which she said pieces of her soul were pierced with hot needles.

'On most days, she looked like a ghost and I'd say she lost at least a couple of stone in weight during the hearings. She'd always smile and was pleasant outside the court, she left the snarling to the law. Inside, she sat at the front of the court with her lawyers, you could see the tension on her face,' said John Hiscock, adding, 'I'm sure they gave her something to calm her down, some sort of tranquilliser, because the evidence was some of the most invasive I've ever heard in a court. All the reporters in court expected her to have a breakdown or a tantrum.'

She did take strong sedatives but they were negated by the energy and blood racing to her head and heart, and around and around again. Her mind was spinning and she had goose bumps beneath her quiet tailoring and calm demeanour. The lunchtime sandwiches went uneaten. She sat quietly, being ignored by Lord Justice Ormrod. Her glances toward Arthur were not returned as he avoided eye contact by brushing imaginary cigarette ash from his shiny, charcoal-grey suit. The odds were short.

I was twenty-five and Arthur was forty-two. He was a transvestite schizophrenic, very sophisticated, and a liar. I was working class and I didn't know much about life.

Arthur Corbett's versions of events, delivered through his clacking teeth, although titillating the crowded public gallery with the messy details of his sexual desires, were not crucial. As a witness, the Hon. Arthur Corbett was forthcoming, revealing and frank about previously taboo intimacies, about his fantasies and his inadequacies. His much-quoted comment, with Judge Ormrod commending him of this insight, about dressing in women's clothes, marked him in the court's opinion as an honest man: 'I didn't like what I saw. You want the fantasy to appear right. It utterly failed to appear right in my eyes.'

This was all said righteously but it was the medical evidence on what constituted a man or woman that anchored the many days of expert testimony and increased April's anxiety. It was her body being dissected by the evidence, as if it was a new discovery out at Roswell in New Mexico. When Arthur Corbett testified that his love for April was that of a 'normal' man for a woman, the judge thought that silly and of no consequence, even from his 'honest' witness.

During the 1960 trial on whether D. H. Lawrence's *Lady Chatterley's Lover* was obscene, the prosecutor Mervyn Griffith-Jones inquired of the jury, 'Is it a book you would even wish your wife or servants to read?' Decades on that is cited as an example of the establishment being out of kilter with public opinion. It's hard to accuse Judge Ormrod of that during the hearing to annul April's marriage nearly a decade later. 'Sex change' was an alien concept, same-sex marriage not thought of, homosexuality legal for only two years, and the entwinement of April and Arthur beyond the norm. The majority, 'the public', were too unaware even to have an opinion. Yet, given his judicial status, one might have hoped for more compassion from the bench. No matter how many times you read his judgement there is no sense of attempted understanding, awareness that times were changing, that the parameters of human sexuality in day-to-day life were being stretched.

This is the judge on the initial date of April and 'Frank' at the Caprice: 'The petitioner's description of this first meeting contains the key to the rest of this *essentially pathetic* but almost incredible story.'

April suffered what's always the worst hatred, from those who felt deceived. She insisted there was no duplicity in her marriage and indeed it was the entity *April Ashley* to whom Arthur married and with whom he was desperately obsessed. There was much abstract hatred, and fearful outrage. More than sixty years on, as she lay dying, she told of the woman who marched up to her and slapped her. It was such a bruising blow she couldn't go out for three days. With so much that had gone on in her life, that slap about the face still hurt and tingled in her brain.

So also did her most harrowing moments in court, when she was quizzed about her pre-operation body, the size and activity of her penis, the size of her testicles. Which to *April Ashley* never existed. She could offer the court nothing other than:

I haven't the foggiest idea.

She was subjected to a question time about her body, including pre-op, if she'd experienced erections or ejaculated. Judge Ormrod somewhat apologetically acknowledged how distressing this cross-examination was for her. He was long dead, in 1992, but it remained distressing for her.

The annulment divorce was an event which in later life she felt she needed to analyse but often her heart wasn't in it. She'd strive for happier moments – there weren't many – around the court; how she learned to give the 'lovely' photographers their image of the day – they left their cameras locked in an anteroom, allowing them to go into court and listen each day to the testimony – and how they tipped her off about a subsidised bar in the bowels of the court building.

It was 11 a.m. opening time, darling.

Faint distraction from the agony of nine medical experts discussing the very particulars of her body at a public hearing. She endured repeated medical exams, including a 'three-finger test' by a gynaecologist to determine whether her vagina could accommodate a 'normal-sized penis' which she 'passed'. But there was so much more to dismay in a court packed with legal and scientific experts anxious to display their speciality knowledge but unable, it seemed, to show a kindness that the subject of their arguments was anything more than a commodity in an anomalous situation. This line-up was to decide whether April was still a man. If she was, the marriage to Arthur Corbett never happened, two people of the same sex could not form a legal union. The doctors of body and mind paraded, for a per diem, through the witness box, only a couple looking over toward April, and offered their view toward determining, as Judge Ormrod noted, 'the first occasion on which a court in England has been called on to decide the sex of an individual'.

Simply, to which sex did April Ashley belong? It was confusing in 1969/1970 and more than half a century on the debate continues with many, many more shades of an argument echoed long ago in that oak-panelled Court 2.

April's pre-operation life was applied in evidence like a tourniquet, she was breathless as she heard the testimony and the questions of a past she believed she'd eradicated forever.

One of her legal team had insisted on April's mother Ada being considered as a witness on her behalf. She had visited Ada, now living in Manchester and married to Bernie their Liverpool lodger, and her mother's main concern was that her new man's name would not get mentioned in court. April, against legal advice, insisted her mother never get near the high court.

My mother thought Arthur was far, far nicer than me.

She could do nothing to prevent evidence from Dr Vaillant the psychiatrist who gave her male hormones and electric shock treatment in the psychiatric ward at Walton Hospital in Derbyshire in 1953. Dr Vaillant continued to be unhelpful to April. All the medical experts agreed on four medical criteria in assessing the sex of a person: chromosomal factors; gonadal factors (presence or absence of testes or ovaries); genital factors (including internal sex organs) and psychological factors. They were not unanimous on hormonal factors or secondary sexual characteristics. The medical men – they were all men – said April's chromosomal sex was XY, male. There could be no discussion about that: no surgery or hormone treatment could alter the XY equals male equation. April's whole case – that since Casablanca she had been living openly and happily as a woman, as a true female and could not live as a man, in fact, would rather die than do so – was of no consequence to the court. Judge Ormrod said April was not a woman, had not been a woman when she married Arthur Corbett, so that marriage was void.

From his judgement: 'The respondent is not, and was not, a woman at the date of marriage, but was, at all times, a male.'

Mrs Arthur Corbett, future Lady Rowallan, vanished with the verdict:

'*Void ab initio*' ('Never existed in law').

That was cruel and utter humiliation.

I had to go through physical agony to get my dream; for many others it does not involve such an emotional sacrifice. Imagine how much you must want something to do what I did. And I followed my dream in the days when such ideas were thought as practical as flying carpets.

There was more hurt and it had monumental implications for those with acute gender dysphoria for which the only treatment was gender reassignment. For many veteran transsexuals 'sex change' is useful shorthand, simple and explicit. But, according to Judge Ormrod's ruling, it was not a 'cure': 'Intercourse using the completely artificially constructed cavity could never constitute true intercourse.'

On April, and I could never conceive her as anything but a woman, he said, 'Her deportment was reminiscent of the accomplished female impersonator.' Of course, how comfortable her appearance as a woman – she was lucky with her birth body and to transition young – was not a legal factor.

Ormrod set out in UK law that, for marriage, 'man' and 'woman' were biological terms. And if surgery couldn't change biological sex, no transsexual could marry by switching gender.

In 1970, the NHS offered 'sex-change surgery' but with a zany catch-22. The government allowed a man to become a woman through taxpayer-funded surgery but that 'new' woman could not marry a man as she would, for marriage purposes, still be a man and two men could not legally marry. And vice versa. The paperwork problem was as absurd. Passports and similar documents could be changed to the new name and sex – but not birth certificates. All transsexuals hoping to 'pass' as their new sex and having to apply for a passport or needing their birth certificate for whatever reason would be forced to reveal their 'secret'. As April always insisted it is the dream of all transsexuals simply to be accepted as their new selves.

In her brave *Bodyshock* (Columbus Books, 1987), Liz Hodgkinson picked up on that and other repercussions of the precedent set by April's legal trauma:

For all practical purposes, April Ashley, and all subsequent transsexuals, could be considered female but the true, the original sex could never be altered. On hearing the judgement, many transsexuals' hearts sank. Large numbers of them maintained their marriages, legally and properly conducted, confirmed that they really had 'changed sex'. Yet from a medical and biological point of view, post-operative transsexuals cannot genuinely be considered to have changed sex. Nowadays, they must accept this before treatment can be started. Few would argue about this as a medical fact.

Hodgkinson goes on to say that outspoken American feminist activist Dr Janice Raymond coined the expression male-to-constructed-female (and vice versa) to describe post-operative transsexuals and explained at least one always refers to himself as such. She wrote that, though the biology may be clear, the legal position was not. She presumed the birth certificate ruling was intended to stop people pretending to be someone else – a groundless fear, she argued, as most transsexuals desire to be totally acceptable, if possible, in their new sex. There was nothing to suggest such exploitation. The April Ashley case, she wrote, defined maleness and femaleness as a person's ability to have children. She argued it was the ability to marry and function as a natural member of the desired sex, which decided the case in the end. And, astutely, that the judgement questioned what a 'real' marriage might be:

'If a woman has passed the age of reproduction, may she not contract legal marriage? If she's had a hysterectomy is her marriage no longer legal? If a man is paralysed and confined to a wheelchair, unable to have sexual intercourse, may he not legally marry? Is marriage basically a biological or a cultural institution? The questions thrown up by the Corbett case resound still, but the outcome was that a post-operative transsexual may not marry at all, in either the original or the new sex.'

April was aghast at it all. She was skeletal; she lost three stone, nineteen kilos in weight, and had to buy a new wardrobe of clothes. She tried vainly to be upbeat.

Every cloud, darling.

As I said, she was never keen to go over the 1970 trial, which it was in every sense.

After the court case, I was totally, totally and utterly lost. Suddenly, I lost all my confidence as a woman. And I was exhausted. Knocked out.

In later years, April did closely follow the debate and the editorial which resulted from Corbett v. Corbett, much preferring to discuss how others viewed the events which were ever hurtful for her. She knew her lawyers were on her side, they were engaged to be so, but they were as interested in their Christmas holiday plans as the outcome of her case. Judge Ormrod thought it a waste of money. We agreed it took academics to see the travesties, the conundrums and the animosity of the fearful.

Jacqueline Rose, Professor of Humanities, Birkbeck, University of London, in a landmark essay about an ever-changing, as in opinion-of-the-moment, subject was wise and pertinent in the *London Review of Books* in May 2016:

Cruel and outdated as the Corbett case may be, it makes a number of important things clear. The transsexual woman or man is not the only one performing; she or he does not have a monopoly on gender uncertainty; what makes a marriage is open to interpretation and fantasy – there is strictly no limit to what two people can do to, and ask of, each other.

Above all, perhaps, the Corbett case suggests that a transsexual person's enemy may also be their greatest rival, embroiled in a deep, unconscious identification with the one they love to hate; while the seeming friend, even potential husband, may be the one furthest from having their interests, their chance of living a viable life, at heart.

After the annulment, Ashley fell back into penury, where, like many transsexual women, she has lived a large part of her life … Even before the trial, Ashley's career as one of the UK's most successful models had been brought to an abrupt end when she was outed by the press. Up to that point, like many transsexual people who aim to pass, she had lived in fear of 'detection and ruin' (in the words of [Harold] Garfinkel, one of the first medical commentators to write sympathetically about transsexuality).

April thought the impartial, internationally known, Professor Rose, was accurately analytical in her essay, later published in expanded form in her book *On Violence and On Violence Against Women* (Faber, 2021), singling out her point:

Ashley was not, to Ormrod's mind, a woman. This was more to the point, as far as Ormrod was concerned, than asking whether or not Ashley was still a man ...

Ormrod may have found for the plaintiff on the grounds that Ashley couldn't fulfil the role of a wife but it is obvious from Corbett's statements that this was never exactly what he had had in mind ... In this, without knowing it, he can be seen coming close to obeying a more recent transsexual injunction, or piece of transsexual worldly advice. As Kate Bornstein, one of today's best-known and most controversial male-to-female transsexuals, puts it towards the end of her account of her complex (to say the least) journey as a transsexual: 'Never fuck anyone you wouldn't wanna be' (from *A Queer and Pleasant Danger: The True Story of a Nice Jewish Boy who joins the Church of Scientology and Leaves Twelve Years Later to Become the Lovely Lady She Is Today*, Beacon Press, 2013).

April was helped by seeing others understand the madness of what she endured and when we did talk about the high court and the characters, she agreed that her contemporary account, her instant reaction was the raw emotion of the time. She didn't have the time to polish her thoughts, she was front page news and no matter what you hear they don't hold them. On Monday 2 February 1970 Judge Ormrod delivered his judgement.

April did not stay in court. Throughout most of her life she was counselled and looked after by the lawyer Peter Maddock, brother of her great love Edward Maddock, who was by her side almost from the beginning, certainly during the middle, and at the end. To her he was the person 'against whom all other men pale'. In court he could see the horror on April's face as the judge's words disassembled her whole being. With a swift, 'You don't need this,' he took her arm and led her into the Strand.

April wanted her own time and alone she took a taxi to the pre-gentrified Holland Park where she was living in a three-storey house with her friend Joan Foia, Joan's daughter Caroline and her boyfriend John, both of whom were rather taken by April swanning down the stairs from her top-floor accommodation to deliver her rubbish to the dustbins. Tony Singleton also shared the house: 'It's not well known but April lived with us during the divorce chaos from about 1968 and into the 1970s. At first Joan was thrilled to hear Justice Ormrod was in charge of April's divorce/annulment as he and his wife were friends of hers plus he had a good medical knowledge and would have at least an understanding on her side. This, as far as Joan and I were concerned, turned out to be a joke. Joan and I went along to the final day's summing up with some trepidation as we were all now very aware, from comments April made, of Justice Ormrod's negative attitude toward her. But we were still horrified at the various summing-ups that were made and particularly the final decision.

'We got home well before her arrival, where we'd set up daffodils on both sides of the forty or so steps to her room, daffodils in vases, milk bottles, wine bottles, anything we could find. The idea had been to celebrate her winning but it was three flights of stairs of commiseration flowers. When she did eventually arrive she muttered, 'It didn't go well, I don't think he likes me,' and went straight up to her rooms. I suspect she hardly saw the daffodils. But she invited Joan up and Joan spent a couple of hours. Joan never told me what they talked about. Joan never spoke to the Ormrods again. What never came out at the time was that Ormrod's ruling was somewhat guided by the thinking that, by definition, a woman must be able to give birth; ironically, his wife Annie was unable to have children.

'April seemed broken by it – no, that's wrong. Nothing ever broke April. One of the attitudes I loved about April was her ability to see things amusingly and positively whenever things were going somewhat awry. Thankfully, she didn't have time for true shock, she was so busy after the verdict doing her newspaper story.'

Arthur Corbett missed his day in court, his victory which meant he did not have to give April anything, no divorce settlement. That 2 February morning he'd been found in a coma at the Villa Antoinette, a victim it was believed of a nasty fall. April, bombarded by questions from waiting newsmen as she left the court, explained she would not be dashing to be by his side while he recovered. There was a scuffling press conference but April said little, committed as she was to an exclusive telling of her courtroom experience, in return for five thousand pounds. It was quickly done. It reminds us how far April soared above her circumstances only to be sabotaged by the time and place she was living in.

On 8 February 1970, the *Sunday Mirror* printed April's conversations with accomplished interviewer Ronald Maxwell. It's important for it reflects, despite the journalese, what she felt in the moment – in that it conveys more of the hurt than did later and more considered talks she had with friends and commentators. It also, in the introductory presentation, shows the subliminal awe of the story itself. Incredible – as in Judge Ormrod's review from the bench.

Under the headline, 'April Ashley's own story: exclusive' was: 'I _am_ a woman'.

The introduction ran: 'She is beautiful. She walks with the elegance and grace of a fashion model. Yet in the eyes of the law she is a man ... despite her sex change operation.'

April then explains, as she often did to me, that she could not live as a man because, in her view, she'd never really been one. What stunned readers of the time was that anyone could be so open – shameless was one view, so brave, another – about a subject so remote from their daily lives. She explained she was not made from medicine or science but benefited from new learning in both. Her surgery, on a small part of her anatomy, synchronised her body with her mind.

Astonishing is the confidence she displayed after such a battering of a knock back from Judge Ormrod's ruling. She was adamant in repeating her point in the article, that she could only function as a woman. Rather than feeling transformed, she felt complete.

April does not hold back intimate detail in the interview. She goes into areas she would later shy away from both publicly and privately. She talks of, pre-operation, falling in love with Tony, and he with her, a psychological time bomb.

Be it the shock of the court decision and her mental turmoil, she spoke most frankly about issues which had no ongoing mass market forum. It was a trailblazing opportunity. When we talked about the article she chose a quiet smile:

I got things off my chest.

When April later reflected on what had been her instant reaction to the case and her comment that it was free of bile, hurt but no recriminations, she acknowledged that after it all the most ongoing feeling was one of disappointment.

I was not bitter for myself so much as for all the poor other transsexuals who could not be legally married. Just because Arthur and I made such a farcical mess of things it doesn't mean it couldn't have worked between two other people. Of course, there are hundreds of trans-sexuals living quietly as wives but because of my legal precedent they had to live in terror that one day the men who pardoned them will turn. That seems terribly unfair.

Thirteen

Monstered

'Wheresoever April stood, on any stage, that was always
centre-stage.'
Tony Singleton, actor, June 2022

April never regretted her deal with the *Sunday Mirror*, and the
cash provided some short-lived insurance, or what she said and
how it was presented. Indeed, so many years later she felt she
should have been more robust.

> My rights were violated for years. Britain is the most civi-
> lised country on Earth, but so backward about sex. I love
> my country – I grew up in Liverpool during the war when
> it was being bombed flat – and my heart will always be
> British, but the government condemned me to being a
> freak who lived in exile. If the judge's decision had gone
> the other way, it would all be very different. Arthur was
> left free to rob me of *every*thing, our house, even my
> thirty Balmain evening gowns, which he did.

She never did forgive him the Balmain gowns.

On the late Sunday evening of the day her *Mirror* story was
read by millions, she appeared on *The Simon Dee Show* on
London Weekend Television, recorded on the Saturday. She
had about her an unexpected calm. She admitted a little blusher

helped around the eyes, disguised the cost of sleepless nights, but the telltale is in her voice which so very often must catch itself. At the time the always-pleased-with-himself Simon Dee was a very big deal indeed. With April on his show – it's on YouTube – were John Lennon and Yoko Ono making their first ever joint television appearance Also on, eerily, was the black rights activist Michael X who would be charged but not tried with the 1972 stabbing to death in Trinidad and Tobago of his lover Gale Benson, the daughter of April's benevolent friend Leonard Plugge. Michael X was hanged in Port of Spain for a separate murder in 1975.

April said she was uncomfortable for myriad reasons and Lennon, rather than his usual greeting of, 'Hello, here comes the fucking Duchess,' was literally wrapped up in Yoko. It was their 'bed-in' period. Everyone on the show was a huge celebrity of the day and it showed the interest – that is, curiosity – about April that she appeared with them.

Everybody wanted to see the freak.

Which, stoically, she later employed to her advantage.

Peter Maddock again rescued April, this time from the doldrums, but she thought they made one misstep. She was at a dreadful low, was all but mainlining tranquillisers, as her severe weight loss emphasised. The hopes that her life was resolved and her future happy were like snow that doesn't settle. Ongoing at the time of the court case were plans for April, with her *Sunday Mirror* money, scant savings, cash from other investors and Peter's help, to open a restaurant at 8 Egerton Gardens Mews called AD8 on 2 March 1970, which turned out to be four weeks after the high court judgement. Peter advised April to rest and rehabilitate at a Hampshire health resort. It proved disquieting.

I did the wrong thing. The walls were paper-thin and I heard this man in the next room saying, 'You'll never guess who's in the next bedroom? That monster April

Ashley.' With hindsight, it would have been much better had I gone off to Greece or Spain and got laid every night. It would have been much better than sitting in a room brooding all on my own. For me, everything came to a screaming halt and I was humiliated in front of the world. It was a big mistake.

Yet, April was the fighter her father knew never stayed on the canvas. She went on display at AD8 ('A' for April, 'D' for partner Desmond Morgan), which was one of those 1970 places, and there were many, many, where much of the menu was 'nestling in a bed of green peppers'. For most, Elizabeth David remained anarchistic. 'The food was terrible,' Peter Maddock admitted in 2022, 'but not many customers came to eat. The opening launch coincided with the judgement in the divorce case. We'd invited one hundred or so people to the opening party but hundreds more showed up uninvited, plus a phalanx of reporters and photographers. April stationed himself in the restaurant lobby, with a glass of champagne, and greeted the guests. And although devastated by the court judgement she looked spectacular. Ever the trouper. And no one had any idea of what she was going through.

'An hour later, a traffic jam had built up in Brompton Road and three young policemen arrived. The leading policeman told her: "April, we must ask you to shut down this party."

'She took a step back and, fixing him with her famous stare, said, "Well, I can't see any easy way to do that. Can you?" They looked at each other and she said, "In the meantime, would you like a glass of champagne?"

'Bizarrely, they stayed to the end of the evening. Well, those were different times, more relaxed times.'

They were there to be entertained in the basement premises, where guests were met with echoing chatter, thick unfiltered cigarette smoke and April in glorious form as the elegantly dressed host. She was the novelty. On that opening evening, dozens of inquiring Londoners crushed in to take a look. It was hot and humid and the cube of ice in a drink melted before the cocktail left the bar. None of that or the rubbish food deterred names of the day from turning out, from opera singers to ambassadors, rock'n'roll stars (Keith Moon her favourite) to a couple of important and lively people from the Ministry for Works and Pensions, somewhat uncivil servants. April was generous to those she saw hungry for food or company. Also naughty. 'What did you say your name was?' she asked a disgruntled Mick Jagger.

'The restaurant became a celebrity hangout: stars like Ava Gardner, Nureyev and Liberace came to dine and came back,' was Peter Maddock's accurate remembrance.

Tony Singleton most readily agrees. 'Joan and I went often and I suspect it was popular not so much for the food but for the amazing atmosphere and wide-ranging clientele. April sitting at the piano belting out a few numbers while passing out shots of icy vodka sprinkled with pepper from a silver tray next to the keyboard. The music and the audience got louder as the booze flowed. It never seemed to run out.

'One evening Sammy Davis Jr came in and introduced himself to April and her friend, inquiring who they were. April replied, "This is Giovanna Princopessa di Bavaria and I am the Lady Rowallan."

'He replied, "You've got to be kidding."

'April put on her top elegant-amused-high-horse look and told him, "She was and I will be," and they all fell about and had a fabulous evening together.'

Resident in London, Ava Gardner, the former Mrs Mickey Rooney (1942/43), Mrs Artie Shaw (1945/46), Mrs Frank Sinatra (1951/57) and expert on bullfighters and tequila, was a regular and a pal. Exhausted, April would sit at a corner table with the American actress and over a gallon of something put the universe to rights.

In the morning I never remembered how we saved the world.

Booze became a warm blanket and one evening – over the years the number varied in the telling between eighteen and thirty-two – she ordered a dry martini before dinner to be told by the AD8 staff that she was well into double figures. *Are you counting?*

It was a hectic life, advertising AD8 by scooting around parties and first nights and brandishing the brand; on meeting Princess Margaret at one such affair, and through the fermented haze between them, vainly inviting the late queen's younger sister 'to dine'. April met and entertained many of the short shelf-life gossip column names of the time and some everlasting giants like Francis Bacon and Lucien Freud. Her more anonymous friends were steadfast.

She had little to do with the economy of the restaurant business: her job was to smile and be seen, to be the champion of a frivolity she was not experiencing. She became a 'face' on television and the questions always returned to Casablanca. That was her 'selling point' – along with the absurdity of her situation following the high court ruling. She was adrift, a human *Mary Celeste*.

In 2023, the Scottish government found itself in disarray after introducing the Gender Recognition Reform (Scotland) Bill and, due in part to this proposed legislation, the first minister and Scottish National Party (SNP) leader Nicola Surgeon left office. Gender, and the switching of, is a worldwide trending topic. In the UK, headlines shouted about a Scots offender who 'identified' as a woman being sent to a women's prison. Given that, April's onscreen conversation with the always-admired interviewer Mavis Nicholson half a century earlier, on 3 October 1977, is prophetic:

Biologically, I'm male. For all intents and purposes, I'm male, except for socially, I should be accepted as female. Sort of leaves you in limbo, because I don't know where I stand to this day.

'Did you tell me that you are not legally supposed to go into a ladies' lavatory, for instance?'

Yes, I think that would be true.

'And what if you were to become a criminal in any way? Which prison would you be sent to?'

I'd be quite fascinated.

'Would you think that might be a man's prison? Not a woman's prison?'

I think it would have to be solitary confinement, otherwise there would be a riot.

Almost exactly four years earlier, on 19 October 1973, she was interviewed by the sharp and sympathetic Russell Harty on his popular ITV chat show and introduced 'as the man who had had the effrontery to undergo an operation to become a woman. Since then, she has undergone the even more painful business of divorcing the man she married and being told by a judge that she didn't measure up to being a woman anyway. Well, she's here to tell us where she stands tonight. Ladies and gentlemen, Miss April Ashley.'

You must imagine a much amused look on April's face. And on Russell Harty's, whom we must credit for taking the role of his guest's 'straight' man. She told me there was no rehearsal, no pre-planning of questions, simply chemistry.

'When you decided to do that, was your mother alive at that time?'

My mother's still alive. At the last count. We're not very close.

'What was her reaction to your operation?'

She thought I'd had a nose job.

'You decided at a very early age that you were female?'

I didn't decide it. I don't know who decides it. A god perhaps. It's terrifying as you grow up because you know one thing should be happening and another thing is happening.

'Are you still an object of curiosity?'

Oh, I think so. Why do you think they're [the audience] *all staring at me so intently?*

'Well, a lot of them may be surprised that you are so beautiful to look at.'

Yes. And I must point out to them that I've had nothing done [hoots of laughter from the audience and April] ... *well, nothing has been touched on my face at all. My nose is my own. My mother's ignorance has nothing to do with it. Everything else is natural. And you know, this is something else which absolutely kills me: they talk about a female trapped in a male's body. Well, I think if I went home to bed with some of these people they'd be quite amazed because there's certainly nothing male about my body.*

'Does that mean you can enjoy absolutely normal sexual relations with the man?'

Yes, but [by law] *biologically I'm a male. But socially, I'm female. Now, if a man knows that I'm biologically a male, and goes to bed with me, he is a homosexual. But if a man goes to be with me as a woman, and I've done it, and doesn't know the darn thing about it, he thinks he's made a big score – Christ, she's gorgeous.*

'You are beautifully groomed; your dress is beautiful and your face. Do you take a lot of time over your makeup?

I used to take very short time to do my makeup but last year I broke both my wrists.

Puzzlement.

I fell down the stairs at a certain nightclub in London [Tramp].

'That's a very mundane ... I thought it was skiing or something.'

I broke both my wrists – by the way, I wouldn't do anything as mundane as skiing – and this one's deformed permanently, and makeup takes an hour and a half every day. Every day I work at my restaurant. Every day.

'How do you view the prospect of old age from where you sit now?'

I long for my autumn years. Hear the violins! I long to get away from that April Ashley image, from the press, I long for a little cottage in the country.

'A thatched cottage?'

No, no, no. God forbid. I'd hate a thatched cottage. Think of all the mice running around ... no, give me something Cotswolds-brick, something solid.

'And you in a lovely poke bonnet.'

No, no. I'd have my lovely long hair, even when it's white.

'Give or take a year, we're roughly the same age. When we're eighty, shall we have a get-together? More atomic conversation?'

We'll have champagne.

They never could. Russell Harty died, aged fifty-three, in 1988, from liver failure brought on by hepatitis. April sent condolences from California.

The year after her Harty interview, the end of April's five-year contract with her AD8 partners loomed and there was tension and there were tantrums.

I got a little Gordon Brown with the dinner plates, darling.

There was not going to be a happy ending. And every evening there was the chance of a crass customer.

I'd have people poking me in the chest to see if they were real. They'd pull my hair to see if that was real, which could be very painful. I even had a man put his hand up my skirt to see if there was anything there. He was quickly ejected. One had to go through all these ridiculous small insults, which doesn't make for an easy life. I was so gaunt and grey. I was working seven nights a week until my doctor said, 'April, you're far too thin. You should have a holiday.' I was packed off to Barbados for a month. It was marvellous. The moment I got back there was all the stress of the restaurant again. My energy evaporated.

She felt AD8, close to Harrods in Knightsbridge, was cursed. There, she learned of the death of Edward Maddock and that shock added to her deteriorating health. Champagne, Valium and the hypnotic Mandrax comprise a destructive mix. She escaped into a little acting, including playing Countess Dracula, something of a disturbing metaphor for her escape into the dark.

When April spoke of her post-court London adventure, there was little bitterness, more disappointment that relationships and business partnerships had not flourished as they might. She never blamed others and I think she believed she wasn't, and couldn't have been, at the top of her game after her divorce and legal vaporisation. That had been a real punch in the gut. Her restaurant 'partners' isolated her and she negotiated, but her heart wasn't in heavy deal-making. It was a bullying job anyhow. She had some months to go on her contract – she'd sunk her five thousand pounds of Fleet Street cash, a few hundred more, and seven days a week for more than four years into the business – and the offered pay-off was three thousand pounds. It was quite a sum in 1974 – five thousand pounds a year was an impressive salary – but she fervently believed it didn't reflect the April Ashley contribution, the attraction. She spoke about her ousting many times, and maybe it was the years gone by, the time for melancholy reflection, for she didn't rage about the phrase they used to kick her out. She was advised to accept the cash settlement because no one would want to employ 'a middle-aged sex change'. It was brutal, and it was factually correct.

I started applying for jobs in shops.

Being April, 'the shops' included Simpsons of Piccadilly and Fortnum & Mason.

Sometimes, I would get very polite letters back saying, 'Sorry, we don't need anybody,' or I would get quite blunt letters saying, 'We don't want people like you working for us.'

When April had appeared on Russell Harty's 1973 pro-gramme, another of the guests was Albert Hammond, who had co-written 'It Never Rains in Southern California', a sun-and-freedom-seekers' escapist anthem which, half a century later, he continues to perform to audiences' delight. Albert – who by one of fate's whims was my neighbour in Los Angeles for many years – remembers enthusing April with his talk of life by the Pacific Ocean. She seemed, he said, captivated. Being contrary, she went to Wales.

'There was a side to April that loved the glamour, the opera, the first nights ... and the Dom Pérignon. But there was another side to her that longed to be in the country, in a cottage with a wood fire burning, and a couple of dogs. And that's what's happened after four years: she decided to go to Wales,' explained Peter Maddock.

Yet, April had heeded Albert Hammond's counselling and via California, where she spent some weeks being a little bored, went the long way to Hay-on-Wye on the Welsh side of the border, in Powys, where in April 2023, they celebrated her life with 'April Day'. There were talks about her life at Hay Castle and the revealing of a new portrait of April, a conceptualised, 8-foot-by-10-foot image of the photograph on the front of this book, by Caris Jackson.

It was commissioned by the redoubtable 'Flaming Ladies of Hay' who, along with most of the town, have direct memories of her and enjoy recounting tales of one of their more flamboyant residents. She remains a raffish mascot for the town she saw as a sanctuary from her life spiralling out of control. When she arrived in Hay she weighed under nine stone (fifty-seven kilograms) and, by 1975, when she first met Vera Taylor she had suffered at least three heart attacks – one generous quake and two after-shocks. That was where her legend of thirty-two martinis before dinner began. Oh, and the stress, she explained to Vera, was the other factor. She was all but penniless and surviving on toast, and a rented television set for entertainment; she was a total TV soap addict and would cut you off – *Bye, darling* – if the theme for *Coronation Street* and, later, *EastEnders* and *Emmerdale* began.

Vera Taylor and her husband Gerald, a hugely successful antiques dealer, owned Winforton Court, a fourteenth-century, H-shaped, timber-framed and stone manor house which April immediately knew was her sort of place.

Perfect for me to haunt, darling.

And as she recovered her health, and appetite, she often did, turning up in style at their five-foot-wide, oak front door which was always open to her. Vera Taylor has a marvellous photograph of April playing snooker in the games room. 'She was dreadfully competitive but it was fun having her at the house,' Vera said when we lunched in London in May 2023. She never lost touch with April and felt she understood her more than most. In a straightforward way. 'She just wanted to be a woman and was a woman. Simple as that. It's become so political now. Different generations. I'm eighty-two-years old: when I was young it was sort of happy and love-and-peace and people lived how they wanted to live, none of this complication. Fortunately, I'm in the country in France. And there's not much fuss and in a village near me there's many women waiting to have the operation. Oh, April started something – I have to smile. She was always about equality, ahead of her time. I knew her for more than forty years, not one dull moment.

'We used to laugh about the absurdities that life presents to us: Queen Victoria supposedly saying lesbians didn't exist when Disraeli brought in some homosexual legislation making it illegal for men. "What about the ladies, ma'am?" and Victoria said there was no such thing. Chaps were criminalised if they did it, and women with women didn't exist. I mean, talk about equality, you can't even become a criminal.'

Vera said that when they first met, April was, of course, full of stories from her seven weeks' touring around the west coast of America. 'It sounded as if they'd rolled out the red carpet from San Francisco all the way south to the Mexico border. If April was at one party there was always someone there to invite her to the next. She was interesting and fun. And people were fascinated by her presence, people like the actress Elizabeth Taylor who you'd have thought had herself to be fascinated by.'

I was working from Los Angeles during April's California 'tour' and such was her VIP status in Hollywood circles that she was invited to a reception organised by the British Consulate, as were the Fleet Street correspondents, along with UK-linked stars like Cary Grant who found her 'elegant and graceful'. Which is not bad from Cary 'Mr Elegance' Grant. Yet, April said that glitter-around schedule was a mirror of her London life and she was aware she'd slowed down. She flew home.

'April spent a lot of time, several months, getting into good health before she truly started getting about in Hay,' said Vera Taylor who was in London for the May 2023 coronation of King Charles III. 'April loved Charles, especially being the Prince of Wales,' Vera grinned. 'She was very much a monarchist …

'She'd been through so much at that time that she was careful with people, friendly but careful. Not everyone knew her background but most of us did. When she first came to my house, I think she gave me a bit of a test. She wanted me to accompany her to the lavatory to do a wee. So I did, and I just sat by the basin and she did a wee. She didn't expose herself or anything and then we went downstairs again. And that was it. I felt she was testing my reaction but I only thought she was a remarkable person and over forty years that proved very true indeed. Nothing was said but I feel it was for me to accept her as a woman. I never had a moment when I thought April was different. Why would I?

'The business was Gerald and Vera Taylor Antiques, and we had a big barn and April loved the grandfather clocks we sold. She loved the house and the antiques, loved all the grandeur. She had friends but she didn't go out a lot socially at first. She kept a lowish profile and walked her dog, Flora. She said she wanted a quiet life after all the nonsense in London.'

The quiet life for April was not as others imagined such a thing.

'She did have her men around Hay. She'd talk to me about it but we never got into detail – "He did this", "We did that", that sort of thing. She picked up a German tourist which was great, because he didn't know anything about her and they made love and things. She always said Welshmen were very "thorough". That's what she said, what I remember. Whatever did she mean? Oh, we didn't go into *that*.

'But she could be very naughty. We had a big bash for the Queen's Jubilee in 1977 and my brother-in-law Philip Taylor found himself alone with April. She asked him: "Philip, have you had your Jubilee fuck? And if not, shall we?"'

'One of our young clockmakers had the same experience. She was going through a very stricken period at the time and the visits to our house gave her companionship – and food and plenty to drink. You wouldn't know she was on her uppers because she had such stunning outfits: long dresses and a huge diamond ring. We'd wear long dresses and play billiards in our games room where ['Hanging'] Judge Jeffreys was said to have held one of his Bloody Assizes in the seventeenth century.

'April was fun with a great sense of humour but she could be difficult. She was always kind to and defending the working man, old people and animals. And she could be a capricious diva. My late husband Gerry and I took her to London for a visit and we'd had a day of it. We were driving down Park Lane and April announced that she wanted to go to the Park Lane hotel for drinks. Gerry could see the bottles of Dom Perignon being ordered – and paying the bill. He said we'd rather not and should get going. April said she would jump out of the moving car if we didn't go. She made such a scene it was safer to stop in the middle of Park Lane, I had to direct the traffic around us, and April leaped out of the car, stood tall, and marched off on her own. She did indeed order bottles of champagne. And drank them. She couldn't pay the bill and was arrested that evening. Of course, we had to bail her out of that and drive her back to Hay.'

Moment of madness, darling.

'Gerry adored her, he was very gregarious and jolly and used to egg her on to do her *Madama Butterfly* dance. She's done it for you, I'm sure. He loved that. He got on terribly, terribly well with her but he used to hide when he could see the champagne bottles arriving in twos. We'd have two or three rounds at the Blue Boar and she'd say, "Oh, darling, stay on," and he'd excuse himself because he knew he'd have to pay for the lot.'

When I go into the Blue Boar, I'm never given any prefer-
ential treatment. I have to wait my turn. And in fact – as
a male-orientated place for fishermen, farmers, horses,
horse-dealers, dads – sometimes you in fact have to wait
until all the men have been served. It's an extraordinary
thing. But they'd sometime sneak out a Glenmorangie on
the bar for me in desperate times.

'She seemed to have this ability to find people who are helpful
or kind. I introduced her to friends in Glendale (California)
and a doctor among them supplied her with hormone stuff for
the rest of her life. People wanted to help her.

'I'd meet her most market days, Thursday mornings, and
we'd go for a drink and a talk. She was friends with an older
lady called Molly. April did look after people. She herself was
a real person, and if you cut through to the real person, and
exposed yourself as a real person, that's all that mattered. You
were friends.

'But it was not all easy going. Some people were wary of
her and children would taunt her in the street as "that lesbian
lady". She tried to get some work and did get a little job dis-
tributing leaflets but the other employees – they weren't even
working together – objected to April when they found out –
and you couldn't not find out – that she was wonderful and
gracious and different. Maybe they were frightened of her and
she lost her job.

'Attempts to get off the dole through catering and waitressing work failed when some of the other staff discovered her past
and made her feel a freak. She seemed to take such knocks as
a matter of course. Yes, you're right, she could change sex but
not people's attitude. And she knew that, and she learned. She'd
had quite an education by the time I met her.

'Although April was an extravagant character, she was full
of good old-fashioned advice and she told me once when I
confided a problem that one should never bear grudges. During

her life, she was often treated badly by the press and society as an individual. Her advice to me was to simply put this offence out of your mind and, therefore, it doesn't exist and so cannot harm you. It is advice I remember and by then she was the Duchess of Hay, so it was a royal command.'

April's title, First Lady, Duchess of Hay, was bestowed on her by Richard Booth who rivalled her in attracting attention if not in the grand manner of wit. Because of her fondness for his aunt, Viva King, April was eager to be helpful to Booth who rented her a small apartment – 'on a corner near the toilets and the town clock', recalled Vera Taylor – above a book-antique shop, Number One, The Pavement. Richard Booth opened his first bookshop, the Old Fire Station, in Hay in 1962 and turned the town into the world's biggest centre of secondhand books. He bought up books from famous families and homes in the UK and by the ton from American universities at basement prices. A little bonkers and with not much business acumen, he succeeded where perhaps he might not have done. His idea had legs and in time there were thirty or so secondhand book-stores in Hay and a still-thriving literature festival and, always, festivities around Hay Castle, which he owned. He saw April as a publicity machine, an added attraction, for the town and the idea. She was happy to do so for she paid no rent in return for her marketing effect: a grace-and-favour arrangement.

On April Fools' Day 1977, wearing a DIY crown and a fake ermine robe, Richard Booth declared Hay's independence and himself the ruler. April was anointed the Duchess of Hay. Vera Taylor was Duchess of Winforton and her husband Gerry, Minister of Foreign Affairs. American tourists were sold titles – if they were nice. Passports were issued to those with local addresses.

The eccentric bibliophile moved to Hay when his family inherited the nearby Brynmelyn Estate, which was eventually passed to him. Booth bought the decrepit and crumbling Hay Castle and the parties there rivalled medieval banqueting. April was a regular guest of honour, Marianne Faithfull a more reluctant one. The castle was terribly damaged by fire in 1977 and gave him and April another dinner table story: he was sound asleep when the blaze began and roared through the castle and he said 'as king', he mistook the sound of crackling flames for the cheering of his subjects.

He was a mostly benevolent ruler. We were sitting by the swimming pool in the south of France when April began reminiscing about Castle Hay and the fire, thoughts provoked by the local television news of wildfires across Provence. She admired Richard Booth's cool and his willingness to turn most situations into marketing opportunities. She accepted that he'd done just that with her: turned her into a tourist attraction.

Because I'd met Richard through his Aunt Viva, he was indulgent toward me. I had very little money and I had a deal with Richard that whenever I did jobs for him, PR jobs, I didn't have to pay my rent, which was seven pounds a week. I did the very first interview for him for the *New York Times*, one of the most important papers in the world. He said: 'Oh you talk to them for me.' I went down and I did the whole thing. The man kept looking at me. He didn't know who I was at all but it went frightfully well.

I ended up doing so many jobs for him that I hardly ever had to pay rent. That allowed me some spending money. I went out once a week perhaps and I had to buy a round to begin with but thereafter there would be glasses of Glenmorangie sitting on the counter, often a whole row waiting to be drunk. I liked the malt whisky, it tasted like lemon sherbets. I had fabulous clothes so I didn't need to buy any clothes. I was a gypsy girl sipping lemon sherbets.

It was not all happiness between Richard Booth and April: he appeared on the 'shit list' she kept current throughout her life;

there were some permanent entries but time and mitigation removed you as quickly as irate moments placed you on it in the first place. April became disenchanted with Booth who made lavish promises, almost all tied to publicity stunts, and didn't deliver. Relations deteriorated when he sold some paintings April had left with him for safekeeping. She was furious and did not speak to him, although relations calmed in later life. She castigated herself for being bitter about his antics.

Such a waste of time and effort.

'I remember her being heartbroken when she was told Richard Booth had died. She was very sad,' said Bev Ayre. It was 2019 and Booth was eighty years old. Vera Taylor added, 'One of the things for April was she did tend to fall out with people and not be in touch with them and then at the end, "Oh, what a shame, I never really got to talk to them." She did have such fond memories of Hay, she had the time of her life there.

'I was in Hay in April [2023] and someone told us they were seventeen years old when they met April there. They were a punk and they said they felt that April was the most archetype punk in that she would walk through the middle of Hay with her head held high and she wouldn't give a shit what people were saying about her.'

When I arrived in Hay I couldn't get over all these people. They were waving to me and smiling at me. But not speaking. It took more than one year and then gradually people started to talk to me. We'd chat and by the time I left, ten years later, I knew the whole town, I spoke to everybody and they'd grown quite fond of me by then so it was very nice. Doing shows for all the locals. We'd have such fun and I'd get rip-roaring drunk.

Fourteen

While The Sun Shines

'I learned courage from Buddha, Jesus,
Lincoln, Einstein and Mr Cary Grant.'
Peggy Lee, 1963

I'll tell you a lovely story, darling.

I had a journalist come down from London to interview me when I was in Wales. She said: 'Do you have any
private letters that I could read?' It was in the middle of
winter. I said I had boxes full upstairs.

'Do you want to go up and have a look?

She said, 'Oh please, yes.'

It was freezing. I had this whole top floor and there was
just nothing in it. Very tall, late Victorian house. I took her
up some hot soup as I thought she must be frozen. She
said it was wonderful. My soup, not the attic.

She came down and said, 'May I ask you a question?
Do you ever get depressed?'

I said, 'Not very often, no. Not enough to be worried
about.'

She said, 'I have never, ever, known anyone who is
more loved than you.'

'If ever you get depressed, go and read your own letters.'

I had never thought of it. She said she had interviewed
hundreds of people, and she had never seen such lovely

letters. I thought that was a lovely thing to hear that. She wrote a very nice article.

Of course, not everyone was a fan. She had her share of poisoned pen letters, a pushback from locals who thought she was a touch too 'Duchess' in her attitude – *better than a touch too common* – and she did disgruntle some customers late in the evening at the Blue Boar Inn, to the dismay of landlord Christopher Fry and his wife Liz, who explained, 'We had to ban April from drinking port. A lifetime ban. We stopped the port, kept her on the Glenmorangie. Champagne and whisky and gin, she could handle them all in the same evening. But when she began supping the port, it was fireworks. She was uncontrollably rude.'

April did have her moments but that said, there was rarely malice in her wonderland of remarks. Once in a Saturday morning market in Provence we were searching for kitchen table coverings – cheap and cheerful French breadbasket affairs – when the smug imported tones of middle England shrouded the fun: 'Oh, not the quality you get at Harrods.'

Arriviste!

It was more loudly spoken than muttered and had the required effect.

We were in the Chelsea Arts Club one evening:

Let's sit in the corner at the bar, darling, everyone will come to see me.

Indeed, there was soon a queue of people and champagne bottles by the bar.

Many of her adventures flourished at the club off the King's Road in London. One with Grayson Perry who was knighted in the 2023 New Year Honours for services to the arts. April called him her 'toy-boy lover', fondly recalling them living together in Hay. Sir Grayson, an Essex boy born in Chelmsford in 1960, met April at James Birch Fine Art, a gallery in World's End, the wild west of the King's Road. From the age of fifteen, he'd lived with his transvestite alter ego, Claire and, as the winner of the

Turner Prize in 2003 became very publicly associated with that lover of dolly dresses, big hair, cartoon bows and a blonde wig. April said it was lust at second sight when they next met.

He walked up to the bar at the Chelsea Arts Club and said, 'I only have to look at you to get an erection.'

Few even such close friends of April ever saw her without makeup. Grayson Perry said he never did, even when they were living together. He told Jane Preston, the director of an astute television documentary on April broadcast in 2022, that it was a daily surprise that she'd appear looking perfect.

'I remember her getting up – she was always up before me – and she would arrive fully quaffed, made-up, kind of seductive, kind of bit vampy. You know … "Dahhhling." This is a long time ago. I can just remember there was a lot of alcohol involved, lunchtime drinking, evening drinking, I was under no illusion that this was going to be a long-term relationship, put it like that.' April was a little more circumspect when we talked about her affair with Grayson.

I certainly found Grayson fun. There was no angst in our relationship. We used to go to galleries and have drinks and dinner. It was a very normal male–female relationship as far as I was concerned. It was in Hay that it all ended. One evening we were leaving the house to go to dinner at the pub. Nothing special. On the doorstep, he said, 'Oh, I can't go out. I don't want to.' I asked him what was wrong, but he just looked confused. I'd said I'd arranged to meet friends and was going with or without him. I tried to persuade him not to be silly, but he got something in his head and was stubborn. I left him to it and went off for the evening. The next day, we said our goodbyes, and that was the end of the affair. It had been a sweet and gentle relationship. I was a little upset that it finished abruptly like that. But he was so young, and only just really finding himself as Claire.

He would go to the Beaumont Society and I think they must have helped him. I know they have been wonderful for many people; they're Britain's biggest support network for transgender, transvestite, transsexual and cross-dressing people.

I think he's done brilliant work in ceramics, especially with the autobiographical images of himself and Claire and his family. He must be proud of what he's achieved.

The break-up didn't slow April's social life. One Hay landlord recalled, 'We'd have a lock-in at closing time which was exclusively for the locals, people who'd been in the pub for the evening. April turned up at the locked door wanting in and we told her no: "If you can't be here during opening hours, you can't come in after them." I served some drinks, glanced around in the bar and turned to face April waiting to be served. "Evening, darling, the usual, please." She'd climbed through the tiny window in the pub toilet.'

April was never a supporting player in her story. In any story. 'April was always helpful to lost souls,' said Vera Taylor,' and that's how she started looking after Charlie. He truly began to depend on her and I think, in turn, she got a boost from being able to do some good for him. She'd gone on the dole and tried out at a few jobs; she was always willing but nothing seemed to suit. Charlie became a mission for her even if he wasn't always easy.'

Charlie was Charles Simpson, eighty-four, cantankerous, mischievous, selfish, naughty and a wonderful match for April. She met him through a mutual friend's mother, Brenda, and started to help him out in his garden. They most happily suffered as they battled against each other and their many unseen foes. For April, some foes were real and close, such as an aggressive landlord. By this time, Richard Booth had sold the building she was living in. Her new landlord said she could stay on and, as her arrangement had been quid pro quo, Brenda invaluably advised her to nevertheless get a rent book and have it signed off each month, making her a sitting tenant.

A saviour, for the new owner – who'd said, 'Oh, April, it's no problem, you can live there and we won't even put the rent up' – suddenly comes bursting in one night, without even knocking, and was so drunk and he wants me out and I said, 'Oh, you do. I'm sorry to tell you ...' and thank God for Brenda. I had my rights.

Had these people *spoken* to me and said, 'We bought the building April, would you mind moving on?' I would have. Instead, they put me in a corner. I said, 'If you wanted me out you only had to be polite because nobody is going to speak to me like that.'

Then Charlie begged me to go and live at his house, which I was very reluctant to do. I went over and I saw how big the house was upstairs, because I'd never been upstairs. He said, 'You can have the front bedroom. My bedroom's at the back.' It was huge. What was nice was, although his bedroom was next to mine, you had to go down a flight of stairs and up a flight of stairs to get to his room.

I looked at it and I said, 'As long as I can paint it whatever colour I want.'

He said, 'Do whatever you want to the house.'

I moved in and people were happy about that – especially the council because I'd taken a care package off their books. They knew that I really cared about older people. Right up until the end it was OK. Charlie was fine. He could be an absolute bastard but I understood that even then. You get old, you get selfish and sometimes it comes out as nastiness. It could be so difficult. Very demanding. I would cook him lunch and put a little supper on and he would go to bed earlier, so I had the sitting room to myself. I had the front sitting room and he had the back sitting room first of all. Then, as he came to rely more and more on me we would sit together in the evening. I looked after him until he died. He left the house to me. He gave me half the house about two or three years before he died. It was a big shock; he had to get the doctor's permission, the solicitor's permission. He had to be compos mentis.

By the way, darling, if anyone had told me how difficult the last eighteen months would be I would not have taken it on. It was horrendous. Charlie would fall out of bed, he would fall down the stairs, and having to carry quite a big man up the stairs, and the fact that he was naked, was not easy. Then, having to get him back into bed again. Making sure he bathed and was clean and all of those sort of things, it was hard work. When he died, I thought to myself: 'You deserve the house.' I had bloody well worked hard for that house.

From that point – when everyone found out I had inherited the house – they all seemed to approve because by then they realised what a demanding job it had been. Charlie left me the house and I was so stupid. He wanted to leave me his money, too. It wasn't an awful lot – about ten thousand pounds – and I said, 'No, you must leave that to your daughters.' The house was not their house. The house belonged to Charles's second wife, not their mother and because they never came to see him, I felt that was OK. It had nothing to do with them the house. I made a point of telling Charlie's solicitor: 'Don't allow him to leave his money to me.'

It would have been helpful for April to have taken the money for, as she always agreed, she was not a natural homeowner. Bills were pests. And they arrived on a regular basis, week after week, month after month. While she was useful about the big

In wartime Liverpool, April felt trapped in herself and by the bombs dropping on the city, the most attacked area of Britain outside of London. The memory never left her. © *Shutterstock*

Before they began destroying her home city, the Nazis raided and shut down the Institute for Sexual Science in Berlin, the headquarters of pioneering Dr Magnus Hirschfeld, who ran the centre from 1919 to 1933. He was a hero to April.

Happy Days: pre-operation Toni April on the top far right with the off-duty Le Carrousel troupe she felt so at home with. That's Bambi one over to her right.

Happier days: for post-op Miss April Ashley, the carefree superstar model, happiness arrived like a long, warm note on a flute.

April with the delighted
what she called 'my freedom'
highlighted all across her face.

April with the look *Vogue* and the top photographers craved.

Anyone even thinking of giving April a ticket in 'Swinging' 1960s London got a warning look.

April being introduced to Sir Winston Churchill at the final matinee of *Fata Morgana* in April 1964. There's Sarah Churchill to her father's right and the young David Hemmings [to Churchill's left] gently smiling toward April, while director Ellen Pollock oversees the introductions.

April and actor friend Tony Singleton having fun in a London railway station photobooth in 1968.

Apprehension across her face, April arrives at the High Court in London on 2 February 1970 for a historic verdict which would distress her and change her life and that of many thousands of others for decades.

Opening night at AD8 and a thin-faced April, in the aftermath of her court ordeal, with [left] her dear friend Joan Foa, aka Giovanna Principessa di Bavaria to April, and restaurant partner Desmond 'Dizzy' Morgan, welcoming entertainer Lionel Blair.

April with Martini in hand. One of April's favourite remarks, though she seldom adhered to it, was, 'Martinis are like a woman's breasts, one's not enough and three's too many.'

April modelled for an exhibition of jewellery staged by Tony Singleton at the Christopher Hull Gallery in Motcomb Street, Belgravia, London, in 1971. *Photograph by Eddie Kalish*.

Glamour was forever associated with April and few saw her without her 'face' on. She maintained that like Norma Desmond, she was always ready for her close-up.

April in her glory in the south of France with the fading grandeur of the château where we spent many hours talking artfully concealed.

On 12 December 2012, the woman who began life as a boy made a grand appearance at Buckingham Palace where the Establishment validated the long and often cruel road she had taken. King Charles III, then Prince of Wales, presented her with an MBE. © *PA Images/Alamy*

Images courtesy of Tony Singleton and Vera Taylor unless otherwise noted

Victorian house and garden, there was always something going wrong with the heating or the cooker or the ancient pipes which brought in the water supply. And there were the vet's tablets for whippet Flora's exceptional wind. Somehow, with the house she also took possession of a shotgun. We never did discuss – rather, she never explained – how, but she said the two policemen who mattered in town knew about it. She'd handled a gun before when she lived in Spain.

> I went into Gibraltar with Tim Willoughby and he said, 'April, you live right in the middle of nowhere, you have to get a handgun.'
> He got me a Luger and I took it – and I immediately put it down. Tim said, 'What's wrong?'
> I said, 'I'd kill Arthur.' No, the minute I put that Luger in my hand I said, 'No. I'd shoot Arthur.'

A shotgun in Wales was an altogether different matter. She had problems with youngsters running and jumping across an ancient wall she shared with the next door bank.

> I told the cops about these kids who used to run across my back wall which, from my side, was only about four feet high. These little buggers were running across this wall and ruining it. I came out with the shotgun and I must have looked like a madwoman and I shouted: 'You fuckers. You go over that wall one more time, you'll be dead!' I never saw them again.
> Then one morning I came out and part of the wall had fallen. I thought, My God, what am I going to do? This is terrible. This beautiful wall, thousands of years old. Just then the telephone rang and this voice said, 'Miss Ashley?'
> I said, 'Yes. Is that you, Mr Hughes? [The bank manager] I've just seen the wall.'

> He said: 'Well, I'm just ringing you up to reassure you that it's the bank's responsibility, not yours.' I thought it was my responsibility. He said, 'The bank owns the wall.' I still wanted to shoot the little fuckers.

And film-makers wanted to shoot her, in a film of her life. The director-producer-scriptwriter Mark Ezra was keen to tell her story on screen. In 2021, shortly after April died, he recalled the plan in awry letter to *The Times* in London. He explained he'd been introduced to April at the Chelsea Arts Club in early 1982 and she'd invited him to visit her in Hay-on-Wye to talk about a film of her life. The movie biography was to celebrate the sixties, April's turbulent story, her marriage to Arthur Corbett and Judge Ormrod's decision that April, 'while a woman for many legal purposes, did not qualify as a woman for purposes of marriage.' That year, in December, he wrote, he and April a flew to Marbella, to ask Arthur Corbett, by then Lord Rowallan, to sign a waiver legally agreeing not to oppose Ezra's planned film. He offered to the *Times* readers another wonderful only-April memory:

'When we arrived, bearing two bottles of champagne which April, somewhat nervously, hoped might lubricate his signing arm, Rowallan appeared to be living in some penury. He struggled to find more than two cracked glasses and directed me to his bathroom, where I discovered an old tooth mug, green with mould and slime. In the event, April and I shared her glass. After about twenty minutes I left the two of them to discuss old times and thrash out the basis of an agreement. I spent forty minutes or so wandering the beach front before returning to find April flat on her back in the middle of the road, waving the signed agreement in triumph.'

The distinguished film-maker was not the only one who wanted to put April onscreen, and she was tempted by the bubbly life in London but wary of the TV talk shows which she felt were simply curious to see *an aging tranny*. She was most certainly a 'name' on that circuit. What will be shocking in the modern cancel-culture environment are some of the 'names' who appeared with her in a documentary/fantasy produced by Alan Yentob, the BBC's former creative director and controller of BBC1 and BBC2, for the *Arena* programme. The film was about a country lad homeless in London and seeking fame and fortune, who is taught how to 'lig' – to freeload. In a pun on the George Bernard Shaw classic, it was to be called *Ligmalion*. The colourful chancer was played by Tim Curry, renowned as the self-proclaimed 'sweet transvestite' Dr Frank-N-Furter from the original *Rocky Horror Show*. April was to play herself.

Who else could do it?

The cameo appearances were the added attraction: Lady 'Bubbles' Rothermere, wife of the proprietor of the *Daily Mail*, Lord Montagu of Beaulieu, singing about the stately homes of England, Gary Glitter, Baroness Thyssen, cookery presenters Fanny and Johnny Cradock, media monster Robert Maxwell, Alexei Sayle as John Bull and Sting as Machiavelli. It was crucified by critics when it aired on Easter Monday 1985. April predicted that.

You didn't need to be Sherlock Holmes, darling.

Still, she loved her performance as herself – *I am the Duchess of Hay, clothes do not make the man* – filmed at Clyro Court, part of Baskerville Hall overlooking the Wye Valley, built in 1839 by Thomas Mynors Baskerville for his second wife, Elizabeth. And, yes, Arthur Conan Doyle was a family friend who learned of the legend of the hound of the Baskervilles. He set the great Holmes and Dr Watson adventure in Devon to 'ward off' tourists swamping the hall and next-door Hay.

April's Australian adventure, and she told it in exclamation marks, was more louche than you'll find in the pages of Conan Doyle. As always, she was tempted by travel and making an entrance. The television talk show host Michael Parkinson in the 1980s enjoyed the benefit of wintering Down Under and hosting his eponymous programme there. April immediately accepted an invite to escape from the Welsh weather and from the ongoing and increasing pressures of home ownership.

When we were sitting in the sunshine in Provence she suggested if the climate in Hay was more clement she'd never have moved. Yet, even when she talked about the day-to-day in Hay, her body language reflected the weariness of it and you expected a sigh at the end of every sentence; the Parkinson opportunity was irresistible, her accommodation at the Sebel Townhouse on Elizabeth Bay was five-star.

Word soon got around that she was in Sydney. Elton John, a friend since AD8, called and they had dinner. She deployed her wit for Parkinson and then left the luxury surroundings of the Sebel House to stay with her friend, Geoffrey K. She was in no rush to return to Hay.

I'd fallen in love with the bar of the Sebel Townhouse. I would, wouldn't I, darling? So most nights after dinner, we'd pop in a cab and go and have a nightcap at the bar there. One night I was sitting at the bar and talking to the barman who by then was one of my best friends in Australia. Geoff and I had had quite a bit to drink and were in a good mood. Suddenly, this huge crowd of young men arrived. One of them stood out because he was incredibly handsome and had this mane of hair. He kept looking at me and smiling. And I kept looking back and smiling. And then one by one, all of his friends disappeared and I was alone at the bar with him and Geoff. I went to the loo and when I came back Geoff was standing over in the corner.

This young man, Michael Hutchence, said to me, 'Come to my room for a bottle of champagne.'

I couldn't resist it. I couldn't resist him. I said, 'That would be very nice. What about my friend, Geoff?'

'Oh, he'll wait for you.'

He was staring into my eyes intently and shaking. I went over to Geoff and said, 'I'm just going to go off and have a bottle of champagne with this lovely man. Is that all right?'

'Yes, darling. Oh, I'll wait for you. I want to hear about this one.'

I didn't have a clue who Michael Hutchence was. We went upstairs and had champagne and suddenly I was naked. And he was naked. He had the most incredibly beautiful body and he had the most enormous whanger. I was barely able to cope with him, but I did. He wanted to do it every which way. He was certainly desperate for sex. There was no conversation as such, just sex. It would be very rare if I didn't tell someone my history, but not in this case. As with all one-night stands, there is little point in telling. These men don't find anything different about me because there isn't anything different. They always thought they'd hit the jackpot. I didn't know about Michael's reputation as a sexual adventurer. He certainly didn't display any foreign sex toys to me. He had enough of his own. More than enough. He was wonderful. A man who wouldn't have disappointed any woman. I could barely handle him at all. I am really shy but I love a man with a sense of humour, who is very sure of himself sexually. It was hugely enjoyable, pleasure for pleasure, and no ulterior motives. Michael was an absolutely beautiful man and I was flattered – who wouldn't be?

We relaxed afterwards, had a couple of more glasses of champagne, and he was very pleasant. And then we kissed goodbye and he closed the hotel room door. I was in such a good, high mood I wandered back to the bar swinging my knickers around my finger. Geoff was waiting. 'Do you know who you've been to bed with?'

I didn't and he explained it all to me. Michael had come in with band members and some of his road show, the entourage and they'd taken off one by one so he could be alone with me. When I was in the loo, he'd asked Geoff politely if he'd get lost and Geoff had said no, but he'd stand out of the way while he tried his luck. He got lucky. But I had no idea of his identity. As I explained we'd been endlessly at each other, not talking. Geoff said, 'He's the lead singer of INXS, one of the world's most successful rock groups.'

Of course, I followed his career and life after our night together and he had such interesting lovers, among them Helena Christensen and Kylie Minogue. The whole saga with his lover Paula Yates was so tragic. Her husband Bob Geldof appeared with me in *Ligmalion*. As was his suicide in 1997, so sad, alone in a hotel room. When he died so young – he was only thirty-seven – his sexual antics got more attention than his music. Why such a man would kill himself is impossible to answer. He was God's gift to everybody. We are all complex people.

As was her situation in Hay. 'April would have stayed in Australia much longer, for she did have such a good time,' said Vera Taylor, 'but her responsibilities with the house brought her back to us sooner than she wanted.

'April had many friends but she kept us apart. I don't know who she went to see in London, she kept one unit quite separate from another unit. I tend to introduce people to each other and hope everybody gets on really, which is why I used to have parties, introduce people who then became friends. April enjoyed her freedom, being able to move about without question. I think throughout her life she had been trapped in situations and she began seeing the house as another trap she needed to escape from.'

Indeed, that foreboding Victorian house on the hill became as appealing as the Bates Motel, and the bank owned more of it than she did. She was also getting fed up with expectations of her, especially by twee television producers who thought they knew what she was or, rather, should be all about.

When a television company came to the house to film me for a documentary, they told me, 'Just go about your normal business and we'll film you.'

'Well, I'm going to mow the lawn now.'

'Oh, can't you do something more feminine, like wash the dishes?'

'But I don't wash the pots. I hate washing dishes. I get someone else to wash the dishes. I'm going to mow the lawn.'

'Like that?'

'Like what?'

'In jeans? Couldn't you wear a dress or something?'

'But I don't wear a dress to mow the lawn. It's a crazy idea. I wear jeans and Wellington boots to do that.'

April was never what most anyone expected. In her older, winter age, there were flashes of annoyance at ignorance, and she'd abandon her usual grace and articulacy in reply to nasty, thoughtless and, in the thoroughbred twenty-first century, with transsexuality so socially and politically sensitive, increasingly fetishising inquiry. You could clearly see that weighing her down, the weight of the awfulness. Never for long, for she was a great one for over the horizon.

PART FOUR

First Lady

'First you are young; then you are middle-aged; then you are old; then you are wonderful.'
Lady Diana Cooper, 1892–1986

Fifteen

Climate Change

'As soon as I stepped out of my mother's womb I realised that I had made a mistake – that I shouldn't have come, but the trouble with children is they are not returnable.'
The Naked Civil Servant, Quentin Crisp, 1968

April attained her half-century in Hay-on-Wye. There was champagne, and there were decisions to be made. She'd had an architect nose around the house and suggest improvements, a couple more bedrooms, a new bathroom, a sitting room, which was good, professional thought but it would cost more than the equity she maintained in the property. She consulted Mr Hughes at the bank.

He thought some income from running a bed-and-breakfast business would bring in enough money to keep her and her home afloat. April looked around her Victorian surroundings and said she thought her mind then was working at a crazed angle, gone through the gears to a stubborn position. Now or never.

There are some moments in your life when you can do something and there are other moments when you can't. I decided it wasn't my time to be a bed-and-breakfast landlady and it was such a small amount in those days, just a couple of pounds a night. Did I really want all these people roaming around the house? I wasn't ready for that.

It wasn't the work that frightened me. It was the idea of facing all these bloody strangers knocking on your door, coming in, sleeping in your bed and then having to get up and do the breakfast. It didn't seem like a solution to my feeling, of a sort of claustrophobia with Hay and the house. What decided it was my own stupidity. I was asked to appear on a couple of talk shows. I did one in London for ITV with Larry Hagman, who was big on *Dallas* at the time. And the wonderful American character actor George Kennedy. The other I did in Birmingham with Engelbert Humperdinck.

When the car brought me back from Birmingham, I thought to myself that *They just want to see what you look like at fifty, you stupid bitch. Why did you do all of that?* I should have refused them all. They paid you nothing, anyhow. That evening, I settled down with my dog and my beer which I always had in the evenings when I wasn't going out. I put the television on and I couldn't see anything. The first thing I did the next morning was to shoot around to the doctor's. I thought I'd gone diabetic.

Dr Wilson told me, 'No, April, you're fine, go and get your eyes tested.' Suddenly, I needed glasses. I'd always worn shaded glasses but that was just because I liked everything to look soft. There I was at age fifty, I had this huge Victorian house and vast gardens I used to do myself. And I was sitting there thinking I'm going bloody blind. It wasn't joined up thinking. If I was lucky I would come out with about thirty thousand pounds. I wasn't going to win a race for the house with the bank. That wasn't a contest.

I wanted a new beginning. I always wanted to live in America. I just decided I was going to sell everything.

Flora would be looked after by friends. I had a garage sale but I wasn't much good at bargaining. I gave the whole bloody lot away and made a hundred pounds out of all the stuff in the house. I packed up all my personal bits and I got on a jet plane not knowing when – or if – I'd be back again. I flew to New York and into Hell's Kitchen.

It was in San Diego where April remembered most of her American adventures for me and it was easy listening while looking out toward Japan and watching the sun slip down over the Pacific. Hell's Kitchen got short shrift.

That address turned out to be more appropriate than I would have liked. I went with a friend who turned out to be a terrible drug addict. He used to disappear all the time. It was Christmas and he was nowhere to be found. My answer to this was to have a party. I had the nice apartment we'd been given to myself and invited a crowd of people that I knew in Manhattan. On the off chance, although convinced he'd be too busy, I contacted Quentin Crisp. He'd become so famous after the screening of *The Naked Civil Servant* on television. I said, 'Quentin, can I give you a small party?'

He was delightful. 'Oh, April, darling, that would be lovely. But being Christmas time would that be OK? It's a strange thing. Everybody thinks celebrities are visiting at Christmas and you always end up spending Christmas alone.'

He had nowhere to go. It was astonishing. He arrived, this most charming man with his bouffant and lavender. He had just the most exquisite mannerisms and everybody loved him. It turned out not to be too Scrooge a Christmas for any of us. At about quarter to midnight, he said to me, 'Oh, April, I have to go. I have to catch the tube.' He didn't say the 'metro'.

I said, 'Would anybody here like to drive Mr Crisp home tonight?' Every hand shot up.

We met and talked a lot while I was in New York, which wasn't too long as it turned out. By New Year's Eve, I was gone to California: this mad girlfriend of mine, Jane, the daughter of a longtime friend who I knew in Rome, turned up and asked me to go with her. We moved into a bungalow on Sunset Boulevard, where Marlon Brando used to take all his women, just down from the Chateau Marmont. It was charming but every day I had to walk down and carry a gallon of wine back for this crazy friend. She wanted cheap wine and it came to about three dollars for a half gallon. Yes, darling, the Gallo gallons. It got so tiring, walking back and forward for that drink.

I've never driven a car in my life but the few times my friend did take me out, I watched carefully. I got up one morning, and she said, 'Are you going for the wine?'

I said, 'This time, I'm going to drive so I want the keys to your car.'

'But you can't drive, no keys.'

'That's OK. No wine. I'm going back to bed.'

She threw the keys at me. I got behind the wheel of the car and couldn't get it going. Our neighbour, Jeff West, saw me and said, 'Oh, April, you have to put it into "park" if you want to start the car.'

I drove beautifully to the shops. I drove back perfectly and parked perfectly. The only thing is I didn't put it back into 'park' and, when I was getting out, the car started rolling forward. Happily, there were bollards.

I took four lessons and got my California driver's licence. And I got married again.

April was to be very much part of the British scene in Los Angeles in the 1980s and you'd see her at parties and Hollywood functions. She was a good guest at anything. She was also always hoping to get a break into television or film.

Character roles, darling.

Novelist and actor Jackie Collins was a fan and she gave April some worthy marketing advice: if you are taking the trouble to get out the full glamour, said Jackie, attend at least half a dozen parties, do the Beverly Hills circuit, and make sure you get your photograph taken at each. Screen appearances, work of any kind for a non-US citizen, would require a work permit, a Green Card. You could get one of those through marriage.

I became friends with Jeff, who ran a nightclub called the Pink in Santa Monica, not that many blocks from the beach. His club attracted quite a crowd and had a reputation of being a New York style club: people like David Bowie and his wife Iman and a gallery of all sorts of actors and actresses. I would go for breakfast with him once in a while. It was just a friendship. Always. He was gay and he had a very nice boyfriend. He and I became friends. It was very nice. We laughed a lot and got on very well and things like that. Jeff was a gorgeous, big Texas man with jet black hair and green eyes. He explained the problems of my friend, who wasn't just on the wine but also severely involved in drugs. I was always naive in this area: drugs were something I never got into and I wanted nothing to do with; in those days, people were snorting cocaine off the counters of hamburger bars on Sunset Strip – ketchup, my favourite, was so passé.

My friend got more and more unwell and I went over to Jeff's and told him, 'She won't get out of bed: she's drinking a gallon of wine every day.'

'You don't know why those men come to the door? They're all drug dealers. She's a drug addict. Some of them fuck her for a line of coke, that's what she's doing.'

Oh my God, this little girl I knew from all these years before, her mother that I adored? Suddenly, it all fell into place. As did my life.

Once again through kindness of a friend.

My lovely LA friend Michael rang up and said, 'Would you like to borrow my house in Palm Springs?' He was going to Colorado. By this time, I'd bought a little Honda and I said that it would be marvellous. I said it would be nice to get away for a little while, and it would be nice to just be quiet.

I got to Palm Springs. I was on the terrace and I rang Jeff up and said, 'What are you doing?' and he said, 'Nothing.' I asked him what was wrong. He said, 'You've no idea what's going on.' I said, 'I was just ringing to see if you would like to come and spend the week with me in Palm Springs.' He said, 'Oh, God. It's a miracle.' He said he would tell what was wrong when he got there. I asked him when he was leaving and he said, 'Right now!'

Half an hour later the telephone rang and it was Jane. She had become such a shrew, I think. 'You've no idea. I'm going to have that son-of-a-bitch put in prison.' I asked her what she was talking about. 'That Jeff West. I'm going to get him.'

I could not get out of her what he'd done. I decided not to tell her that he was on his way to stay with me. By then I knew Jane and I knew that if you told her anything trouble would follow.

Jeff arrived. They'd had a terrible row. She'd called the police on him and everything. It was all over something so stupid. When he got to Palm Springs we had a glorious week together. In the evenings we'd cook marvellous meals. He was a good cook, too. Where we were staying was called 'The Lake' because there were lakes everywhere. I came out one morning and in all my igno-rance I said to Jeff, 'This water has gone from blue to black almost overnight. It's so strange there are no fish in these lakes.'

He said, 'April, it's like going to lavatory when you pull the chain. That's what they do. They just pull a chain, the whole things empties and then they fill it up again!' Hundreds and hundreds of lakes. It was a huge complex.

Then we went back to Hollywood and I got in and Jane said, 'I don't know where that swine has got to, but I'm going to get him.'

I said, 'Jane, before you say another word, I have to tell you Jeff has spent the last week with me. When you rang up I'd already asked Jeff, and he'd left about half an hour earlier. There was no way I could get in touch with him to stop him from coming. He just came and I let him stay because I'd invited him. I didn't know you were going to have a row. I didn't know you were going to fall out with him. I don't know what you fell out with him over.'

Well, she started on me. She started screaming and shouting and everything and Jeff heard us. He came over and knocked on the door and he said, 'April, if you want to, you can come and live in my house.'

They were all the same, those little cottages. He said, 'You can come and rent my place if you want.'

I said, 'OK.'

I said to Jane, 'I'm off.'

She flew into an almighty rage and she wouldn't speak to me.

Years later, 2000-and-something, I was staying at the Chateau Marmont and I got the driver to take me down to Hayvenhurst where her apartment was, right there in the middle of Sunset and Santa Monica, and pop in and say, 'Hello.'

I knocked on the door and I hear the television on full blast. She wouldn't come to the door. Just then this other woman, who lived next door to her – who was also English, and whose cat I used to look after when she went away – came out and said, 'April. How wonderful to see you.' I asked her how Jane was doing and she said, 'I haven't spoken to that woman in years. I wouldn't speak to that woman.' I felt very sad for her and she was the one who got me married to an American, which was very helpful indeed.

Jeff was the American in question. While April and he were sharing his home, he offered, 'I'll marry you if you like, you can get a Green Card much quicker.'

On 13 July 1986 the Most Reverend John Gregory, the thirty-fourth captain of the *Queen Mary* – the wartime-troop-ship-turned-tourist-attraction dry-docked at Long Beach, California – married them in his private quarters. He knew all of April's history and delighted her with, 'Will you the beautiful April, take ...' Although the ceremony was spurious in intent, Gregory nevertheless made it special, looking her in the face and telling her, 'What's important is to be happy.' She was: it was a marriage which gave her freedom as opposed to the previous relationship which had emotionally compromised her and left her floundering. April was as unconventional as ever. There were three people in the marriage, April, Jeff and his boyfriend Lee.

She was hopeful for the future. Her diary entry for her California wedding day reads:

Sunday the thirteenth of July 1986. What a day. The ceremony on the *Queen Mary* was so lovely that I got quite carried away by it all. We all got very drunk, but it was a super day. The captain was charming. There's a chance I might have a small part in *Cagney & Lacey.* I do hope so; it might open up a whole new life for me.

When news of the wedding emerged, the *Daily Mail* in London made contact with Arthur Corbett, who was still on the Costa del Sol. He told gloriously indiscreet diarist Nigel Dempster, 'I don't suppose she'd be allowed to do it [marry] in Britain, but American law must be different. I'm retired from being a barman and I'm certainly not getting married again.'

In 2022, there was a salutation from Jeff West at April's memorial service in Liverpool: 'What a privilege that I should have met and known and shared a portion of my life with this extraordinary human being, this champion, this woman. April had the grace and elegance of royalty and the heart of a showgirl. I always remember that she was there. Someone said there should be a rule that everyone in the world should get a standing ovation at least once in their life. I hope those of this memorial will stand and give her a final standing ovation.'

Of course, we did.

Although the 1980s greed-is-good days were all around her in Hollywood, April was struggling for funds. She had to work and that Green Card was a necessity. The US Immigration and Naturalisation Service is a cumbersome beast and with California sitting on the Mexican border it has little time for niceties, but plenty of bureaucracy. First, the couple had to convince the authorities they were cohabiting.

They didn't ask if we were in love.

They had to 'perform' for April's Green Card, prove they were living together, that this was not the marriage of convenience that in reality it was.

They were frightening beyond words. They sat us in two opposite rooms asking the same questions at the same time and it's nerve-racking because you can see one another. One of the questions was, 'Do you have a real Christmas tree or a fake Christmas tree?'

I said, 'Oh, we had a real Christmas tree.'

He said: 'Where did you buy it?'

I said, 'I don't know. I have a feeling it was somewhere around Melrose Place on Melrose.'

Thank God for the old memories.

Then he said, 'Have you ever met your mother-in-law?'

I said, 'No, but I speak to her at least once a week on the telephone.'

This was true. She'd ring Jeff and if I picked up the phone she'd always say, 'Oh, hello, April.' She knew the situation. I was able to say honestly that we did talk.

Then he said, 'When was the last time your husband saw his mother?'

I said, 'Oh, he went home just for one night or two nights for Christmas.'

They said, 'Why didn't you go?'

I said, 'We couldn't afford it – the two of us to go for such a short time. We didn't have that much money.'

Bloody Jeff had forgotten totally that he had gone home for Christmas and told them, 'Very, very recently but I can't remember when.'

I thought he'd blown it. I was nervous, like a kitten, I couldn't sit still. We went to lunch and came back as soon as the blinds went up on the counters. There seemed to be thousands of people waiting. It's a cattle call. We saw this funny little man come out and say, 'Mr and Mrs East and West ...'

I said, 'Jeff, we've got it. He wouldn't dare joke.'

We went over and saw him. He said, 'Everything's fine. We'll let you know. You just go down to the centre there and they will get you a Green Card.'

It wasn't that easy. When I went to get it, it hadn't arrived and a year later I went and they said it had been sitting on the shelf. I'd been waiting all that time and every time I went down there it was, 'No, not here for you, not here for you.' I had to be there six o'clock in the morning to get a number. If you didn't get a number, you didn't get a chance to see them.

I went in one day and ran up to this window and I said, 'Excuse me. Before you start, may I just ask you one question?'

She said, 'Get to the back of the line and wait until your number is called.'

I did and about four o'clock in the afternoon my number was called. I went to her – it was the same woman. She came back and she said, 'I can't understand this. This card has been here for more than a year.'

I said, 'I knew. I could have let them know that this morning when you started work because I jumped in the moment you opened. I was the person.'

She said, 'I can't remember. I can't remember anything. You had to wait for your number.'

I said, 'But, yes, you could have saved me a whole bloody day, had you just been a little bit courteous and a little bit nice. You're not a nice woman.' She gave me the card and I just walked away.

The pantomimes began in getting a job. The first job I went for, and I got it instantly, was as a hostess at the Ports O' Call in San Pedro. It was one of those touristy places: you see all the ships, a big, big restaurant hanging right over the water. Rather nice.

To be a hostess in an American restaurant, you're a dogsbody. You're dogs' meat. I couldn't switch off being the owner of AD8 to just being a servant. It was difficult. Very, very difficult indeed for me to switch. Being the hostess, you're on the reception and have to tell the girls where to take the guests. You have to give each waiter equal tables. It's quite complicated; it took me a little while to get it because if you didn't give them equal ... oh, boy, they would come screaming at you. It was one thing having the waiters screaming at you. They wanted equal amounts of sittings so they could make their livings. That was understandable. People screaming at you because they want window tables was another thing.

I'd say to them sometimes, 'Well, I'm sorry you're going to have to wait about twenty minutes. If you're prepared to wait that long, then you'll have a lovely window table.'

They would say, 'Thank you very much.' They weren't all shits. An awful lot of them were. I'd go and look out of curiosity, those people never even looked out of the window. The way they spoke to you. Some of them were common and so rude. I quietly told them, 'You're not getting a table, goodbye.'

I had this lovely Lebanese man as my boss. When he met me he said, 'Oh, April, you look so beautiful in your own clothes. Don't worry about the uniform. I don't want you to buy uniform. I want you to be in your own clothes. You look so elegant, you give something to this restaurant.'

I did put on a show, I was so very arrogant in those days. I was still wearing lovely clothes and dresses and high heels and all of that. My boss was promoted to the big chain and the new boss was a Germanic shit. He had a German name too. He came in the very first day, took one look at me and said, 'Why are you dressed like that?'

I said, 'Well, Mr Salman wanted me to wear my own clothes because he thought I made the place look elegant.'

He said, 'I want you out first thing tomorrow morning to buy a uniform. You buy a uniform and you buy flat shoes and you dress like everybody else.'

I said to him, 'There's only one problem.'

'What's that?'

I said, 'At this moment in time I do not have enough money to buy a uniform, so you're going to have to wait until my pay day.'

He said, 'That's just not good enough.'

I said, 'Well. Are you going to pay for it?'

He said, 'I most certainly am not.'

I said, 'In that case you're going to have to wait.' I was totally broke.

I'd only been working for a few weeks for him and then the usual thing happened to me: 'Aren't you famous in your own country?'

'I'm quite well known, but I wouldn't say I was famous.'

From that moment on, everything changed. He was rude beyond words. When I went for the schedule – I used to work full-time – I went up to him and said, 'You only have me down for two days?'

He said, 'Yes. That's all I need you for.'

I said, 'I can't live on two days. I was employed as a full-time person. I can't live off two days. It won't pay my rent.'

He said, 'I don't give a damn. Go and get another job.'

I was a bit worried. I was very careful with money at that time, when the month's rent had been paid. Then I went in another day and I looked at the schedule and I only had two half-days. I went to him again.

I said, 'Now you've only got me down for two half-days. Do you think I can live off eight hours work a week? That's not fair. I've been here for five months and I work very hard. I never leave on time and I've never been late once.'

'Not my problem,' he said. I knew then it was time to start looking for another job.

No, darling, you could sue for unlawful dismissal. I don't know why I didn't do it because one day he was sitting there having lunch and there was an ice bucket and I wish to this day I'd poured the bloody ice bucket over his head. I knew I had to leave anyhow. I knew I had to get a job. The man knew who I was and I also knew that the next time I was sent a schedule I was going to have half a day. He was determined I was going to go. This was just after buying the uniform too. I don't know whether it was because he'd just been promoted and suddenly got into management, a big restaurant. He was certainly on a power trip.

Hesitantly, I asked April if she'd retraced her teenaged sailor steps in San Pedro, not directly mentioning the doctor's surgery on West 6th Street where George Jamieson had been treated kindly. It was remarkably alien to her, the very idea that she'd had any detailed memory of San Pedro. She was much more comfortable launching into memories of her other Californian adventures.

I got another restaurant job in the area, at the Williamsburg. It was where people stood in a big line to be seated and to pay and my idea of being a hostess came as a terrible shock. Also, I knew I always had problems with numbers, I did not realise fully until I started doing that job that I was totally dyslexic. I didn't realise this. I had always put it down to just being stupid. They would all want to pay at the same time. I kept giving them the wrong change and I thought it was because there was so many of them rushing at you, charging at you. Then the bloody telephone would go and you would have maybe twenty people waiting to pay you, screaming at you that they needed to get back to work and this sort of thing. You picked up the telephone and you had to say, 'Good afternoon. My name is April. This is the Williamsburg restaurant, how can I help you?'

If my boss wasn't around I'd say, 'Hello. Williamsburg.'

Suddenly, one day there was a lot of people, maybe thirty and I answered it, 'Williamsburg.'

'April. This is Mr Williamsburg. What are you doing? You know exactly what you've got to say, you're not saying it properly. What do you have to say?'

I said, 'Mr Williamsburg, there are thirty people waiting to pay for their food. They're screaming at me.'

He said, 'I don't care. What do you have to say?'

I said, 'Good afternoon. My name is April. This is the Williamsburg restaurant. How can I help you?'

He said, 'That's what I want to hear every single time.'

I said, 'Mr Williamsburg. When you have thirty people in front of you it's too much to say.'

He said, 'Don't argue with me.'

I said, 'OK.'

I put the telephone down and then the phone rings again immediately. It's Williamsburg impersonating a caller and trying to catch me out. I'm in a tizz and don't realise.

'This is Mr Caruso. I want to talk to Mr Williamsburg.'

I said, 'Well, he's not here, Mr Caruso. He just telephoned me from somewhere.'

I didn't realise he had just telephoned me from the kitchen in the restaurant. I thought he'd telephoned me from home or something.

Mr Caruso said, 'No. He's there and I want to speak to him now.'

I said, 'Mr Caruso. I have thirty people screaming at me wanting to pay for their food. I am sorry, I cannot speak to you. Mr Williamsburg is not here. I have to go. Please excuse me. Goodbye.'

Mr Williamsburg comes right up to me and that's when I twigged that he used the phone in the kitchen. He said, 'You're fired.'

I said: 'OK. When?'

He said: 'Take the money off these people and then come into the office.'

I went into the office and he was there with the assistant manager who, to his credit, said, 'I think you should at least give April a second chance.'

He said, 'No. She's out of here. She won't answer the telephone properly.'

I said, 'Mr Williamsburg, when you have thirty people screaming at you to get out, why waste your breath on all of that? They know where they're ringing and I do say, "The Williamsburg," and I'm very polite. It's not as if I'm impolite.'

'No,' he said. 'You do not say it the way I want you to say it, and so you're fired.'

The assistant manager started, and I said, 'Don't bother. I'm out of here. I'm leaving now,' and left.

What happened next was unbelievable. I found a hostess job at the Marriott hotel at Long Beach airport, where they insisted you buy this uniform the colour of yuk and wore flat, hard plastic shoes that [meant] when you got home in the evening your feet were screaming louder than the customers. I was supposed to be being trained to be the cashier but the girl said to me, 'I can't be bothered to train you, I really can't.'

I said, 'But you have to. I won't know how to do it otherwise. It's all new to me, this stuff. It's totally new. I've only done it once before and that was a different machine. This is a totally computerised machine.'

I was sitting at home, getting ready to go to work and the phone rings and it's my boss: 'Oh, April, Fanny – or whatever her name was – is sick today so you'll have to go on the cash tonight.'

I said, 'Mr Johnson, I do not know how to do it. I do not want the responsibility of it. The girl has not trained me.

I've only seen her do it about two or three times because I'm so busy seating people. I don't know how to do it.'

He said, 'It doesn't matter. You'll figure it out. You're on the cash tonight.'

My heart was in my mouth and I'd been there about a week and all these little old people were coming in and I'm very sweet with old people. I love old people. I'd always give them an extra cup of coffee. They would say, 'We do love you. You take great care of us ...' and stuff like that. Saturday night on the cash, all these old people. With this cash register, you punched in how much the meal cost, waited for a few seconds and it would compute the tax, and a few seconds on tell you how much to give them in change. I was so nervous. I was giving them back what they were supposed to be paying.

The next day my boss called me to the office and he said, 'Miss Ashley, we are missing three hundred dollars (and something).'

I said, 'What?'

He said, 'We are missing about three-to-four hundred dollars.'

I said, 'Do you think I stole it?'

'Oh, no, we don't think you stole it at all, but we want to know where it is.'

I said, 'Oh my gosh, I don't know.'

'Go away and try and figure it out and let me know. You're missing quite a chunk of money.'

I go down to the canteen and I'm sitting there and, by this time, the whole of the hotel knows, all the staff knew. All these lovely waiters are coming up to me and said, 'April, do you think you'll get fired?'

I said, 'Of course I will. At least they don't think I stole it.'

They asked me if I wanted them all to go out on strike. I said, 'No.' They said they would all go out on strike because they had a union. They said they could stop them from firing me if I wanted them to. I said I wouldn't want that to happen. I said it was my mistake, whatever I'd done. I said, 'Ah, I know what I did! If you excuse me,' and I ran and ran, jumped into the lift and went up to my office. I charged in, I hardly knocked on the door and I said, 'I know what I did! I know where the money went.'

He said, 'Sit down. What did you do?'

I said, 'I didn't wait for the seconds to tell me to give the change. I gave them back what they were paying for their dinner. I was actually giving them back that amount of money.'

He said, 'That's what you think you did?'

I said, 'I know now. I'm talking to the waiters downstairs and it suddenly hit me right out of the blue. I didn't wait for the few seconds that it took for the computer to work out how much the change was.'

He said, 'Go back to work and I'll work it out.'

About half an hour later he calls me back up to the office and he said, 'Right down to the penny you are right. You are fired.'

I said I knew I was going to be fired and I said I was sorry and there was one extraordinary thing. I said … all those lovely old people who said they loved me and – I said – not one of them, not one of the sons-of-bitches, turned round and said, 'April, you've given us too much change back.' Not one of them. They were all crooks, the lot of them.

I said, 'Goodbye, and anyhow I am awfully glad: this fucking uniform is so ugly. These shoes are killing me.'

He said, 'Well, there's nothing I can do about that. That's Marriott's policy. You are absolutely right, to the penny.'

I said, 'Who cares? Goodbye.'

He said, 'I wish you the best of luck,' and I said, 'Thank you very much.' He was quite nice. It was so funny. But these geriatric crooks … oh, my.

I got in my car and I drove home and I thought, *What am I going to do now?* It wasn't easy. I will never work in a restaurant again. It's so humiliating. It's just so degrading, the way people talk to people in restaurants. In America they do. They do. They are dreadful. Whenever I went to a restaurant in America, I would always leave as big a tip as I could, because I knew what they went through.

April was now living on her own. She and Jeff West had separated, an amicable divorce followed, so there was an urgency every month to pay her rent and have enough to live on. The memories of existing on toast and baked beans in Hay were at the front of her mind and she worked at finding employment.

I went for hundreds of jobs but that's when I started suffering from ageism. Even though I was fifty something, I was still very glamorous. I was very slender and I moved like a rocket. I would leave the young girls standing. It was not easy finding a job. I think a lot of them wouldn't employ me because I was more than nineteen years old. I think there was a lot of that. I seemed to be running around like a headless chicken. In Los Angeles everyone seemed to know who I was and it was nice to get invited to parties – Elizabeth Taylor, Harrison Ford, the big names were always kind, but celebrity didn't pay the rent.

Her personality and presence helped when she decided to get a job with Greenpeace – *saving this, that and the other* – a movement she'd supported for many years. She'd moved to the lower profile city of San Diego and drove up the Pacific Coast Highway to Greenpeace's office in Venice, California. The recruiter, as April told it, was keen.

The assistant manager was this young lad – they were all so very young – who thought I was the most glamorous thing in the world. He said, 'Oh, yes, we'll give you a job right away. When can you start? Do you want to start tonight?'

I said, 'It's at night?'

'Oh, yes, we go out about four o'clock. We get a bite to eat and then we can go canvassing.'

I went out with him. I was so shocked. Going out and knocking on people's doors. I didn't do it alone, of course, not for the first week. You'd say, 'Good evening. My name's April and I'm with Greenpeace and we're here fundraising.'

I couldn't get over it. People started writing cheques out for me. I'm on my very first night and I made my quota. You had to make a quota, which was $110 a night, otherwise you didn't keep the job. Afterwards, the regulars were impressed that I'd done that. They were saying my first night alone and I'd made my quota. Then, I went through a period where I couldn't get a penny out of anybody. OK, I was being paid peanuts but by the same token I was doing a job and I wanted to do it well.

Americans are very odd. They will tell you any kind of lie to get you off their doorstep. They are very honest generally in their own right but to get you off their doorstep they will tell you anything. I pledged to change that. I started doing a lot of research about sharks and whales, things that I was interested in. I wasn't interested in the pollution or going in regattas and what have you. I discovered I'm not really an environmentalist, I'm a conservationist. When I started talking whales and the sharks and saving the dolphins and keeping the oceans clean, people would become fascinated. Sometimes they'd be so fascinated that they would let me talk for hours and then they wouldn't give me a penny. But they liked me.

Brazenly, April called at the impressive home of the American tycoon, Occidental Petroleum's Armand Hammer, who died in 1990. Unknown to April, he was already very ill, but his butler heard the Greenpeace pitch and told her: 'What I would do if I were you is I'd drop a note to Dr Hammer.' She did, and two days later back came a letter with one thousand dollars.

It wasn't always easy going. One Black colleague was working a rich, right-wing area and the police arrived: 'Whatever you do, go and hide yourself because you'll be killed.' One woman used a water hose on two Sri Lanka members, shouting, 'Get off my doorstep!' Raising money could be deadly.

I was beginning to be one of the better earners and gaining my confidence and I was doing more and more research and it got to a point where people would really listen to me and what I had to say. Even if they didn't give me a *lot* of money, they would give me money. But you had to be careful. I can't remember them all now, but the most dangerous was ... when I almost lost my life ... was in Santa Monica. At one door, this man opened the door and was blind drunk. He reached behind the door and grabbed a spear gun. Those things go right through you at that range and I said: 'Oh it's all right. I get the message.' I walked down the stairs and I looked back up and he still had the gun pointed at me. It could have gone off. I was so badly shaken I couldn't work that night. I had to go and sit for four hours and wait to be collected.

One evening, I was waiting to be picked up by the Greenpeace van at Palos Verdes, one of the richest places in America. It's one of those cities that chooses not to have lights. Why I do not know. The houses are so far apart because they're great palaces. It's pitch black and not a star in the sky and suddenly these car headlights pick out my silhouette and the car is driving toward me at what seems like a hundred miles an hour. It was so quick, I couldn't have jumped out the way and at the very last minute the car swerved away and above the engine I heard all these kids shouting and laughing.

One evening, a girlfriend dropped me at home and I'm waving to her and these kids came out of nowhere and go for me with knives, try to rip my stomach open.

There were some pretty hairy moments. It was late at night, you see, when you finished; you were meant to work until nine o'clock at night, but by the time the van picked everybody up it was later. One night a young woman was raped. She was very brave. She came back to fundraise. Inner strength and belief in yourself is remedial.

Sixteen

California Dreamin'

'There never seems to be enough time.'
'Time In A Bottle', Jim Croce, 1973

Despite the fevered moments, April found life with Greenpeace purposeful and was content living in San Diego, a city where many rehearse before attempting to compete in Hollywood, where everyone's a player. She never did get to appear with Tyne Daly and Sharon Gless in *Cagney & Lacey* but would commute up to Hollywood for auditions. If her funds allowed.

Her apartment on Second Avenue, guarded by an orchid tree, was small, a nomad's living quarters, as though you were in a hotel for a few days and scattered your suitcase items around the room for the moment. Things didn't seem permanent but April was. And the cat, Lily Ashley-Buttufuco-John Wayne-Bobbit-Harding-Gululi. She knew the city and we'd go off to Croce's restaurant, owned by Ingrid, the widow of the singer Jim Croce, where April's favourite meats got involved with tortillas and the rest of a south-of-the-border menu. She worked for a time at an art gallery over the vertigo-inducing bridge in Coronado with a view over Glorietta Bay, the surrounding grounds all colour, blue and purple agapanthus, hummingbird sage, pink morning glory and a rainbow of fuchsia.

Her apartment was itself a madness of plants but she wanted a garden, a little house down at the tip of Coronado where

California confronts Mexico. There the beaches were immaculate and inviting and we'd repeat the Joan Rivers classic: a place where you can lie on the sand and look at the stars and vice versa.

Lunch at the Hotel del Coronado was a treat. A Victorian beauty of a place, it's often been used for the movies, hosting Marilyn Monroe, Jack Lemmon and Tony Curtis for Billy Wilder's *Some Like It Hot* (1959) and Peter O'Toole for *The Stuntman* (1980). I spent some days with O'Toole during filming there but my stories, which took place after surgery had claimed half his stomach and he wasn't drinking, could not match April's 'Hellraiser' O'Toole experiences in Spain. Still, she wanted to see where the filming had gone on. We also walked to the jetty where, in *Some Like It Hot*, Joe E. Brown takes off in a boat with Jack Lemmon, in drag, who reveals that he is a guy, providing Brown's besotted Osgood Fielding III with the film's classic last line: 'Nobody's perfect.' For April, the environment, the tropical trees, shrubs and flowers, a colonnade – terraced in grass to the beach – had her dreaming of everlasting happy days. Someone tracked her down there and portrayed as rather withdrawn but she later addressed that.

People sometimes make me out to be sad but I am rather jolly. An embittered old woman is no good to anybody.

And she was fun, other than when cornered while trying to find a parking space. Her vanity was always pleasured by compliments. She'd tell everyone listening of the customers who admired her professionalism, her manners and how she appeared to them.

A man came into the gallery and said to me, 'What is it like to be extraordinarily beautiful?' Things like that blow you away, because all you're thinking is, I've got another four hours to go, my feet are killing me, shall I take another pill to stop the cramps in my legs … ?

As well as Greenpeace, I did some television advertising work for the racetrack – that awful drunk Bing Crosby opened it – and I got about: jobs in the art galleries, a jewellery shop – diamonds are a girl's best friend – and I worked as a tour guide around where our martini bar is. To everybody, I was just April. They thought I was a bit eccentric because I tell the truth. I tell their bosses what shits they are and the Americans find that stunning because they are very politically correct and I am very politically incorrect. I have never hidden what I think and where I am. If the Queen can be in the telephone book, so can I.

As ever, the missing part of her circle of happiness was that she never completely felt she was *Miss* April Ashley. Her rights had been denied her. She wasn't noisily political but over the decades had written 'thousands and thousands of letters' to people seeking advice on sexual identity issues.

Strangely enough, although it was transgender, it was also gay and lesbian people writing to me and women desperate for divorces, married women who just needed permission from someone to leave the marriage – I never had any from men, by the way, but dozens from women.

In the San Diego apartment, she kept an extra mattress for unexpected visitors, those she called her 'runaway trannies'. There, as she did in England and France, as she would explain as an octogenarian, she always went about her life while working to establish her full human rights –as a person. But no hysteria.

I thought the best way I could do it was by example. I wasn't about to live in a twilight world. I wanted to live in the real world. Previously, I told it all through amusing anecdotes about what I suppose was a glittering and glamorous life. Times, and I, have changed. I understand my life so much more now and people are willing to listen and to understand. I am invited to talk to audiences all over the world to explain what happened to me and what happens to many people. It is right for me to explicitly explain the trauma that I – and many others – go through. At the same time there has been a lot of heartache and soul searching. But I will not be miserable about it for my life has also been mad and glorious fun. I don't think there is a foreign capital I have not visited or a foreign diplomat who has not tried to lure me into bed. And sex you could call me an expert on for I have seen it from both sides of the fence. Those who seek me out for advice tell me I'm inspiring across the gender gap, for my life shows that if you have the willpower to live as you believe you have the right to, then you can achieve.

She often said, although it's hard to contemplate, that she could have remained in Liverpool and lived on benefits, especially as a heart attack survivor, and she would have received housing and a full pension at age sixty-five. Around the time the Labour Party won the 1997 election, her mind became more focused on establishing her legal status. I was by then living between California and the UK and regularly commuting and she wanted to get hold of the newspapers so she could read about the new Westminster players. They were added to my shopping list with the Maynard wine gums, the Dazzle blue eye drops from Boots and the occasional Mason Pearson hairbrush. She sensed times were changing but being progressive never equates with swift progress; the magic word is rarely 'now'.

What I think bolstered April's ongoing activism was that her principal nemeses were dead. Perhaps subliminally, even after all the years, she remained fearful of the power of the Courts of Justice. She decided to write to Britain's new prime minister, Tony Blair.

I explained that for forty years I'd held a passport in the name of Miss April Ashley and I would like a new birth certificate to go with it. I'd been in the body I always wanted for four decades – wasn't it about time? That bloodsucker, the awful Justice Ormrod, was dead and so was Arthur, of a stroke on 24 June 1993. I was in San Diego when I heard he was ill and flew to Spain to see him. When he saw me, he burst out crying. He still had all my photographs and he said that I was the only one he had ever loved.

I had to wonder what he cared about. He abandoned his wife and four children for his sexual urges. He didn't care about me. He admitted he cheated me. He knew he did wrong, he said so on his deathbed, he defrauded me and harmed me. He asked me to forgive him. I didn't, but I did, if you understand.

For all the leads in their life, things have not worked out too well for Arthur's family. Johnny, his son, who never took to me, sold Rowallan Castle and its seven thousand acres in 1988 to pay death duties. He was married three times and maybe he's happier now.

Going to see Arthur brought back all the horrors of the divorce from me. I remembered at the height of the divorce proceedings being in Sloane Square one day and seeing this woman coming my way. She was very well-dressed and I thought, 'Oh my God, I can't remember her name' and she was coming directly towards me. Instead of saying anything she hit me across the face, didn't say a word and carried on walking; that happened at least three times, people just bashed me in the face. I was in a pub once dressed in Chanel and looking extremely elegant and all these young lads told me they're going to beat me up. But this was the beginning of the Blair years – Britain was a different place, wasn't it? Hadn't things changed? Legally, not for me.

The rules were still spelled out by the Birth and Deaths Regulations Act of 1953 which regarded birth certificates as records of fact at the time of birth; did people like me exist? Ormrod's law meant transsexuals could not marry, had difficulties with employment law and, if they committed a crime, could find themselves in the wrong prison. The regulations were more enlightened since my surgery in 1960 but not in certain, very important areas.

April was adamant she still loved her country but believed that dithering, not-wanting-to-offend governments (which rings modern bells) condemned her to being a freak living in exile. As if to emphasise that, she never heard a word from Tony Blair. She tried the deputy prime minister – at least she had known John Prescott personally when she was George Jamieson and the burly politician had been in the merchant navy. He was to be of great help and encouragement.

Playing amateur psychologist was another parlour game we shared and April did believe that the lack of formal documentation, a birth certificate in the name of April Ashley, was a lifetime trauma. Enforcing this feeling of not 'being' was a sensation of being alone in the world in terms of blood ties, of family. In one of our analytical sessions, she offered:

I've felt like an orphan for most of my life. In fact, I had officially been one since 1974, though I didn't find that out until ten years later. My bloody mother! She never wanted children. She pitted one against the other and she was wicked to everybody. She died in Swansea. [April's sister] Marjorie, who called her 'That Woman!', had apparently tried to contact me, though I never heard anything. In 1984, the telephone rang and this voice said, 'Hello, Auntie April?'

'First of all, don't call me Auntie,' I replied. 'And who are you?'

'I'm Maddie.'

'Hello. I remember you; you came to London to stay with me. You're Marjorie's daughter. How are you?' I asked her, friendlier now. 'How's your grandmother?'

'Oh, she died in 1974.'

'What did she die from?'

'Cancer,' came the reply.

That didn't come as a surprise, after her factory work during the war. I didn't know how to feel. I still don't. This woman scarred all of our lives, the whole family.

There were more family shocks. I opened a friend's website in London and I got an email from my great-nephew; I emailed him back but it didn't work and I got terribly upset about it. I said, 'Oh, God, this family vendetta is going to go on into a third generation, how stupid.'

My great friend Peter Maddock listened to my concerns about not being able to contact the boy and said, 'Oh, don't be silly, darling, I'll put an advert in the *Liverpool Echo*.' They all lived around Liverpool and Manchester. Apparently, all his friends rushed into the pub and said, 'Is this you, Scott?'

I couldn't sleep one night in my apartment in San Diego and was dozing on the couch at four o'clock in the morning when the phone rang. A voice said, 'Are you April Ashley? Why are you trying to get hold of my son?'

I said, 'Just a moment, who are you?'

'Well, I'm your nephew.'

'Oh, who's your father?'

'John.'

'Freddie?'

'We called him John.'

'Oh my goodness. It's four o'clock in the morning here. Could I have your phone number and I'll ring you back a little later?'

Because my eldest sister always had problems, I said, 'By the way, how's Theresa?'

He said, 'Oh, she's dead.'

'What did she die of?'

'I don't know, she died years ago.'

Four hours later, the phone rang again and somebody I didn't recognise said, with real cruelty in their voice, 'Oh, by the way, Roddy, Ivor and Marjorie are also dead.'

'Holy mackerel. How did they all die?'

'I don't know, except for Ivor, who died of emphysema.'

That didn't surprise me, because Ivor smoked about fifty packets of cigarettes a day.

I got on the phone to Peter, crying my eyes out. 'It's like a holocaust,' I told him. 'My whole family's gone. I don't know how they've gone. I don't know how they died ...'

He said, 'What are you whingeing for?'

'Wouldn't you?' I asked him.

'When was the last time you spoke to those people?'

'Well, it's more than forty years ago.'

'Well, what are you whingeing for?' he asked me again. 'I'm your family, shut up.' He was right, and so practical.

Then, out of the blue, I got an email: 'By the way, Roddy is not dead.' It was from Roddy's daughter.

I wrote back and said, 'Where do you live?'

Back came an email saying, 'I've had a talk with my husband and we don't think this conversation should continue. We don't think we should have anything to do with you any more.'

They're grown-ups. They've got children of their own. They can make up their own minds. But to write an email just to say they don't want anything to do with me ... I would ring John and I had the courtesy to call him John. He didn't use his second name until he was about thirty, when he decided that he hated the fact that he had the same name as my father, Freddie.

'Hello, John, how are you?' I would ask.

'Fine,' he would reply.

'How's your family?'

'Fine.'

'How's life?'

'OK.'

He would never, ever call me by my name and never get into a conversation. I stopped calling. There was no point when somebody didn't want to know you.

In family terms, I've been alone since my father went. Friends are what kept me going, believing in myself. And men and women have always been different in their reaction to me. I've had some foul-faced bitches being rude to me. I've always found with men it is to do with sexuality. I've never yet met a man who is comfortable in his own sex who has ever been rude to me. Those men I've always been comfortable with. I always get a good reaction from them. If you get a man who isn't comfortable in his own sex, it doesn't work for some unknown reason.

April's considered and forthright attitude to life was not always shared and her values and, without doubt, who she was, clashed with some Greenpeace workers. The organisation promotes itself as 'a family' and April comforted herself in this perhaps naively, given her own immediate family's disdain of her.

In Greenpeace everyone hugs everybody. I had young men who would come in and hug me and then, when they'd been told who I was, wouldn't come near me. They wouldn't even say hello to me, they would walk straight past me. When they worked with me I'd say: 'Darling, this is your route and you've got this street, this street and that street.' We had cards with all that information on it and they would almost snatch the map out of my hand. You could see that they had been told and you knew that they didn't like you.

Then I had one who accused me of making sexual advances. You'd have to die laughing, darling. He was a sexist beast. Instinctively, I didn't like him because he looked at your breasts all the time, at the breasts of all the women. He wouldn't look you in the eye. He said I made a grab for him when we were driving – at seventy-file miles an hour on the freeway. They sent a team from Washington to investigate. Happily for me, everybody but one girl said they wouldn't believe that 'April would do something like that'.

I said to the investigators, two men and a woman, from Washington, 'Listen, if I was going to go for somebody it wouldn't be that creep. There's too many attractive young men in this office. If I wanted a toy boy, there's quite a few I could have had, but I didn't. The only time I ever had anything to do with a person with Greenpeace and he's left Greenpeace and I would not go to bed with him. There was a bit of fiddling and that's it.' The last woman was laughing and she left, she gave me a big hug.

They ruled on the day that it was all nonsense. I went into the office and I said, 'Ladies and gentlemen. Sitting right here among you is this man here. He's the biggest little shit of a liar in the world. [Name omitted] you are a disgrace to your sex, you are a disgrace to anything. To think you tried to destroy somebody and their career by lying, you little shit. You're nothing more than a little shit.'

I knew I would be fired immediately but I didn't care. Awful little shit. They said I couldn't say that and they fired me. Then they stopped me getting unemployment too. They said that I had done it on purpose. In America if you get yourself fired on purpose, you didn't get unemployment. That was the end of Greenpeace for me. It was awfully sad because I should have stayed.

I was miserable and took to my bed. The stress of it all had worn me down; being accused of being a sex pest knocked me out for a time. But I had rent and daily life to pay. It became difficult. Peter Maddock, who always knew when I was in trouble – I never had to ask for help – was somehow alert to my perils. Peter said, 'You're in San Diego, you can't get out of bed, you seem to be totally isolated. Come to France. You can either go and live in Chesney's flat in Nice or you can live in the mountains where it's full of magic.'

With Lily Ashley-Buttufuco-John Wayne-Bobbit-Harding-Gululi, the aging male cat, no quarantine in France, she arrived with little luggage – *my life is in storage, darling* – at Nice airport and headed toward the hills for the twenty-five-minute drive toward Tourettes-sur-Loup and the hospitality of Chesney, a most accomplished chef and cheerful host. There's a swimming pool and a medieval charm about the property. Chesney enlarged an outside guest area and put in a bathroom – *being English, I love a bath* – which became April's apartment, small but adequate for her and the cat.

This was her sanctuary beneath the cloudless air of Provence, an escape from the ooh-la-la of Nice and the up-the-road of Monaco, Somerset Maugham's 'sunny place for shady people', where she could reflect. It was pleasant, only a short drive from the medieval hill town of St Paul de Vence, and close to the small hotel and restaurant, Colombe d'Or. The name means 'golden dove'. A young Provençal called Paul Roux began the business and in 1931 hung a sign outside reading, '*Ici on loge à cheval, à pied ou en peintres*' ('Lodgings for men, horses and painters'). Matisse arrived first. And, just as artists had followed him to the Côte D'Azur for what he called 'the silver clarity' of the light, they stepped in his footsteps to St Paul de Vence. Léger, Braque, Chagall and Miró were regulars, paying for the meals and lodgings with paintings, some of which became priceless masterpieces. Picasso turned up in the 1940s, a barefoot Bardot after him. Jean-Paul Sartre, Simone de Beauvoir, James

Baldwin, Charlie Chaplin, Cocteau, Truffaut, Orson Welles – all are names in one of the most eclectic visitors' books I've ever seen.

Matisse wrote that life, art, should be part of somewhere that offers 'a soothing calming influence on the mind, something which provides relaxation from fatigues and toils'. At Colombe d'Or, a portrait by Matisse looks down on you in the dining room. April liked to survey the scene before making her entrance.

A big one.

At the Tourettes-sur-Loup property, there's a stairway from the flat down to the terrace with its glazed doors into the dining room of the main house. Most evenings when I was there April would, on cue, appear at the top of the stairs in elegant finery, conjuring Gloria Swanson as Norman Desmond in *Sunset Boulevard*. By then, for April, it was the horizon which was closer. She'd slowed down, no longer the rocket girl of California, but was as determined as ever. We talked a lot in the day but she missed dinner many times and we'd pick up the conversation later in the evening in her apartment when vodka from her freezer made her more relaxed. When she was in San Diego and nearing her sixtieth birthday, April had made notes about writing her life story[6], a follow-up to a volume she had published in 1982. The notes, which are now in her archive held in Liverpool, read in part:

> I know this is time for me to write my autobiography and tell my whole story, having lived in the States for ten years as an ordinary person working for Greenpeace. Part

---

6 I worked with her on this book but, sadly, through misunderstanding, April and I, believing we had the right, used material from her earlier book which provoked copyright problems. *The First Lady* was withdrawn from sale and the litigant financially compensated.

of living in the States is that you become absorbed in a country where people do share painful memories, and resulting triumphs. But I am a private person, and to bear my soul again in print, I needed a reason, a compelling reason. That compelling reason presented itself with a telephone call from Seattle. A voice said: 'Are you April Ashley? You saved my life.'

As a child, this person had found on a rubbish dump the *News Of The World* newspaper containing a two-page story on my life. This was their turning point; they'd stumbled on something and knew they were not alone. In every country in the world today, there are thousands of young people, boys and girls, who cannot live in their skin, who cannot live with the sex that nature assigned them. They become freaks, outcasts, figures of fun, despair: self-mutilation and suicide often follow in the wake of this rejection. Unable to live a lie. I was the first person in Europe to challenge the system and to change my sex from male to female. Even today in the States, society may accept a homosexual Marlboro Man, but is far less forgiving when a change of sex is concerned. Male to female or female to male. My story is about winning against the odds. Yes, you can change sex and lead a valid life. You can have friends or a home, a career, respect. I've done it.

It was a decade after she'd written those words when the world of bureaucratic paperwork caught up to prove that for her. In Provence, the postbox for the property is up the long driveway linking to the potholed mountain road; in 2005 April was reluctantly keeping fit strolling up and down that pathway several times a day.

Had there been post?

Seventeen

Happy Birthday

'You are a very remarkable woman.'
Noël Coward to April Ashley, 1970

The Negresco hotel was buzzing. As ever, the grand art deco geometry of the place complemented by the Mediterranean light, the atmosphere, only heightened April's delight. It was a genuine champagne moment.

In September 2005, April received her birth certificate in a large, official, brown envelope from HM Government, identifying her as female and revealing that her father had been a tram driver before going off to sea.

That detail tickled her as much as anything.

Transgender issues were by then, issues taken more seriously by cultural groups and administrators. April's example – her high profile a magnet for interviews – had boosted the campaign for legal reform. She always emphasised her lack of scientific expertise; what she could do was tell her story, her story of survival which began at a time which fewer and fewer could imagine. Back then she was living science-fiction. Now, the law was legislating fact.

In 2002, the European Court of Human Rights ruled in Christine Goodwin v. the United Kingdom that the human rights of transgendered individuals were violated by the ban on changing gender in official UK documents. The Blair government, with John Prescott in the wings, introduced a bill to allow that.

After heated debate in the Houses of Parliament, the Gender Recognition Act (2004) was passed, becoming law on 1 July 2004.

Attitudes were changing. That year, Nadia Almada, a transsexual, won the *Big Brother* television show in the UK. The story of Colin Bone, who at age sixty had gender reassignment, made the newspapers because of who he was rather than the surgery. A gynaecologist, he returned to his post as a consultant and medical director at an NHS hospital, the Queen Elizabeth hospital in King's Lynn, Norfolk, as Celia MacLeod. He'd been a guest of the royal family at Sandringham and met the Queen, although never treated any of the royal family. April was fascinated by his case, loving the royal connection:

> What intrigued me, of course, was the life he must have led for all these years, even with a supportive wife. He said he had been aware of 'ambiguities and confusion' since he was a schoolboy: 'When I was nine I acted the part of a princess in a school play and I was extraordinarily reluctant to take my costume off afterwards; it just felt right.' The lesson, I feel, is that it is never too late to become the person you want and need to be. To find that happiness.

She herself was often the catalyst for those, like her, looking for the courage to face their dilemma and have reassignment surgery. In May 2023 a former heavy-hitting alpha male, now living as Jen following surgery and cohabiting with her former wife of forty years as 'sisters', met me for lunch to talk about the inspiration which April's life had gifted. After an afternoon talking, Jen said she'd rather ponder and write down what she felt and sent me this:

'I was fourteen years old when April was outed to a newspaper by a "friend" and the world found out that this beautiful model was born with male body parts. It was a bad time to be "trans". So shortly after the war, when "men were men", people were ill-informed, there was no social media through which a balanced debate could be argued and homosexuality was a crime. She was derided, ridiculed and abused. My own father described her as 'something', an 'it', a freak with no entitlement to be treated with any sort of respect. This, for a boy struggling to convince himself, apart from the rest of the world, that he was really a boy, was hard listening. I had no overt feelings of gender dysphoria then, just a total dislocation with my male peer groups and how they acted, and whilst joining in with the derision, something inside me stirred with empathy.

'When finally, the years of overwork, the strain of constantly having to prove myself, the physical demands of working exhausting hours all finally caught up with me, so gender dysphoria emerged as an unstoppable steamroller. My feelings of disgust and revulsion with what I was doing was only mitigated by the thoughts of those who had gone before me, who lived in far less tolerant times, who had stood up as their authentic selves in the face of such derision and hostility. If they could overcome, so could I. April gave me a backbone.

'A couple of years later, convinced that full transition from male to female was my only hope of survival and a normal life, it was time to face the world. April became not only my backbone but also my inspiration. We, as characters, were totally different. She enjoyed flaunting and revelling in her released femininity and always looked gorgeous. I was reserved and could in no way be glamorous nor flamboyant, but we were joined together by the need to be ourselves and to hell with what anyone else thought. If she could do it then so I could I, living in a far more enlightened society. I never met her, but I came to love her. I came to be inspired by her courage in the face of so much ignorant hostility. I came to be grateful for her dignity that so contributed to the acceptance I was now the beneficiary of. I came to be reassured by her unwavering conviction of who she was and what she was doing. Most of all, I admired her poise, intellect and outrageous demeanour that so demolished her prejudiced detractors. In the most miserable times of my transition period, when faced with hostility and derision, I could almost hear her whispering to me, "Go for it, Jen, demolish them". R.I.P., April. Thank you. Jen x'

In her lifetime, April received a great deal of such applause. She never spoke of suffering more or less than anyone else with gender dysphoria. Her mantra was that each individual was born human. She took responsibility for her life, she didn't franchise it out.

She gave much of the credit for legal reform to Stephen Whittle OBE, who changed sex after being born a woman and married his partner in 2005. At that point they'd been together for twenty-six years and had four children conceived by sperm donor.

I, and all other transsexuals, have lived in a legal limbo until these past years. Stephen Whittle and his colleagues at Press for Change helped introduce equality. It's taken such a time for people to realise that transsexuality is not a psychiatric condition. Just as the Earth is not flat. But it can be heartbreaking.

Professor Jacqueline Rose, in her 2016 *London Review of Books* article, picks up on Stephen Whittle's foreword to the first *Transgender Studies Reader*, in which he lists as one of the new possibilities for trans people, opened up by critical thought, the right to claim a 'unique position of suffering'. She comments, 'But, as with all political movements, and especially any grounded in identity politics, there is always a danger that suffering will become competitive, a prize possession and goal in itself.'

April had enough of suffering. When she received her birth certificate she thought about cash.

I went to the pension people in Newcastle and enquired if I could get my pension backdated. It caused quite a telephone tussle until they

*found a nice supervisor. I felt like James Bond, certainly some sort of
spy, as my files are all coded and top secret.*

In the end, the pension wasn't backdated.

There is privacy by law, too, as a birth certificate can be
amended to show that a transsexual who was born a man was
born a woman and vice versa, and that people marrying or
beginning a new relationship, cannot discover whether their
partner is a transsexual if the partner chooses not to tell them.

April was lucky in her birth certificate quest, another
example of loyal friends, people who want to help, she had a
way of attracting them. John Prescott had helped her, but so
did others:

Dr Neville Rosedale was wonderful. He was eighty-two
when I contacted him in 2005. He'd been my gynaecologist since 1960. He and his wife Pat have been good
friends to me, but I'd lost touch when I was in America.
To get my new birth certificate, I needed to prove I'd had
the operation – I needed paperwork. I had an old London
number for Neville, but tried it anyway with the new
code. And there was his voice on an answering machine,
sounding as calm and reassuring as he had forty-five
years earlier. I left a message. He called me back.

'Records? I've got them all, going back to when we
first met.'

He sent them off to the gender recognition panel and
I believe that's why I got my birth certificate so quickly.
Most people would have cleared such stuff out but
Neville is a noble man; he had all the details of my exami-
nations over the years.

As always, Peter Maddock held my hand throughout. We went to one of those lovely Nash houses behind
Oxford Street in London to swear an affidavit that all my
information in applying for my new birth certificate was

244

true. There was a very lovely Indian gentleman behind the counter and he read and reread my information. He was fascinated by it.

Peter, who likes to get on with things, said, 'I'm Miss Ashley's solicitor and I can sign that for you.'

'Oh, no,' replied the official. 'It would give me great pleasure to sign the document.'

And he did, with a smile. It was one of those lovely moments.

On 11 August 2005, the UK's General Register Office let me know that they had received a copy of my full gender recognition certificate – and could make a new record of my birth. Which they did.

And forty-five years and four months after I became the woman I wanted to be, I had a piece of paper to prove I really am April Ashley. I felt free at last.

Her new status inspired April and brought on a new era in which she was even more of a standard bearer for fairness in life. As she often said, she didn't endure the physical and mental agonies, the pain and the cruelties, on some whim. She played down, even in her final days, her role as an inspiration and, in many cases, life-saver for thousands of others worldwide challenged by the same dilemma. She didn't want to preach; she was always willing to counsel and help. Each person, she insisted, is an individual. Still, her influence was abundantly clear – look at the record-breaking exhibition of her, *Portrait Of A Lady*, at the Museum of Liverpool. Despite her, sometimes guarded, self-deprecation, she was a star. And she knew it. When, in 2017, the new (now former) and 'enlightened' UK *Vogue* magazine editor Edward Enninful invited her to be on his magazine's cover with the model Kate Moss she inquired about payment.

Oh, it would be April's honour.

She discovered Kate Moss was getting ten thousand pounds for her part of the 'honour' and the email went back: 'No fee, no me.'

April had, many, many years before, sworn never to be exploited. She had an aura about her. She attracted people and conversations and studied looks everywhere I went when I was with her. Not because of who she was, but the way she held herself, the confidence, the grace of a distinguished lady. Her interests and her friends, like her life, were eclectic. She was as happy discussing the plot intricacies of *Coronation Street* with wryly amused guests at La Colombe d'Or in the south of France as explaining navigational tactics about crossing the Pacific in a yacht with the commodore of the San Diego Yacht Club and bemoaning the table manners of The Beatles and The Rolling Stones at her London nightclub.

Becoming April Ashley at age twenty-five had only been the beginning – her extraordinary life followed.

A round of media appearances in London included a late afternoon interview and then an early morning Radio 4 appointment. We went to the Chelsea Arts Club to meet some friends, which translated to whoever was at the bar, and April took her place on a high stool with champagne arriving from stage left. With her makeup and hair to do – *radio or TV, one must look the part, darling* – she had to be up around 4 a.m. to be ready for her car. The evening slipped on. It was 10 p.m. when I suggested we might call it an evening, with the radio show in the morning.

'Gerald hasn't come over to see me yet.'

Gerald?

Loudly: 'The baldy little man with the big ears over by the snooker table.'

'Do you know him?'

'No, but he's giving me the eye.'

'Gerald?'

'Oh, I don't know his name. He looks like a Gerald. Little eyes.'

I went off to arrange a car for April, foolishly working on the premise if it was waiting, clock ticking at the front door, she'd get going. I also made a couple of phone calls and returned to the bar.

'Oh, this is Charles and he's just treating me to a little champagne, aren't you, darling?'

There, of course, was Gerald, now Charles, with a big grin on his face. I think we made it out by nearly midnight, she sang a little *Madama Butterfly* before we dropped her off at Peter Maddock's flat. She was enunciation and subject perfect the next morning with Libby Purves on *Midweek*.

In his 2021 letter to the *The Times*, telling of their trip to see Arthur Corbett in Spain, Mark Ezra also wrote that April 'had a very low tolerance of alcohol … just a couple of glasses would send her head spinning' and there was an element of the first drink or two adding to the gaiety of her moment but from then on she could maintain an even keel into a long night. Unless, of course, from stage-left came a bottle of port.

Very happily for April, and her legacy, two people did appear – and took centre stage – in her later life, after she left France and returned to London, back down the Fulham Road where, in the early days of her adventures, finding a shilling for the gas meter had been a triumph. Bev Ayre and Louise Muddle, promoters of Liverpool, stars themselves in the furtherance of Liverpool's place in the world and of all things April. As Peter Maddock says, they are 'the keepers of the flame'.

April was contacted in 2008, the year Liverpool was named European Capital of Culture, to participate 'in conversation' as part of the city's celebratory events. It was organised by Homotopia, an annual international LGBTQ+ art festival in Liverpool, and April nervously agreed to go back home, seeing another opportunity to promote transgender rights. She and Ayre had a remarkably April-style first encounter at the city's Hope Street hotel. They'd arranged for Bev to go to April's hotel room to discuss her appearances in the city's St George's Hall, where Dickens had performed his Penny Readings – *follow that, darling* – and finalise arrangements. There was one problem when Bev arrived.

April was stuck in the bath.

Bev was perplexed. This naked, quite elderly, stranger was marooned in quickly chilling bath water: 'I told April I was a lesbian and played hockey so it shouldn't be a problem for her.' She, as it were, dived in and helped the struggling April from the bath and into a robe and a nearby chair.

Well, now we're introduced, let's have a nice gin and tonic.

When April retold the story, she admiringly recounted: *She put her arms around me and pulled me like a cork out of a bottle.*

It was the beginning of a beautiful friendship. Bev and Lou and April became a Chekov trio, three sisters. April's cultural 'event' sold out and during her visit there were conversations about staging a full-scale exhibition detailing her life story. Bev and Lou worked for Homotopia and they said April became the 'grand dame' of that family, returning each year to the festival whether or not she was featured. In time, she saw 'the girls' and Liverpool as the safe hands for her story, for her legacy and, after much hard work and time, and the involvement of the Museum of Liverpool, the triumph of their work, *April Ashley: Portrait of a Lady*, opened on 27 September 2013. Bev recalled they arrived at the title after April turned down a string of ideas. Eschewing emails and the telephone, Janet Dugdale, director of the Museum of Liverpool, had lunch with April at the Hope Street Hotel and she recalled: 'I looked at the menu and she looked at me. And I said, "Oh, well, I was thinking maybe a salad." She looked at me again. "OK, gin and tonic."' That 'lunch' resolved every question and Bev said, 'That was her, the title and it was, and is, the largest exhibition about an individual transgender person in the world.'

What astonished everyone – none more so than April – was the popularity. By the time it closed on 1 March 2015 more than one million people had visited. At her memorial in 2022 Bev Ayre pointed out the 'broad conversation' that *Portrait of a Lady* had begun:

'The exhibition was quite theatrical and we used a photograph of April looking out and over at you welcoming you into the museum and then into the exhibition, which was on the first floor. I think it was incredibly brave, especially for April, living through a period of great societal change, to be so open, to go between private and public, which I think she did so well. She supported people, often quietly, she did the right thing, she used that kind of icon, legend, status, or whatever, to help by making that personal public. For me, April was enormously brave, dangerously witty and strikingly beautiful. I'm thinking about her legacy. We need to be proud custodians and use it to continue to reflect wonderful change, but also to have a good time.'

April was all about a good time. Even as a new VIP.

It was her friend Simon Callow, the renowned actor and writer, who campaigned for public recognition of her in 2012 and to her tremendous delight – a crowning moment – she was awarded the MBE for services to transgender equality. On 12 December that year the woman who began life as a boy in Pitt Street made a grand appearance at Buckingham Palace, where the establishment validated the long and often cruel road she had taken. The Prince of Wales presented the MBE and she said that she and Charles talked about his aunt, Princess Margaret. April, escorted by Simon Callow, looked regal in a broad-brimmed black hat – *cost more than one pound, darling* – and a purple shoulder shawl. She most certainly dressed for the occasion and Simon Callow observed her happiness: 'For all her cheekiness, her naughtiness, her anarchy, her tendency to be outrageous, she was a terrifically conservative person in many ways. I don't mean the big "C", I mean, the small "c" and she loved tradition. She loved institutions. And she wanted to be acknowledged by them.'

The occasion didn't blunt her vocabulary when on the day she offered a word about the past and her divorce from Arthur Corbett.

I wish he was alive, the old bugger, to see me here in Buckingham Palace receiving an award.

It was as April Ashley MBE that she went off on Christmas holidays with Bev Ayre and Lou Muddle. Lou tells the story of those Christmases in the closing years of April's life. She looked spectacular but the scaffolding – the knees and hips – were wobbly and one kidney was all but gone and the other very much on the blink. Still, mustn't grumble, was the attitude. And how.

The Christmas adventures were so good, so fast, somersaulting over each other, that Lou made notes as on 8 December 2013 in Polperro, Cornwall: 'Our cottage fridge contains three bottles of champagne, Bloody Mary mix, gin and two bottles of claret; there's also a couple of fish cakes and some eggs. Monday 9 December 2013: although the thermostat is set to twenty degrees April said, "My teeth woke me up chattering – thank God I still have teeth."

'Halfway through watching *The Wicked Lady* starring Margaret Lockwood, April picked up a phone and made a call to Somerset. She handed me the phone and said, "Say hello to Julia Lockwood," Margaret's daughter.

'Tonight we drink champagne with hibiscus flowers, then April's ratatouille with claret. The cottage is now like a sauna as April can't sleep because of the cold. Thursday 18 December: we watched *A Time in the City* [2008, Terence Davies documentary on Liverpool] which she loved, music and pictures of her Liverpool. We were going to a quiz at the Ship Inn but April was insistent we watched *The Firefly* [1937] with Jeanette MacDonald and Alan Jones, a black-and-white MGM musical, a costume spy story set in Spain under Bonaparte, but with songs. Christmas Eve: literally, as we stepped out the door, there were carol singers in Victorian costumes, it felt like a

Richard Curtis script. We were the only guests in the restaurant to begin with, then another couple arrived, who ended up in a sing-off with April. He sang Jim Reeves, Lee Marvin and Elvis. April sang a song about lesbians and Benzedrine. The carol singers came inside and we all joined in. We had more renditions of "The Donkey Serenade" from *The Firefly* before we got home. Christmas Day: April came down and we opened up presents around the tree. April bought us a bathroom set with shells, and a pair each of sequin slippers, in gold and blue.'

By then, April was in glass slippers, a bona fide regal presence wherever she went which, by then was not too far. She'd meet friends like Simon Callow at a local Fulham restaurant. He said the staff would see her making her way outside and her first glass of champagne would be being poured as she walked in the door. Tony Singleton visited her at the first floor flat, up half a dozen stone stairs from Rostrevor Road in Fulham. Then, the balcony windows were always open onto the very alive streets of London.

'In the last few years, both in our eighties, a couple of times a month, I used to totter down on the bus carrying a light luncheon and a bottle of wine to her flat in Fulham. She always had a bottle of champagne standing by so heading home about five o'clock was always a bit of a challenge. And having fun chats about our past and entertaining comments about our latest old age medical problems. Thank heavens we kept in contact during the lockdown a couple of times a month by telephone for an hour or two 'til just before that Christmas when she died. I was always aware that she had put the elegant image on for me but that isn't the image I keep up in my head. I have a collection of photos of April but there are two most important images to me. One must be from one of her *Vogue* shoots in the early sixties, the other is very ordinary: one of her and me in one of those little four-photo strips you get squished in a tube station photo booth, back in 1968. Her with that slightly raised, questioning eyebrow, looking at each other and laughing. That's how I shall always see her.'

It was de rigueur to visit Rostrevor with champagne, even when you knew April's poor health meant she couldn't drink. The bottle would join the dozens of others in a bedroom stash. When I visited in her final weeks I added her favoured pork pies and Scotch eggs to the lunchtime delivery. She'd have a look, a good smell, and the brown bags would find a place in the fridge to be discarded the following day by her carers. She had 'fancies' but her body would not indulge them. It truly was the time of smelling the roses. Her constant complaint concerned the carers who visited twice a day. They were always moving items that little bit beyond reach but, of course, it was April's reach which was fading. Television and radio became dwindling companions, memory and mind as sharp as ever, and enough stored in them to occupy her thoughts. She was bed-bound at her flat for more than year, her health went like a bankruptcy, slowly then suddenly. A bad fall in 2019 saw her stuck in a hospital bed for many, many months and because she lost her mobile phone, and that was some drama, she also lost contact with many people. She struck a deal with the NHS to be allowed home, freeing up a hospital bed for them, in return for the care visits. She worked at normality. When the producer Debbie Mason visited her, a first meeting, she turned her head and pulled back her shoulders.

I've put on my makeup for you, darling.

And, with much effort, she had, meticulously: the pencilled eyebrows the better to be arched. This was the autumn of 2021 and April was poorly, trapped in an ugly, manually cranked metal bed set up in her front room.

She remained alert and bright, telling Debbie Mason her life story or at least all the highlights and delivering, as always, the good lines in readiness for our planned TV series. She was wary of the modern, topsy-turvy world of legal and social confusion over sexual identity, of daily headlines and controversy, preferring that her triumph be viewed as a personal vindication and a rallying landmark. She always saw it in forthright terms without ambiguity.

Hysterical rows created unexpected allies and enemies and much of this dismayed April. Her constant view was that those who truly needed change should be accommodated without prejudice. She knew the new vocabulary but was fluent in past terminology. She was battle-scarred in the gender wars and wasn't inclined to bow down to faddish thought or behaviour. Life was tough enough without being fashionable.

I became a woman but I am a transsexual. That's important.

She 'talked' with her arms, her graceful movements a distraction from her circumstances. Indeed, all you saw was the swan, not the paddling. It was a constant display of that inner strength. Her lifetime was scattered untidily around the room, but if she needed a book, a pencil, she could point to it in a second. As quickly, her mind could turn to optimism, to hope. There was always hope. We talked about physio and her getting out of the bed and walking down Rostrevor to the bakery on the Fulham Road.

They always welcomed me with a 'Good morning, Miss Ashley.' It was worth the walk to hear that. I've always adored the sound of 'Miss Ashley'.

Postscript

MAGIC MOMENTS

'The corn is as high as an elephant's eye.'
'Oh, What a Beautiful Mornin', *Oklahoma!*, Rogers and
Hammerstein, 1943

Disdained and scorned for decades, April was made Citizen
of Honour of Liverpool on her eightieth birthday in 2015,
adding to her MBE of 2012, but I think her greatest joy, her
real victory, was in 2005 when she was officially recognised as
a woman and given a new UK birth certificate to say just that.

I am Miss April Ashley was her anthem.

It was 'sung' with great gusto at her memorial service which
metaphorically took April once again inside the magnificent St
George's Hall in Liverpool, where we gathered on the warm
afternoon of 16 June 2022 to celebrate her life. It was a grand
event and we all said she would have loved it. The lord mayor
of Liverpool, Councillor Roy Gladden, led the dignitaries, and
many of her friends were there to toast her at the event. It was
organised by Bev Ayre and Louis Muddle, now the custodians
of the April Ashley archive estate. We had a theatrical start with
'Oh, What a Beautiful Mornin'' opening the proceedings, as it
does the show *Oklahoma!*

Simon Callow, who had known April for the previous
fifteen years and made several television appearances with
her, was a suave master of ceremonies. He easily introduced

people and stories from her life. He spoke for most of us when he talked to us of 'the story of someone who, against virtually impossible odds, determined to lead the life she knew she was born to live, fuelled by her absolute conviction, despite being born and baptised a boy, that she was a woman and that she would correct what nature had got wrong, to liberate herself into being the woman she knew herself to be. The scale of the ambition is breathtaking. She had this unique, elfin charm, wicked wit, and a kind of sinuous physical charm. She matured into a grand dame of a sort one rarely encounters outside of the royal family – and very rarely there nowadays. She reminded me of an opera singer of the golden age. She had about her not only majestic deportment but profound theatricality.'

He talked of April as an exemplar, someone who had shown and also led the way for others. He also noted that what always irritated her was a lack of respect. He had his very own April story. They had both been invited onto one of those early evening television chat shows but April had conditions: there must be a bottle of chilled Bollinger waiting for her arrival and she must be delivered in a Daimler. The TV budget couldn't meet her demands.

In time, society did meet her needs. Peter Maddock spoke of how 'from the late 1970s, April became a beacon of hope for the transgender community' which was strongly represented in St George's Hall. As was the church, by Father John Williams, a naval chaplain, who led April's funeral when she was buried next to her father in Ford Cemetery, Liverpool, on a frosty and sunny January morning in 2022. April's loves were with her at the end. 'The Last Post' was performed by the graveside. 'My Sweet Lord' by George Harrison was played during the funeral and, so perfectly, was Maria Callas, singing '*Un Bel Dì, Vedremo*', a fluttering-eyelashes farewell to a very special Madama Butterfly. A champagne cork was popped by the graveside.

By the celebration of June that year, her plot had settled in the graveyard and people had clearly paid respects. In St George's Hall, more than one hundred guests who'd gathered from all over the world to commemorate her life were treated to a couple of glasses of champagne each. It was all, every sip, from April's stash.

Sparkling even in the beyond, her own requiem.

Three early evenings before she died, we were talking on the phone about her planned television series and she said:

It has to be fun.

And, knowingly, in the moment, she added,

For I've had fun. So much of it.

Night, darling.

Acknowledgements

It was a pleasure to know April and through her meet so many wonderful and clever people. Most appear in the preceding pages and I want to thank them for their time and help in an attempt to get something of April presented to those who will have heard of her but not know her. Bev Ayre and Louis Muddle who care – I use the word advisedly – for the April Ashley Estate are brilliant champions for April, her legacy and her future influence on those who may face decisive lives. Their kindness to me has been outstanding, as have been the memories of Vera Taylor and Tony Singleton. Peter Maddock, who April adored and respected, and, perhaps, knew her better than anyone, is also a superb custodian of her memory. In her final months April enjoyed the company of film-makers Debbie Mason and David Stevenson and our gatherings brought a bonus, more stories and memories from her, and further perspective for me. Only added to by other members of the film team, Sukey Venables-Fisher and Esther Springer. April provoked discussion and attention all her life and her time-clock running out didn't stop that. We never stopped talking about her. Duncan Proudfoot at Ad Lib was encouragingly enthusiastic and, along with his colleagues Rob Nichols and Mel Sambells, deserves applause.

Salutations to all.

Suffolk, England, July 2023

Appendix

JUDGMENT

This is the court ruling – *void ab initio* – that April Ashley didn't exist, a most debatable judgement given the life she lived. April argued that the verdict was as socially disastrous as that against Oscar Wilde who was convicted of gross indecency – 'the love that dare not speak its name' – in May 1895.

There is a fascination in reading the detail, discovering what was in Judge Ormrod's mind, the Establishment thinking, with decades of hindsight. It remains on a level with the *Lady Chatterley's* trial and, 'Is this a book you'd want your servants to read?'

Judgment

Corbett v. Corbett (otherwise Ashley)

PROBATE, DIVORCE AND ADMIRALTY DIVISION

ORMROD J.

Hearing dates: 11, 12, 13, 14, 17, 18, 19, 20, 21, 24, 26, 27, 28 NOVEMBER, 1, 2, 8, 9 DECEMBER 1969, 2 FEBRUARY 1970

Nullity – Incapacity of wife – Wife registered as male at birth – Wife later undergoing sex-change operation – Provision of artificial vagina – Whether wife a woman for purposes of marriage – Whether wife capable of consummating marriage.

Nullity – Declaration – Marriage void – Wife a man – Power of court to make bare declaratory order – RSC Ord 15.

Headnote

In September 1963 the parties went through a ceremony of marriage. At that time, the petitioner knew that the respondent had been registered at birth as of the male sex and had in 1960 undergone a sex-change operation consisting in removal of the testicles and most of the scrotum and the formation of an artificial vagina in front of the anus and had since then lived as a woman.

In December 1963 (the parties having been together for no more than fourteen days since the ceremony of marriage), the petitioner filed a petition for a declaration that the marriage was null and void because the respondent was a person of the male sex, or alternatively for a decree of nullity on the ground of non-consummation. The respondent, by her answer, asked for a decree of nullity on the ground of either the petitioner's incapacity or his wilful refusal to consummate the marriage; and, by an amendment made during the trial, pleaded that the petitioner was estopped from alleging that the marriage was void and of no effect or, alternatively, that in the exercise of its discretionary jurisdiction to make declaratory orders under RSC Ord 15, the court, in all the circumstances of the case, ought to refuse to grant to the petitioner the declaration prayed for in the prayer to the petition. On the medical criteria for assessing the sexual condition of an individual, the trial judge found that the respondent had been shown to be of male chromosomal sex, of male gonadal sex, of male genital sex and psychologically to be a transsexual.

Held – (i) Marriage being essentially a relationship between man and woman, the validity of the marriage depended on whether the respondent was or was not a woman and, the respondent being a biological male from birth, the so-called marriage was void (see p 49 a, post).

(ii) With regard to non-consummation (assuming the marriage to be valid), the respondent was physically incapable of consummating a marriage as intercourse using the completely artificially constructed cavity could never constitute true intercourse (see p 49 h, post).

Introduction
Petition
This was a petition by Arthur Cameron Corbett praying for a declaration that the ceremony of marriage which took place in Gibraltar on 10 September 1963 between himself and the respondent,

then known as April Ashley, was null and void and of no effect, because the respondent at the time of the ceremony was a person of the male sex; or in the alternative for a decree of nullity on the ground that the marriage was never consummated owing to the incapacity or wilful refusal of the respondent to consummate it. By her answer, the respondent asked for a decree of nullity on the ground of either the petitioner's incapacity or his wilful refusal to consummate the marriage. By an amendment made during the trial, the respondent pleaded that the petitioner was estopped from alleging that the marriage was void and of no effect or, alternatively, that, in the exercise of its discretionary jurisdiction to make declaratory orders, the court in all the circumstances of the case, ought to refuse to grant the petitioner the declaration prayed for in the prayer to the petition. The facts are set out in the judgment.

Judgment

ORMROD J. read the following judgment. The petitioner in this case, Mr Arthur Cameron Corbett, prays, in the first place, for a declaration that a ceremony of marriage which took place in Gibraltar on 10 September 1963 between himself and the respondent, then known as April Ashley, is null and void and of no effect because the respondent, at the time of the ceremony, was a person of the male sex. In the alternative, he alleges that the marriage was never consummated owing to the incapacity or wilful refusal of the respondent to consummate it and asks for a decree of nullity. In her answer, the respondent denied the allegation that she was of the male sex at the time of the ceremony and asserted that she was of the female sex at that time. She denied that she was incapable of consummating or had wilfully refused to consummate the marriage. In para 5 of the answer, she admitted that for many years she had been regarded as a male but had undergone an operation for the construction of a vagina before the ceremony of marriage, and alleged that the petitioner was aware of all the material facts before the ceremony took place and was, therefore, not entitled to a decree of nullity on the ground of incapacity or wilful refusal. In para 6, she alleged that the petitioner had achieved full penetration on several occasions but withdrew after a very short time without ejaculation, either because he was incapable of ejaculation, or because he was unwilling to do so, and then became hysterical. Paragraph 7 contains an implied averment that the marriage was in fact consummated, and then goes on to allege in the alternative that the petitioner wilfully refused to consummate it. Paragraph 8 contains an alternative allegation of incapacity on the part of the petitioner. The prayer to the answer, therefore, asks for a decree of nullity in favour of the respondent, on either incapacity or wilful refusal. By an amendment, made by leave at a late stage of the trial, the respondent pleaded that the petitioner was estopped from alleging that the marriage was void and of no effect or, alternatively, that in the exercise of its discretionary jurisdiction to make declaratory orders, the court, in all the circumstances of this case, ought to refuse to grant the petitioner the declaration prayed for in the prayer to the petition.

A number of technical points arise on these pleadings which I will deal with in detail at a later stage in this judgment. For the moment it is enough to say that counsel for the respondent very frankly admitted that there were formidable difficulties in his way on both limbs of his late amendment to the answer; and that, in my judgment, there is no foundation in law or fact for either submission.

The case, therefore, resolves itself into the primary issue of the validity of the marriage, which depends on the true sex of the respondent; and the secondary issue of the incapacity of the parties, or their respective willingness or unwillingness, to consummate the marriage, if there was a marriage to consummate. On the primary issue, the basic facts are not in dispute; the problem has been to discover them. On the secondary issue, there is a direct conflict of evidence between the petitioner and the respondent, but it lies within a narrow compass. An unusually large number of doctors gave evidence in the case, amounting to no less than nine in all, including two medical inspectors to the court. Each side called three leading medical experts to deal with various aspects of anatomical and psychological sexual abnormality. In the event, as is to be expected when expert witnesses of high standing are involved, there was a very large measure of agreement between them on the present state of scientific knowledge on all relevant topics, although they differed in the inferences and conclusions which they drew from the application of this knowledge to the facts of the present case. The quality of the medical evidence on both sides was quite outstanding, not only in the lucidity of its exposition, but also in its intellectual and scientific objectivity, and I wish to express to all the distinguished doctors concerned in this case my gratitude for the immense amount of time and trouble which they have devoted to it, and for the patient and careful way in which they answered the many questions put to them during the long periods for which some of them were in the witness box. The cause of justice is deeply indebted to them. My only regret is that it did not prove possible to save a great deal of their time by exchanging reports and making available to all of them all the known facts about the respondent's physical condition both before and after the operation, including facilities for a joint medical examination, before the hearing began. Had such steps been taken a great deal of time and expense might have been saved.

The relevant facts must now be stated as concisely as possible. The respondent was born on 29 April 1935 in Liverpool and registered at birth as a boy in the name of George Jamieson, and brought up as a boy. It has not been suggested at any time in this case that there was any mistake over the sex of the child. In 1951, at the age of sixteen years, he joined the merchant navy. Before being accepted, the respondent had what she (I shall use 'he' and 'she' and 'his' and 'her' throughout this judgment as seems convenient in the context) described in cross-examination as a 'vague medical examination' and was accepted. As George Jamieson, the respondent did one and a half voyages as a merchant seaman before being put ashore at San Francisco and admitted to hospital there, after taking an overdose of tablets. He was subsequently returned to this country and became a patient at Ormskirk Hospital. No evidence was available from this hospital but subsequently, in January 1953, at the age of seventeen, he was referred by his general practitioner to the psychiatric department of the Walton Hospital, Liverpool, where he came under the care of Dr Vaillant, the consultant psychiatrist, at first as an out-patient, and later, for a short time, as an in-patient. Dr Vaillant gave evidence under a subpoena issued on behalf of the petitioner, and produced the hospital records which showed that the respondent had been physically examined by one of Dr Vaillant's assistants and that no abnormality had been observed other than that he presented a 'womanish appearance' and had 'little bodily and facial hair'. Dr Vaillant said in evidence that he never had any doubt that the respondent was a male. The hospital records contain summaries of several therapeutic interviews with the respondent, some under the influence of small doses of amytal or ether, in the course of which he expressed an intense desire to be a woman, which, he said, he had experienced since he was a child and gave some account of various homosexual experiences which he had had on board ship. After some six months' treatment, the doctor who had been treating the respondent under Dr Vaillant's supervision reported his conclusions to the general practitioner in a letter dated 5 June 1953, which reads in part as follows:

'This boy is a constitutional homosexual who says he wants to become a woman. He has had numerous homosexual experiences and his homosexuality is at the root of his depression. On examination, apart from his womanish appearance, there was no abnormal finding.'

Unfortunately, it has proved impossible to trace this doctor whose evidence would have been of great value in resolving some of the questions raised by the experts called on behalf of the respondent.

Thereafter, the respondent came to London and did casual work in the hotel trade there and in Jersey until, in 1956, he went to the south of France, where he met the members of a well-known troupe of male female impersonators, normally based at the Carousel night club in Paris and later himself became a member of the troupe. By this time, on any view of the evidence, the respondent was taking the female sex hormone, oestrogen, regularly, to encourage the development of the breasts and of a feminine type of physique. At that stage he was known as 'Toni/April'.

It will be necessary to examine the evidence relating to the taking of oestrogen in more detail later. After about four years at the Carousel [Le Carrousel] nightclub, he was introduced to a certain Dr Burou who practised at Casablanca and, on 11 May 1960, he underwent, at Dr Burou's hands, a so called 'sex-change operation', which consisted in the amputation of the testicles and most of the scrotum, and the construction of a so-called 'artificial vagina', by making an opening in front of the anus, and turning in the skin of the penis after removing the muscle and other tissues from it, to form a pouch or cavity occupying approximately the position of the vagina in a female, that is between the bladder and the rectum. Parts of the scrotum were used to produce an approximation in appearance to female external genitalia. I have been at some pains to avoid the use of emotive expressions such as 'castration' and 'artificial vagina' without the qualification 'so-called', because the association of ideas connected with these words or phrases are so powerful that they tend to cloud clear thinking. It is, I think, preferable to use the terminology of Miss Josephine Barnes, who examined the respondent as one of the medical inspectors in this case. She described the respondent as having a 'cavity which opened on to the perineum'. There is no direct evidence of the condition of the respondent's genitalia immediately before their removal at this operation. I was informed by counsel that Dr Burou had refused to supply any information, or even to answer letters addressed to him by the respondent's solicitors. The respondent, herself, was almost as unhelpful. In evidence-in-chief, she said that she 'thought' that she had a penis at the time when she was in the Merchant Navy. She had testicles at that time. She said, 'I haven't the foggiest idea of the size of my penis' and had no idea of the size of the testicles. In cross-examination, she was asked whether she had ever had an erection and whether she had had ejaculations. She simply refused to answer either question and wept a little. It is a curious fact that, in the further and better particulars under para 5 of the answer, the operation is said to have been for the removal of a 'vestigial' penis and the construction of an artificial vagina. No explanation was forthcoming as to the source of the word 'vestigial', and there is no evidence that the respondent's penis or testicles were abnormal. Insofar as credibility is concerned, I do not think that it would be right to hold that these particular answers reflect adversely on the respondent's credit generally, because the evidence of the psychiatrists is that persons who suffer from these intense desires to belong to the opposite sex often exhibit a profound emotional reaction when asked about the genitalia which they so much dislike. Nevertheless, such unhelpful evidence does nothing to support the suggestion that there was anything unusual about the respondent's sexual anatomy.

Following the operation, the respondent returned to London, now calling herself April Ashley, and dressing and living as a female. In evidence she stated that, after the operation, she had had sexual relations with at least one man, using the artificial cavity quite successfully. In November 1960, about six months after the operation, the petitioner and the respondent met for the first time. He was then aged forty, married and living with his wife and four children, but sexually unhappy and abnormal. In the witness box, he described his sexual experience in considerable detail with apparent frankness and without obvious embarrassment. He was, in fact, an unusually good witness, answering all the questions put to him carefully, and without any attempt at prevarication or evasion. He said that he had had sexual relations with a large number of women before his first marriage and with others, both during it, and after it was dissolved in 1962. He also described his sexual deviations. From a comparatively early age, he had experienced a desire to dress up in female clothes. In the early stages of his marriage he had done so in the presence of his wife on a few occasions. Subsequently, he had dressed as a woman four or five times a year, keeping it from his wife, but the urge to do so continued. With considerable insight he said, 'I didn't like what I saw. You want the fantasy to appear right. It utterly failed to appear right in my eyes'. These remarks are highly relevant to the understanding of the human aspects of this unusual case. From about 1948 onwards his interest in transvestism increased; at first it was mainly literary, attracting him to pornographic bookshops, but gradually he began to make contact with people of similar tendencies and associated with them from time to time in London. This led to frequent homosexual behaviour with numerous men, stopping short of anal intercourse. As time went on he became more and more involved in the society of sexual deviants and interested in sexual deviations of all kinds. In this world he became familiar with its ramifications and its personalities, amongst whom he heard of Toni/April as a female impersonator at the Carousel [Le Carrousel], which he described as 'the mecca of every female impersonator in the world'. Eventually, through an American transvestite known as 'Louise', he got in touch with the respondent and they met for the first time on 19 November 1960 at his invitation for lunch at the Caprice restaurant. The petitioner's description of this first meeting contains the key to the rest of this essentially pathetic, but almost incredible story. By this time he was aware that April Ashley, as she was now calling herself, had been a man and had undergone a so-called 'sex-change operation'. When he first saw her he could not believe it. He said he was mesmerised by her. 'This was so much more than I could ever hope to be. The reality was far greater than my fantasy.' In cross-examination he put the same thought in these words, 'It far outstripped any fantasy for myself. I could never have contemplated it for myself.'

This coincidence of fantasy with reality was to determine the petitioner's behaviour towards the respondent over the next three years or more. The respondent's reaction to the petitioner appears to have been largely passive throughout the whole period of the relationship. After the meeting in November 1960, they saw more and more of each other, meeting daily and sometimes twice a day. He had originally introduced himself to her under an assumed name but soon disclosed his real identity. During these meetings, the respondent gradually 'in dribs and drabs' disclosed the whole of her history to the petitioner, including a detailed account of the operation. According to the petitioner, his original motive in seeking an introduction to the respondent was essentially transvestite in character, but quite soon he developed for her the interest of a man for a woman. He said that she looked like a woman, dressed like a woman and acted like a woman. He disclosed his true identity to the respondent, to show that his feelings had become those of a full man in love with a girl, not those of a transvestite in love with a transsexual. He repeatedly said that he looked on the respondent as a woman and was attracted to her as a woman. On the other hand, it is common ground that, before the ceremony of marriage, nearly three years later, there was no sexual activity in a physical sense between them at all of any kind, although there was the most ample opportunity. At the most, their relationship went no further than kissing and some very mild petting. At no time did the respondent permit the petitioner to handle her naked breasts or any part of her body. The petitioner's letters to the respondent, nearly all of which appear to have survived, whereas all but one of the respondent's have been destroyed, show a similar emotional situation: affectionate, yet quite passionless, with continual emphasis on marriage and the pleasure which the petitioner felt in thinking of the respondent as the future Lady Rowallan. This is not at all the sort of relationship which one would expect to satisfy a man of such extensive and varied sexual experience as the petitioner claims to be. The respondent, however, agrees with his account of their relationship, except that she claims on one single occasion, in a fit of jealous rage in Paris in 1961, he attempted to assault her sexually.

Her description of the incident did not suggest to me that there was anything particularly sexual about it. She said that she never had any real feeling for the petitioner and had been his 'nurse' for three years. She obviously found him a difficult and perplexing person. She says, and some of the petitioner's letters bear her out, that his emotions swung about like a pendulum, from feeling jealous of her as a woman, by which, I think, she meant, jealous of her success in adopting the female role which he often wished he could adopt also, to jealous feelings about other men who were attracted to her. I think that there is a good deal of substance in this view of the petitioner's attitude. Listening to each party describing this strange relationship, my principal impression was that it had little or nothing in common with any heterosexual relationship which I could recall hearing about in a fairly extensive experience of this court. I also think that it would be very unwise to attempt to assess the respondent's feminine characteristics by the impression which the petitioner says she made on him. While I accept his account of his sexual experience from a qualitative point of view, I am sceptical about the quantity of it, but I have no difficulty in concluding that he is a man who is extremely prone to all kinds of sexual fantasies and practices. He is an unreliable yardstick by which to measure the respondent's emotional and sexual responses. As a further indication of the unreality of his feelings for the respondent, it is common ground that he introduced her to his wife and family and quite frequently took her to his house or on outings with them.

By September 1961, the situation between the petitioner and his wife had become impossible owing to his obsession with the respondent, and a separation was arranged. In the meanwhile, with his assistance, she had changed her name to April Ashley by deed poll and obtained a passport in that name. Attempts to persuade the superintendent registrar to change her birth certificate, however, failed. At some stage after the operation, the Ministry of National Insurance issued her with a woman's insurance card, and now treat her as a woman for national insurance purposes. During 1961, she worked successfully as a female model, until the press got hold of the story and gave it wide publicity. Later that year the petitioner decided to live in Spain and bought a villa and a night club, called Jacaranda, at Marbella. In December 1961, they went together to Marbella on the basis that they would share the villa but not sleep together and eventually marry when his divorce came through. The respondent stayed about a week and then left for a while, returning later for about a month and then leaving again. This pattern of coming and going continued for a long time. When she was in Marbella the respondent slept at the villa and the petitioner at the club. She was largely supported by him and he was happy to do so. In 1962, they became the subject of intense press publicity, culminating in a series of articles in the *News of the World* in which the respondent told her life story in considerable detail, most of which seems to have been comparatively accurate. After his wife obtained a decree absolute in June 1962, the petitioner repeatedly pressed the respondent to marry him but she would not agree. She continued to come and go as she wished while he remained at Marbella. Between July 1962 and July 1963 he estimated that they were together for rather less than half the time; their relations remained the same, they slept in separate houses and their 'engagement' was continually on and off as rows took place between them. Nothing of a sexual nature occurred during all this time. In July 1963, the petitioner took the first steps about a marriage. He consulted a lawyer in Gibraltar about it and discussed financial arrangements with the respondent.

It is, I think, obvious that both of them had considerable doubts about whether they could marry, or whether they could find anyone to marry them. In fact, the lawyer in Gibraltar succeeded in getting a special licence for them. They neither asked for, nor received, any legal advice as to the validity of such a marriage. The ceremony was fixed provisionally for 10 September when she suddenly agreed to go through with it and they rushed off to Gibraltar. I think that there can be little doubt that the petitioner was still in the grip of his fantasies and that the respondent had much more sense of reality.

After the ceremony, they returned to the villa at Marbella where some sexual approach was made by the petitioner. It is, however, common ground that the respondent then said that she was suffering from 'abscesses' in her so-called vagina and the subject was dropped, and they continued to sleep apart, she at the villa, he at the club, for the next three or four nights. She then left for London as had been previously arranged, to take some lessons, preparatory to getting into a drama school. It was agreed that she would find a flat in London and he would join her when he could. In fact, he went to London on about 4 October 1963 and stayed about a week in a flat with her. There is a direct conflict of evidence as to what happened sexually between them at this period. He says that she continued to complain of the abscesses. She says that they had cleared up and that they slept together, and that on several occasions he succeeded in penetrating her fully, but immediately gave up, saying, 'I can't, I can't,' and withdrew without ejaculation, and burst into tears. On 12 October, the petitioner returned to Spain; the respondent, who had failed to get into the drama school, remained in London until early December, when she joined him at the villa. Again, there is a conflict of evidence as to what took place between them which I shall examine in more detail when I come to the issues of incapacity and wilful refusal. After about three days, the respondent suddenly packed her suitcases and, immediately and without warning, left for London. This was the end of their relationship. They had been together for no more than fourteen days in all since the so-called marriage. Shortly after her return to London, probably on 11 December, the respondent wrote a letter which is significant, and throws some light of this strange situation and on her behaviour since the marriage. It shows, I think, that reality had broken in on her and that she, quite understandably, could not face the intolerably false position into which they had got themselves. The letter reads as follows:

11 Dec 1963
London

Dear Arthur,

A letter from me. A none too happy one I'm afraid. I have thought and thought, not slept for days. But from all the pain and torture on my mind I see only one thing very, very clear. That is, I will not ever be coming back to you. I don't know what I will do. I don't know how I will live. But I know I won't be back.

The last three years have been the longest, the unhappiest, the most horrible, of my short twenty-eight years. In those three years I have known you!!!! So you must understand that although I don't put all the blame on you, you do seem to have been a terrible jinx on me.

I am paying dearly for my sin of marrying you. The worry and anguish I have felt in the past three years is making me ill. So the only thing I can do is to try to cut you out of my life completely. Then all I have are my earthly problems. A job, a less expensive place to live. Arthur, don't think I expect any money from you – I don't. Because I know I should never have married you. But I do hope you will either let the house or pay whatever rent you think. At least that.

It's so funny, but I felt so much more (although I never really did) secure before I married you than I did after. Then you denying what you had so promised made me feel so sick to the stomach. I could never have stood myself, let alone you afterwards. Then I seem to remember you trying to convince me of other lies of yours in the past. I don't want to sound bitter, but I suppose I am a little. At the moment, my life seems a wreck all over again. I hope this time I have a little more strength.

Arthur, as I am quite a nice person, I will say and do nothing about getting an annulment until you let me know. I can respect that you would not like to hurt your family any more with cheap publicity; in that, I hope, should I ever want my freedom you will respect my wishes.

I hope you sell your land. In brief, Arthur, I hope one day you will find happiness. Although my heart is breaking, I think you had better have Mr Blue. Give my kindest thoughts to Rogelia, Pepe and Jose Luis.

God bless you,
April
P.S. You have better address yours c/of Caroline 73 Queen Gate as I will leave here in a few days.

The petitioner, still living his fantasy, was able to sustain it for a longer period. His reply is written in terms which suggest that he did not take her letter very seriously. There are two other letters written by him in 1964. So far as he is concerned the love affair was continuing despite the respondent's obvious withdrawal. Thereafter, communications seem to have ceased altogether until, on 16 February 1966, the respondent's solicitors issued an originating summons under s.22 of the Matrimonial Causes Act (1965) claiming maintenance. No previous request for maintenance had been made, and in the witness box in the present suit the respondent expressly disclaimed any intention of asking for financial provision from the petitioner. She does, however, maintain that he gave her the villa at Marbella and she has been looking for some means of enforcing her claim to it. Difficulties, however, arose over serving the necessary proceedings on the petitioner out of the jurisdiction, and proceedings for maintenance were started as a substitute for a direct claim to the villa. The s.22 proceedings reached the stage of filing affidavits of means but got no further. The petitioner did not challenge the validity of the marriage in his affidavit but eventually, on 15 May 1967, filed his petition in this suit.

I now turn to the medical evidence and will begin by reading the report and the supplementary report of the medical inspectors to the court, Mr Leslie Williams, FRCS, FRCOG, and Miss Josephine Barnes, DM, FRCS, FRCOG:

'We, the undersigned, appointed by the High Court Medical Inspectors in the above cause, have this day, at 44 Wimpole Street, W1, examined the sexual organs of April Corbett (otherwise Ashley) the respondent. We find that the breasts are well-developed, though the nipples are of masculine type. The voice is rather low pitched. There are almost no penile remains and there is a normally placed urethal orifice. The vagina is of ample size to admit a normal and erect penis. The walls are skin covered and moist. There is no impediment on "her part" to sexual intercourse. Rectal examination does not reveal any uterus or ovaries or testicles. There is no scar on the thigh indicating where a skin graft might have been taken. We strongly suggest that an attempt be made to obtain from Dr Burou, Clinique du Parc, 13 Rue Lepbei, Casablanca a report on what exactly was done at the operation. We also strongly suggest that an investigation into "her" chromosomal sex be carried out by some expert such as Prof. Paul Polani, Dept. of Paediatric Research, Guys Hospital, London.

22nd May, 1968'

Supplementary Report
April Corbett the respondent was examined at 44 Wimpole Street, London, W1, on May 22nd, 1968 by Miss Josephine Barnes and

Mr Leslie Williams. April Corbett had had an operation for the construction of an artificial vagina and the surgical result was remarkably good. It may be noted that the normal vagina is lined by skin which is moistened by mucoid secretion from the cervix uteri. The artificial vagina in this case also appeared to be lined with skin and it was moist, presumably owing to the presence of sweat glands in the skin used to line the artificial vagina. The suggestion in the first report that a chromosome test should be done was because the result of such a test would be one means of making our factual information about the case more complete.

6 July 1968.

The suggested investigation into the respondent's 'chromosomal sex' refers to a method of examining the structure of the individual body cells for evidence of male or female characteristics, which I shall have to discuss in more detail later. The investigation was carried out by Professor F. T. G. Hayhoe of Cambridge who reported, on 31 October 1968, that all the cells which he examined were of the male type.

The expert witnesses called by the petitioner were Professor C. J. Dewhurst, FRCSE, FRCOG, Professor of Obstetrics and Gynaecology at Queen Charlotte's Hospital; Professor Dent, MD, FRS, FRCP, Professor of Human Metabolism at University College Hospital; and Dr J. B. Randell, MD, FRCP, DPM, consultant psychiatrist at Charing Cross Hospital. Professor Dewhurst is the co-author of a book called *The Intersexual Disorders*; and is particularly interested in cases which exhibit anomalies in the development of the sex organs. Dr Randell has made a special study of individuals with abnormal psychological attitudes in sexual matters, particularly transvestites and transsexuals. He and Professor Dewhurst are working together with a plastic surgeon in a team which is studying the treatment of transsexuals by operations similar in character to that which was performed on the respondent by Dr Burou. The experts called by the respondent were Dr Armstrong, MD, FRCP, consultant physician at Newcastle Royal Infirmary; Professor Ivor Mills, FRCP, Professor of Medicine at Cambridge and Professor Roth, who is Professor of Psychiatry in the University of Newcastle-on-Tyne.

Dr Armstrong has written a number of papers on sex and gender problems and is co-editor of a well-known book, *Intersexuality in Vertebrates including Man*. Professor Mills is particularly interested in endocrinology as applied to cases showing various kinds of sex anomalies; that is, in the study of the chemical substances produced by the sex organs and other tissues in the body, and of their effects in the individual patient. Professor Roth has considerable experience of the psychological aspects of such cases.

It was agreed by counsel on both sides that reports, articles in learned journals, and books written by any of the witnesses could be used in evidence without formal proof. It was also agreed that publications by other writers, either in the form of articles or books, should be treated as part of the evidence in the case. This sensible course enabled the relevant material to be put before the court in a convenient and sensible way. It is easier for scientific witnesses to give their evidence-in-chief in narrative form rather than on a question-and-answer basis. It enables them to express themselves in a form to which they are more accustomed and avoids some of the pitfalls of the question-and-answer technique in which the form of a question may inadvertently condition the answer and lead to misunderstanding. It is easier also for counsel and the judge.

There was general agreement among all the doctors on the basic principles and the fundamental scientific facts. Anomalies of sex may be divided into two broad divisions: those cases which are primarily psychological in character and those in which there are developmental abnormalities in the anatomy of the reproductive system (including the external genitalia). Two kinds of psychological abnormality are recognized: the transvestite and the transsexual. The transvestite is an individual (nearly, if not always a man) who has an intense desire to dress up in the clothes of the opposite sex. This is intermittent in character and is not accompanied by a corresponding urge to live as or pass as a member of the opposite sex at all times. Transvestite males are usually heterosexual, often married, and have no wish to cease to play the male role in sexual activity. The transsexual, on the other hand, has an extremely powerful urge to become a member of the opposite sex to the fullest extent which is possible. They give a history, dating back to early childhood, of seeing themselves as members of the opposite sex, which persists in spite of their being brought up normally in their own sex. This goes on until they come to think of themselves as females imprisoned in male bodies, or vice versa, and leads to intense resentment of, and dislike for, their own sexual organs, which constantly remind them of their biological sex. They are said to be 'selective historians', tending to stress events which fit in with their ideas and to suppress those which do not. Some transsexual men live, dress and work regularly as females and pass more or less unnoticed. They become adept at makeup and knowledgeable about using oestrogen, the female sex hormone, to promote the development of female-like breasts and at dealing with such masculine attributes as facial and pubic hair. As a result of the publicity which has been given from time to time to so-called 'sex-change operations', many of them go to extreme lengths to importune doctors to perform such operations on them. The difficulties under which these people inevitably live result in various psychological conditions such as extreme anxiety and obsessional states. They do not appear to respond favourably to any known form of psychological treatment and, consequently, some serious-minded and responsible doctors are inclining to the view that such operations may provide the only way of relieving the psychological distress. Dr Randell has recommended surgical treatment in certain cases, mostly restricted to castration and amputation of the penis, but in a few carefully selected cases, he and Professor Dewhurst and the plastic surgeon who is working with them, have undertaken vagino-plasty as well – that is, the construction of a so-called artificial vagina. The purpose of these operations is, of course, to help to relieve the patient's symptoms and to assist in the management of their disorder; it is not to change their patient's sex, and, in fact, they require their patients before operation to sign a form of consent which is in these terms:

'I ... of ... do consent to undergo the removal of the male genital organs and fashioning of an artificial vagina as explained to me by ... (surgeon). I understand it will not alter my male sex and that it is being done to prevent deterioration in my mental health.'

Professor Roth is doubtful about the therapeutic efficacy of these procedures and has only recommended one of his patients for operation.

There is, obviously, room for differences of opinion on the ethical aspects of such operations but, if they are undertaken for genuine therapeutic purposes, it is a matter for the decision of the patient and the doctors concerned in his case. The passing of the Sexual Offences Act (1967), s.1, seems to have removed any legal objections which there might have been to such procedures. This phenomenon of transsexualism must, however, be seen in its true perspective. It occurs in men and women of all ages, some of whom are married in their true sex and are fathers or mothers of children. In a paper published on the *British Medical Journal* in December 1959, Dr Randell refers to thirteen transsexual men who were or had been married. Some of his male patients, on whom operations have been performed, have been men of mature age; one was a naval petty officer aged forty-two years. All his male transsexual patients, which now number 190, have been biologically – that is, anatomically and physiologically – normal males. Female transsexuals present corresponding problems but they are not relevant to the present case.

It is clear from the account which I have given of the respondent's history that it accords very closely with this description of a male transsexual. Dr Randell considered that the respondent is properly classified as a male homosexual transsexualist. Professor Dewhurst agreed with this diagnosis and said the description 'a castrated male' would be correct. Dr Armstrong agreed that the evidence contained in the Walton Hospital records was typical of a male transsexual, but he considered that there was also evidence that the respondent was not a physically normal male. He said that the respondent was an example of the condition called inter-sex, a medical concept meaning something between intermediate and indeterminate sex, and should be 'assigned' to the female sex, mainly on account of the psychological abnormality of transsexualism. Professor Roth thought that the respondent was a case of transsexualism with some physical contributory factor. He was prepared to regard the case as one of inter-sex, and thought that the respondent might be classified as a woman 'socially'. He would not recommend that the respondent should attempt to live in society as a male. Both he and Dr Randell had been successful in asking the Ministry of Labour to register some of their male transsexual patients as female for national insurance purposes. Insofar as there are any material differences in the evidence of Dr Randell, Dr Armstrong and Professor Roth, I was less impressed by Dr Armstrong's evidence than by that of the other two doctors, both of whom were exceptionally good witnesses. Of the latter two, I am inclined to prefer the evidence of Dr Randell because I do not think that the facts of this case, when critically examined, support the assumptions which Professor Roth had been asked to make as the basis of his evidence.

There was a considerable amount of discussion in the course of the expert evidence about the aetiology or causation of transsexualism. Dr Randell and Professor Roth regard it at present as a psychological disorder arising after birth, probably as a result of some, as yet unspecified, experiences in early childhood. The alternative view is that there may be an organic basis for the condition. This hypothesis is based on experimental work by Professor Harris and others on immature rats and other animals, including rhesus monkeys, which suggests that the copulatory behaviour of the adult animals may be affected by the influence of certain sex hormones on particular cells in the hypothalamus, a part of the brain closely related to the pituitary gland, in early infancy. At present, the application of this work to the human being is purely hypothetical and speculative. Moreover, the extrapolation of these observations on the instinctual or reflex behaviour of animals to the conscious motives and desires of the human being seems to be, at best, hazardous. The use of such phrases as 'male or female brain' in this connection is apt to mislead owing to the ambiguity of the word 'brain'. In the present context, it refers to a particular group of nerve cells, but not to the seat of consciousness or of the thinking process. In my judgment, these theories have nothing to contribute to the solution of the present case. On this part of the evidence, my conclusion is that the respondent is correctly described as a male transsexual, possibly with some comparatively minor physical abnormality.

I must now deal with the anatomical and physiological anomalies of the sex organs, although I think that this part of the evidence is of marginal significance only in the present case. In other cases, it may be of cardinal importance. All the medical witnesses accept that there are, at least, four criteria for assessing the sexual condition of an individual. These are:

(i) Chromosomal factors
(ii) Gonadal factors (ie presence or absence of testes or ovaries)
(iii) Genital factors (including internal sex organs)
(iv) Psychological factors
    Some of the witnesses would add–
(v) Hormonal factors or secondary sexual characteristics (such as distribution of hair, breast development, physique etc., which are thought to reflect the balance between the male and female sex hormones in the body).

It is important to note that these criteria have been evolved by doctors for the purpose of systematising medical knowledge and assisting in the difficult task of deciding the best way of managing the unfortunate patients who suffer, either physically or psychologically, from sexual abnormalities. As Professor Dewhurst observed, 'We do not determine sex in medicine; we determine the sex in which it is best for the individual to live.' These criteria are, of course, relevant to, but do not necessarily decide, the legal basis of sex determination.

The hermaphrodite has been known since earliest times as an individual who has some of the sexual characteristics of both sexes. In more recent times the true hermaphrodite has been distinguished from the pseudo-hermaphrodite. The true hermaphrodite has both a testis and an ovary and some of the other physical characteristics of both sexes. The pseudo-hermaphrodite has either testes or ovaries, and other sexual organs which do not correspond with the gonads which are present. Still more recently, much more knowledge has been obtained about these cases by the development of techniques which enable the structure of the nucleus of the individual cells of the body to be observed under the microscope. Using these techniques, it is possible to see the individual chromosomes in the nucleus. These are the structures on which the genes are carried which, in turn, are the mechanism by which hereditary characteristics are transmitted from parents to off-spring. The normal individual has twenty-three pairs of chromosomes in his ordinary body cells, one of each pair being derived from each parent. One pair is known to determine the sex of normal individuals. The normal female has a pair which is described as XX; the normal male a pair which is described as XY.

The Y chromosomes can be distinguished quite clearly from the X. In the male, the X chromosome is derived from the mother and the Y from the father. In the female, one X chromosome is derived from the father and one from the mother. All the ova of a female carry an X chromosome but the male produces two populations of spermatozoa, one of which carries the Y, and the other the X chromosome. Fusion of a Y spermatozoon with an ovum produces an embryo with XY chromosomes which, under normal conditions, develops into a male child; fusion of an ovum with an X spermatozoon produces an XX embryo, which becomes a female child. Various errors can occur at this stage which led to the production of individuals with abnormal chromosome constitutions, such as XXY and XO (meaning a single X only). In these two cases, the individuals will show marked abnormalities in the development of their reproductive organs. The XXY patient will become an under-masculinised male with small, under-developed testes and some breast enlargement. The abnormality will become apparent at puberty when the male secondary sex characteristics, such as facial hair and male physique, will not develop in the normal way. The XO individual has the external appearance of a female, a vagina and uterus but no active ovarian tissue. Without treatment the vagina and uterus remain infantile in type and none of the normal changes of puberty occur. Administration of oestrogen, however, produces many of these changes. The individual, of course, remains sterile.

The Y chromosome is, therefore, normally associated with the development of testicular tissue in the embryo, the second X chromosome with the development of ovarian tissue. This is, however, by no means the whole story. Whether or not a normal male or female child develops depends on what may be loosely called the maintenance of the correct chemical balance in the embryo. The process may be illustrated by two examples. The first is called the 'adreno-genital syndrome', in which the chromosomal constitution is XX but the external genitalia appear to be male. Gross enlargement of the clitoris produces a phallus which may be mistaken for a penis and fusion of the labia produces the appearance of a scrotum, but no testicles are present in it. This may lead to a diagnosis of undescended testicles in a male, but further investigation reveals that the individual has normal ovaries, a normal uterus and vagina and no actual male organs. This condition is caused by the exposure of the embryo at a critical phase of its development to the effect of masculinising or androgenising substances, either from the mother or from some abnormality in the foetus itself. The individual is, in fact, a fertile female and surgical removal of the abnormal external genitalia will enable her to live and function as a normal woman. In the second example, the external genitalia appear to be female but the chromosomal constitution is XY. Testes are present, usually in the abdomen. In the extreme case – called the testicular feminisation syndrome – the individual appears to be more or less normal female with well-formed breasts and female external genitalia but with an abnormally short vagina, ending blindly, no cervix and no uterus. In another type, the testicular failure syndrome, the appearance of the external genitalia may be more doubtful, with a phallic organ which could be either a small penis or an enlarged clitoris and a short vagina. It seems that in these cases the embryonic sexual organs fail to respond normally to the male hormone, testosterone, which is produced by the foetal testis.

All the medical witnesses accept that these examples are properly described as cases of inter-sex. In each there are discrepancies between the first three criteria for sex assessment, i.e. the chromosomal sex and the gonadal sex do not correspond with the genital condition of the patient. But there is a difference of opinion whether cases in which the chromosomal, the gonadal and the genital sex are congruent – but psychological or hormonal factors are abnormal – should be classified as cases of inter-sex. Dr Randell said that, in terms of sex determination, he would not give much weight to such psychological factors as transsexualism if the chromosomes, the gonads and the genitalia were all of one sex. Professor Dewhurst's views are similar. Dr Armstrong and Professor Roth, on the other hand, would classify transsexuals as cases of inter-sex. Professor Mills, as an endocrinologist, takes a rather different view. In his opinion, patients in whom the balance between male and female hormones is abnormal should be regarded as cases of inter-sex, and he considers that there is sufficient evidence to justify the view that the respondent is an example of this condition.

Professor Mills's conclusion is, of necessity, based largely on inference because the removal of the testicles at the operation in 1960 would, to a considerable extent, affect the hormonal balance at the present time. He thinks that the respondent was probably a case of partial testicular failure, in the sense that, though born a male, the process of androgenisation at and after puberty did not proceed in the normal way. It is suggested that she may be a case of what is called Klinefelter's syndrome, a disorder in which a degree of feminisation takes place about the time of puberty in hitherto, apparently, normal males. The diagnostic signs of this condition are atrophied or very small testicles, some spontaneous development of the breast, a female pattern of pubic hair and very little facial hair. Many, but not all, of these cases are of the XXY chromosome type. To make this diagnosis with any degree of confidence it is necessary to know whether the respondent's testicles were abnormally small or not, and it is desirable to examine a biopsy specimen of them under the microscope. There is, however, no evidence on this point at all. There is evidence from the respondent that spontaneous development of the breasts occurred at about the age of eighteen years, but I am unable to accept her statement that this was spontaneous. It is admitted that she had taken oestrogen over a long period to promote the growth of the breasts. In evidence, she said that she began to take it in Paris at the age of twenty years, but she told Professor Roth that she had started taking it at the age of eighteen years. The Walton Hospital notes record that, on 22 May 1953, she was suggesting that she should take female hormones to help her change her sex. Oestrogen can be obtained quite easily and without prescription. It was suggested that the absence of pigmentation round the nipples indicated that she could not have taken large quantities of oestrogen but, on her own admission, she was taking it regularly in Paris over a period of four years. In the circumstances I am not prepared to accept her evidence that the development of the breasts was spontaneous.

Professor Mills attached much significance to the note in the Walton Hospital records, 'little bodily or facial hair', and to his examination of the face which showed no sign of what he called 'androgenised hair'. In his opinion, this condition could not have been produced by taking oestrogen, nor could he find any sign of the removal of the hair by electrolysis or any other type of depilation. Professor Dent, however, said that he had seen cases in which puberty in boys had been delayed for several years but had then come on, in which there was no sign of male-type facial hair at the age of eighteen. In such cases he thought that oestrogen followed by castration could account for its absence, as in this case. Dr Randell said that he had seen male transsexuals with no sign of facial hair. Professor Mills, I think, was relying largely on his experience of attempting, unsuccessfully, to treat hirsute women with oestrogens. In my judgment, it would not be safe to draw any inferences from the absence of facial hair in an individual who had been closely associated with experienced female impersonators for a number of years.

Professor Mills also referred to two chemical tests carried out on the respondent's urine, both, of course, after the removal of the testicles, the results of which indicated that the hormonal balance in the respondent was strongly female in character. One of these tests, the estimation of the seventeen ketosteroids in the urine, was repeated during the trial in the laboratory at University College Hospital, and gave a distinctly different result. Professor Dewhurst pointed out that this test requires the collection of a twenty-four-hour specimen of urine, and that in both cases the volume of urine supplied by the respondent was much smaller than was to be expected. As neither sample was collected under supervised conditions – the respondent being merely asked to supply the specimen – little significance can be attached to the results, particularly in a forensic as opposed to clinical situation. A similar comment is to be made about a psychological test called the Turner-Miles test which was used on the respondent. This is a questionnaire which is completed by the patient, but in this case the psychologist was not present and, indeed, has never seen the respondent. There is no evidence as to how the questionnaire was completed.

In my judgment, therefore, the factual basis for the Klinefelter syndrome or any other hormonal disorder has not been established, although the respondent may have been a partially under-developed male at the time of the operation. It follows that it has not been established that the respondent should be classified as a case of intersex on the basis of hormonal abnormality.

My conclusions of fact on this part of the case can be summarised, therefore, as follows. The respondent has been shown to have XY chromosomes and, therefore, to be of male chromosomal sex; to have had testicles prior to the operation and, therefore, to be of male gonadal sex; to have had male external genitalia without any evidence of internal or external female sex organs and, therefore, to be of male genital sex; and psychologically to be a transsexual. The evidence does not establish that she is a case of Klinefelter's syndrome or some similar condition of partial testicular failure, although the possibility of some abnormality in androgenisation at puberty cannot be excluded. Socially, by which I mean the manner in which the respondent is living in the community, she is living as, and passing as, a woman more or less successfully. Her outward appearance, at first sight, was convincingly feminine, but on closer and longer examination in the witness box it was much less so. The voice, manner, gestures and attitude became increasingly reminiscent of the accomplished female impersonator. The evidence of the medical inspectors, and of the other doctors who had an opportunity during the trial of examining the respondent clinically, is that the body, in its post-operative condition, looks more like a female than a male as a result of very skilful surgery. Professor Dewhurst, after this examination, put his opinion in these words: 'The pastiche of feminity was convincing.' That, in my judgment, is an accurate description of the respondent. It is common ground between all the medical witnesses that the biological sexual constitution of an individual is fixed at birth (at the latest), and cannot be changed, either by the natural development of organs of the opposite sex, or by medical or surgical means. The respondent's operation, therefore, cannot affect her true sex. The only cases where the term 'change of sex' is appropriate are those in which a mistake as to sex is made at birth and subsequently revealed by further medical investigation.

On that state of facts, counsel for the petitioner submitted that it had been established that the respondent was a male and that, accordingly, the so-called marriage must be void and of no effect. Counsel for the respondent, however, contended that the respondent should be classified, medically, as a case of inter-sex, and that, since the law knew only two sexes, male and female, she must be 'assigned' to one or the other, which, in her case, must be female, and that she should be regarded for all purposes as a woman. He submitted further that 'assignment' was a matter for the individual and his doctor, and that the law ought to accept it as determining his sex. The word 'assign', although it is used by doctors in this context, is apt to mislead since, in fact, it means no more than that the doctors decide the gender, rather than the sex, in which such patients can best be managed and advise accordingly. It was also suggested that it was illogical to treat the respondent as a woman for many social purposes, such as nursing her in a female ward in hospital, or national insurance, and not to regard her as a woman for the purpose of marriage. These submissions are very far-reaching and would lead to some surprising results in practice but, before examining them in detail, I must consider the problems of law which arise in this case on a broader basis.

It appears to be the first occasion on which a court in England has been called on to decide the sex of an individual and, consequently, there is no authority which is directly in point. This absence of authority is, at first sight, surprising, but is explained, I think, by two fairly recent events, the development of the technique of the operation for vaginoplasty and its application to the treatment of male transsexuals and the decision of the Court of Appeal in S V. S (otherwise W) (No. 2), in which it was held that a woman, suffering from a congenital defect of the vagina, was not incapable of consummating her marriage because the length of the vagina could be increased surgically so as to permit full penetration. There are passages in the judgments which seem to go so far as holding that an individual, born without a vagina at all, could be rendered capable of consummating a marriage by the construction of an entirely artificial one. But for this decision, the respondent would have had no defence to the prayer for a decree of nullity on the ground of incapacity. Until this decision, all matrimonial cases arising out of developmental abnormalities of the reproductive system could be dealt with as case of incapacity, and, therefore, it has not been necessary to call in question the true sex of the respondents, assuming that it had occurred to any pleader to raise this issue. Now that it has been raised, this case is unlikely to be the last in which the courts will be called on to investigate and decide it. I must, therefore, approach the matter as one of principle.

The fundamental purpose of law is the regulation of the relations between persons, and between persons and the State or community. For the limited purposes of this case, legal relations can be classified into those in which the sex of the individuals concerned is either irrelevant, relevant or an essential determinant of the nature of the relationship. Over a very large area the law is indifferent to sex. It is irrelevant to most of the relationships which give rise to contractual or tortious rights and obligations, and to the greater part of the criminal law. In some contractual relationships, e.g. life assurance and pensions schemes, sex is a relevant factor in determining the rate of premium or contributions. It is relevant also to some aspects of the law regulating conditions of employment, and to various State-run schemes such as national insurance, or to such fiscal matters as selective employment tax. It is not an essential determinant of the relationship in these cases because there is nothing to prevent the parties to a contract of insurance or a pension scheme from agreeing that the person concerned should be treated as a man or as a woman, as the case may be. Similarly, the authorities, if they think fit, can agree with the individual that he shall be treated as a woman for national insurance purposes, as in this case. On the other hand, sex is clearly an essential determinant of the relationship called marriage, because it is and always has been recognised as the union of man and woman. It is the institution on which the family is built, and in which the capacity for natural heterosexual intercourse is an essential element. It has, of course, many other characteristics, of which companionship and mutual support is an important one, but the characteristics which distinguish it from all other relationships can only be met by two persons of opposite sex. There are some other relationships such as adultery, rape and gross indecency in which, by definition, the sex of the participants is an essential determinant: see Rayden on Divorce, Dennis V. Dennis and the Sexual Offences Act (1956), ss. 1 and 13.

Since marriage is essentially a relationship between man and woman, the validity of the marriage in this case depends, in my judgment, on whether the respondent is or is not a woman. I think, with respect, that this is a more precise way of formulating the question than that adopted in para 2 of the petition, in which it is alleged that the respondent is a male. The greater, of course, includes the less, but the distinction may not be without importance, at any rate in some cases. The question then becomes what is meant by the word 'woman' in the context of a marriage, for I am not concerned to determine the 'legal sex' of the respondent at large. Having regard to the essentially heterosexual character of the relationship which is called marriage, the criteria must, in my judgment, be biological, for even the most extreme degree of transsexualism in a male or the most severe hormonal imbalance which can exist in a person with male chromosomes, male gonads and male genitalia cannot reproduce a person who is naturally capable of performing the essential role of a woman in marriage. In other words, the law should adopt, in the first place, the first three of the doctors' criteria, i.e. the chromosomal, gonadal and genital tests, and, if all three are congruent, determine the sex for the purpose of marriage accordingly, and ignore any operative intervention. The real difficulties, of course, will occur if these three criteria are not congruent. This question does not arise in the present case and I must not anticipate, but it would seem to me to follow from what I have said that greater weight would probably be given to the genital criteria than to the other two. This problem and, in particular, the question of the effect of surgical operations in such cases of physical inter-sex, must be left until it comes for decision. My conclusion, therefore, is that the respondent is not a woman for the purposes of marriage but is a biological male and has been so since birth. It follows that the so-called marriage of 10 September 1963 is void.

I must now return briefly to counsel for the respondent's submissions. If the law were to recognise the 'assignment' of the respondent to the female sex, the question which would have to be answered is, what was the respondent's sex immediately before the operation? If the answer is that it depends on 'assignment' then, if the decision at that time was female, the respondent would be a female with male sex organs and no female ones. If the assignment to the female sex is made after the operation, then the operation has changed the sex. From this it would follow that if a fifty-year-old male transsexual – married and the father of children – underwent the operation, he would then have to be regarded in law as a female, and capable of 'marrying' a man! The results would be nothing if not bizarre. I have dealt, by implication, with the submission that, because the respondent is treated by society for many purposes as a woman, it is illogical to refuse to treat her as a woman for the purpose of marriage. The illogicality would only arise if marriage were substantially similar in character to national insurance and other social situations, but the differences are obviously fundamental.

These submissions, in effect, confuse sex with gender. Marriage is a relationship which depends on sex and not on gender.

I now turn to the secondary issue of incapacity or wilful refusal to consummate the marriage, assuming for this purpose that the marriage is valid and that the respondent is to be treated as, or deemed to be, a woman. I must deal with this quite shortly because this judgment is long enough already. Of the two versions of the events which took place after the ceremony I prefer, and accept, the petitioner's. Although in some ways the respondent's account seems more plausible, and the lack of any contemporary complaints by the petitioner in the correspondence seems surprising, the evidence of the respondent on the question of the alleged abscesses in the so-called artificial vagina was so unsatisfactory and unconvincing that I had little doubt but that on this part of the case she was not telling the truth. The failure on her part to call the doctor, Dr Rosedale, who, she said, had been treating her for this condition at the relevant time, and the absence of any explanation for not calling him, casts further doubt on her reliability. I was, moreover, impressed by the petitioner's frankness in dealing with his letter written on 26 October 1964. This letter is typical of the kind of letter which one often finds in nullity cases and which throws light on the sexual situation between the parties. To my surprise, the petitioner immediately made it clear that he was not referring to the sexual failure. A dishonest witness would have seized on this letter as most helpful to his case. I accordingly, accept his evidence that the respondent evaded the issue of sexual relations, and that he did not press it believing that this aspect of the marriage would come right in the end. I find it extraordinarily difficult, in the peculiar circumstances of this case, to judge whether the respondent's attitude should be regarded as a wilful refusal or a psychological repugnance. I regard both as essentially unreal in this particular case, but the evidence supports refusal better than repugnance. In any event, however, I would, if necessary, be prepared to hold that the respondent was physically incapable of consummating a marriage because I do not think that sexual intercourse, using the completely artificial cavity constructed by Dr Burou, can possibly be described in the words of Dr Lushington in D-E V. A-G (falsely calling herself D-E) as 'ordinary and complete intercourse' or as 'vera copula' of the natural. When such a cavity has been constructed in a male, the difference between sexual intercourse using it, and anal or intra-crural intercourse is, in my judgment, to be measured in centimetres.

I am aware that this view is not in accordance with some of the observations of the Court of Appeal in S V. S (otherwise W) (No. 2) but, in my respectful opinion, those parts of the judgments which refer to a wholly artificial vagina, go beyond what was necessary for the decision in that case and should be regarded as obiter. The respondent in that case was assumed to be a woman, with functioning ovaries, but with a congenital abnormality of the vagina, which was only about two inches long and small in diameter, according to the report of the medical inspectors. This is a very different situation from the one which confronts me. There are, I think, certain dangers in attempting to analyse too meticulously the essentials of normal sexual intercourse, and much wisdom in another of Dr Lushington's observations in the same case where he said ((1845) 1 Rob Eccl at 297):

'It is no easy matter to discover and define a safe principle to act upon: perhaps it is impossible affirmatively to lay down any principle which, if carried to either extreme, might not be mischievous.'

The mischief is that, by over-refining and over-defining the limits of 'normal', one may, in the end, produce a situation in which consummation may come to mean something altogether different from normal sexual intercourse. In this connection, I respectfully agree with the judgment of Brandon J in W (otherwise K) V. W. The possibility mentioned by Wilmer L. J. in his judgment in S V. S (otherwise W) (No. 2) ([1962] 3 All ER at 63, [1963] P at 61) that a married man might have sexual relations with a person, using a so-called artificial vagina, and yet not commit adultery, does not seem to me to be very important, since neither oral intercourse with a woman, nor mutual masturbation will afford the wife the remedy of adultery: Sapsford V. Sapsford and Furtado.

The issue of approbation in relation to the prayer for relief on the ground of the respondent's incapacity was raised by para 5 of the answer, but it was not, in fact, argued before me, so I propose to say no more about it than that, in his evidence-in-chief, the petitioner admitted that he knew all about the respondent's physical condition before the ceremony of marriage.

In the result, therefore, I hold that it has been established that the respondent is not, and was not, a woman at the date of the ceremony of marriage, but was, at all times, a male. The marriage is, accordingly, void, and it only remains to consider the pleas raised by the reamended answer of estoppel or, alternatively, that the court should, in its discretion, withhold a declaration; and the proper form of the order in which my judgment should be recorded. On the issue of estoppel it is important to remember that there is no question here of estoppel *per rem judicatam*, as in Wilkins V. Wilkins. Here the alleged estoppel is an estoppel in pais or by conduct. I am content to follow the decision of Phillimore J. in Hayward V. Hayward, in which he held that the doctrine of estoppel was not applicable in proceedings for a declaration that a marriage was void, and that, in any event, no estoppel in pais could arise in that case, as in this, because the relevant facts were known equally to both parties. The suggestion that a ceremony, which is wholly ineffectual and void in law, can be rendered effectual between the actual parties by some species of estoppel, would produce the anomalous result that any third party, whose interests are affected by this 'marriage', could at any time successfully challenge its validity, relying on the admissions in the evidence given before me. This defence accordingly fails. For reasons which I will give in a moment in connection with the form of my order, the court has, in my judgment, no discretion to withhold a decree of nullity.

The petitioner, therefore, succeeds on the issue of the validity or otherwise of the marriage, and the only remaining question is whether he is entitled to a declaratory judgment under RSC Ord 15, or whether the order of the court should be in the usual form of a decree of nullity. Counsel for the petitioner sought to distinguish the present case from Kassim (otherwise Widmann) V. Kassim (otherwise Hassim) (Carl and Dickson cited), in which I held that, in a case of bigamy, the court had no option to give a declaratory judgment, but must grant a decree of nullity under its matrimonial jurisdiction, derived from the former ecclesiastical courts. He submits that, if he is right in his contention that the respondent is a man, the ceremony of marriage in this case was in fact, if not in intention, a mere sham, and the resulting 'marriage' not merely a void but a meretricious marriage, which could not, in any circumstances, give rise to anything remotely matrimonial in character. Accordingly, the court ought to make a bare declaratory order, recording the fact that the so-called marriage was not a marriage at all. Counsel for the respondent contended that this case could not be distinguished from Kassim V. Kassim, and that, if I was against him on the first part of the case, I should grant a decree of nullity to the petitioner. The importance of this distinction is, of course, that, on a decree of nullity, the court has power to entertain an application for ancillary relief whereas, if a declaratory order is made, there is no such power. I have considerable sympathy with counsel for the petitioner's argument because, on the facts as I have found them, a matrimonial relationship between the petitioner and the respondent was a legal impossibility at all times and in all circumstances, whereas a marriage which is void on the ground of bigamy, non-age or failure of third-party consents, might, in other circumstances, have been a valid marriage. I do not, however, think that these arguments in fact support the distinction between this case and Kassim V. Kassim, the *ratio decidendi* of which was that, in granting a decree of nullity in the case of a marriage which is void for bigamy, this court is exercising its statutory jurisdiction, that is, the jurisdiction transferred to it from the ecclesiastical courts by the Matrimonial Causes Act (1857). The real question, therefore, is whether or not the ecclesiastical courts would have entertained such a case as the present and granted a 'declaratory sentence' on proof that the 'wife' was a man. I have not been referred to any authority on this point, and it may well be that no such case ever came before the ecclesiastical courts, but, in the absence of any indication that they would not have entertained such a case, I feel bound to conclude that this case falls within the statutory jurisdiction of the High Court, derived originally from s. 2 of the 1857 Act. The ecclesiastical courts did in fact grant declaratory sentences in cases of 'meretricious' marriages: Elliott V. Gurr. There is, in my judgment, no discretion to withhold a decree in the exercise of this jurisdiction: Hayes (falsely called Watts) V. Watts, Bruce V. Burke and Bateman V. Bateman (otherwise Harrison).

If it had been a matter of discretion, under either the statutory jurisdiction of this court or RSC Ord 15, I should, unhesitatingly, have granted a decree or a declaration, as the case may be, in this particular case, because to decide otherwise would be absurd in the extreme. The effect of a refusal to do so would merely be to deprive the parties of a record of my decision in a convenient form since the facts, once determined, speak for themselves. In cases where transactions are void *ipso jure* the order of the court effects nothing. It merely records the existing state of facts.

The petitioner, is therefore, entitled, in my judgment, to a decree of nullity declaring that the marriage in fact celebrated on 10 September 1963 between himself and the respondent was void ab initio.

Disposition: Decree of nullity to petitioner.